FLORIDA

A GUIDE TO NATURE AND PHOTOGRAPHY

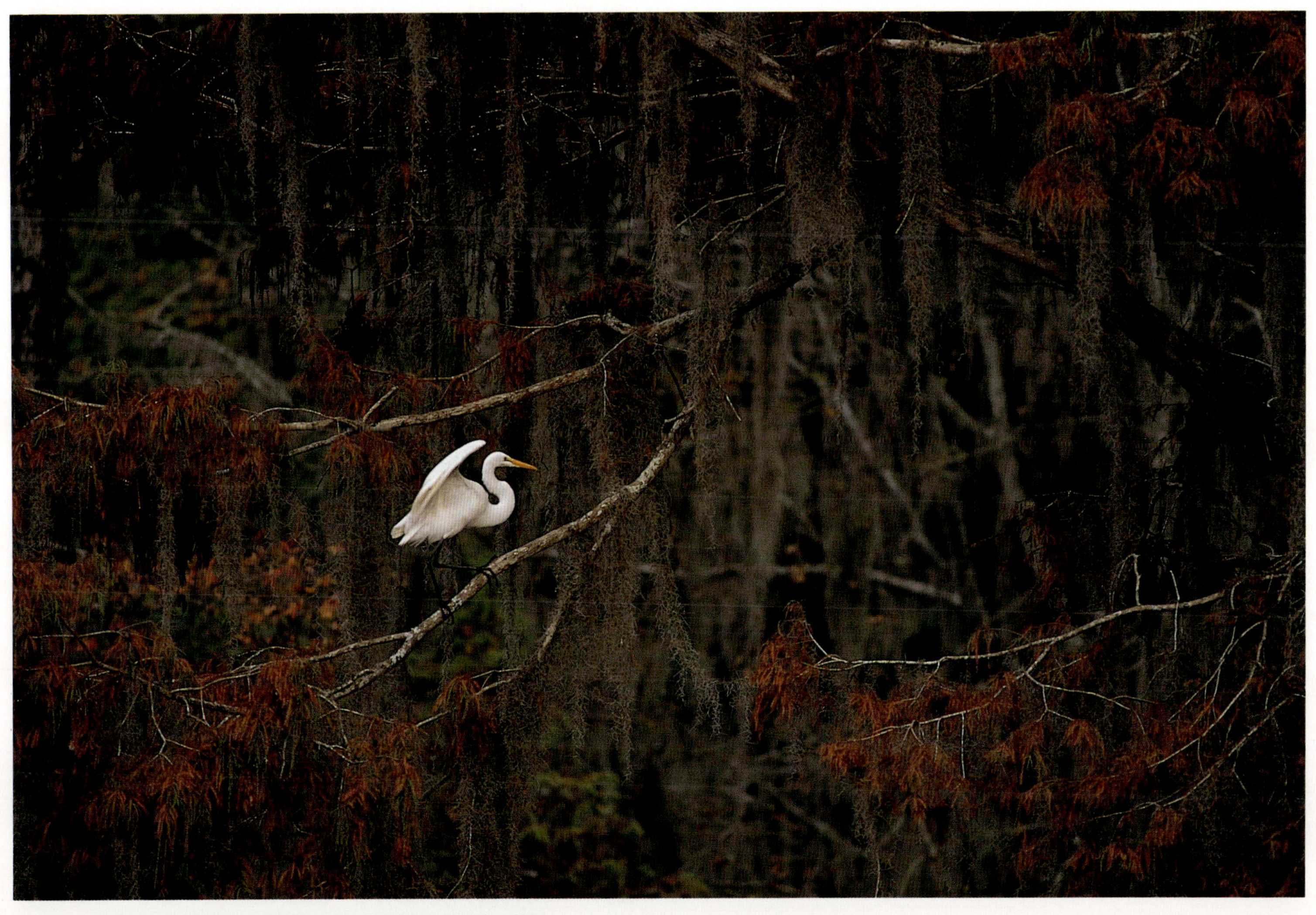

Great egret, Lake Lochloosa, 500mm lens, 1/30 second at f/4

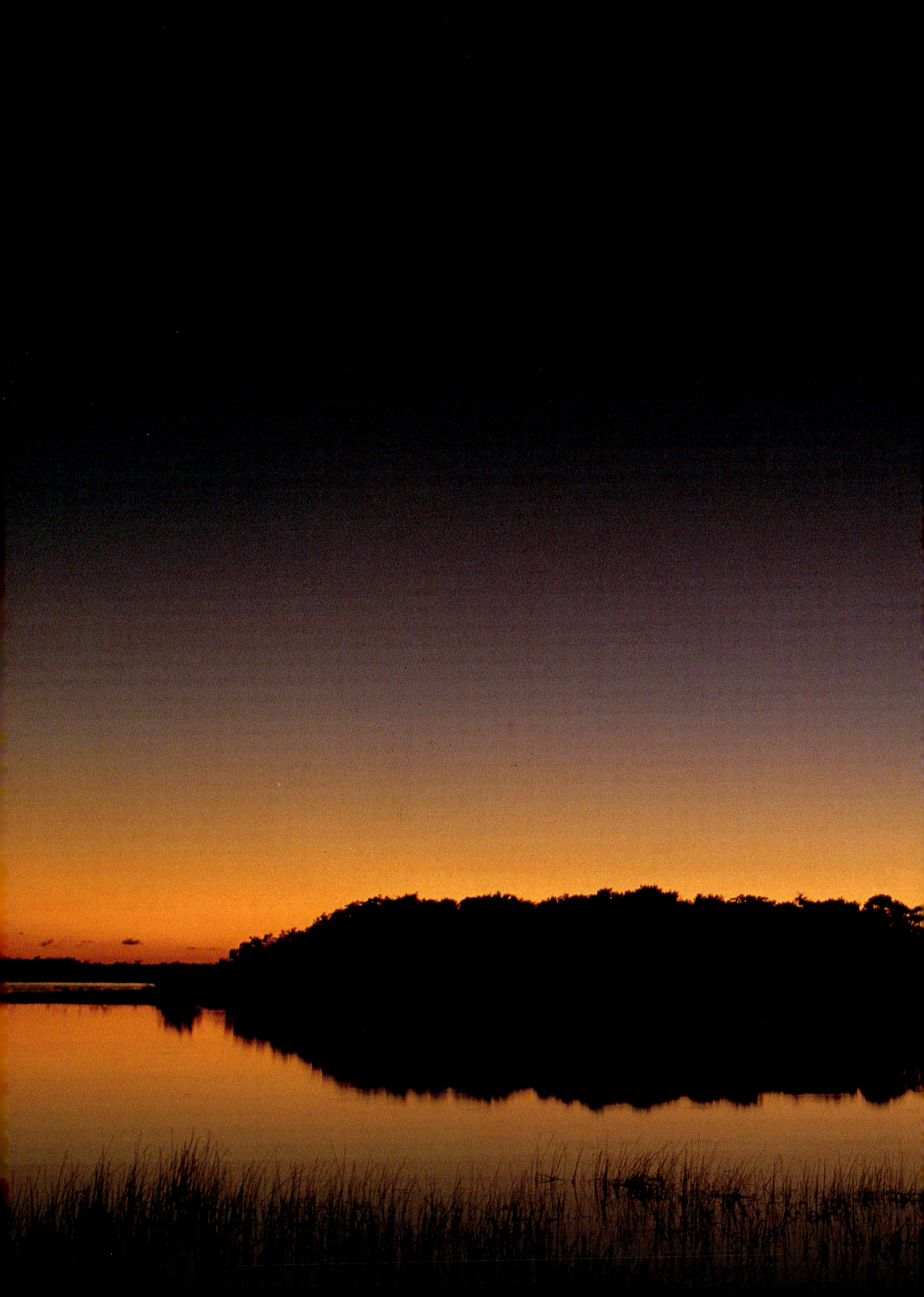

FLORIDA

A GUIDE TO NATURE AND PHOTOGRAPHY

BY JOHN NETHERTON
EDITED BY DAVID BADGER

CUMBERLAND VALLEY PRESS — NASHVILLE

ACKNOWLEDGMENTS

I would like to express my gratitude to the following who helped make this book possible:

Frank E. Carroll, Sara Carroll, Frank L. Carroll, Mark Carroll, Charlie Jarman, Susan Luke, Judy Buchanan, Carole Reed, Pete Garrett, Bob Godby, Sara Keyes and Nina Rubio-Watts.

A special thanks to FUJI PHOTO FILM USA INC. for supplying the film for this project and to Nikon Inc. for the use of equipment.

Also a special thanks to the naturalists and rangers across Florida who assisted me.

Library of Congress Catalog Card
    Number: 90-081715

Graphic Design/Layout:
    The Grafiks Group, Inc.,
    Nashville, TN
Typography: Comtype, Inc.,
    Nashville, TN
Printed by Dai Nippon, Tokyo, Japan

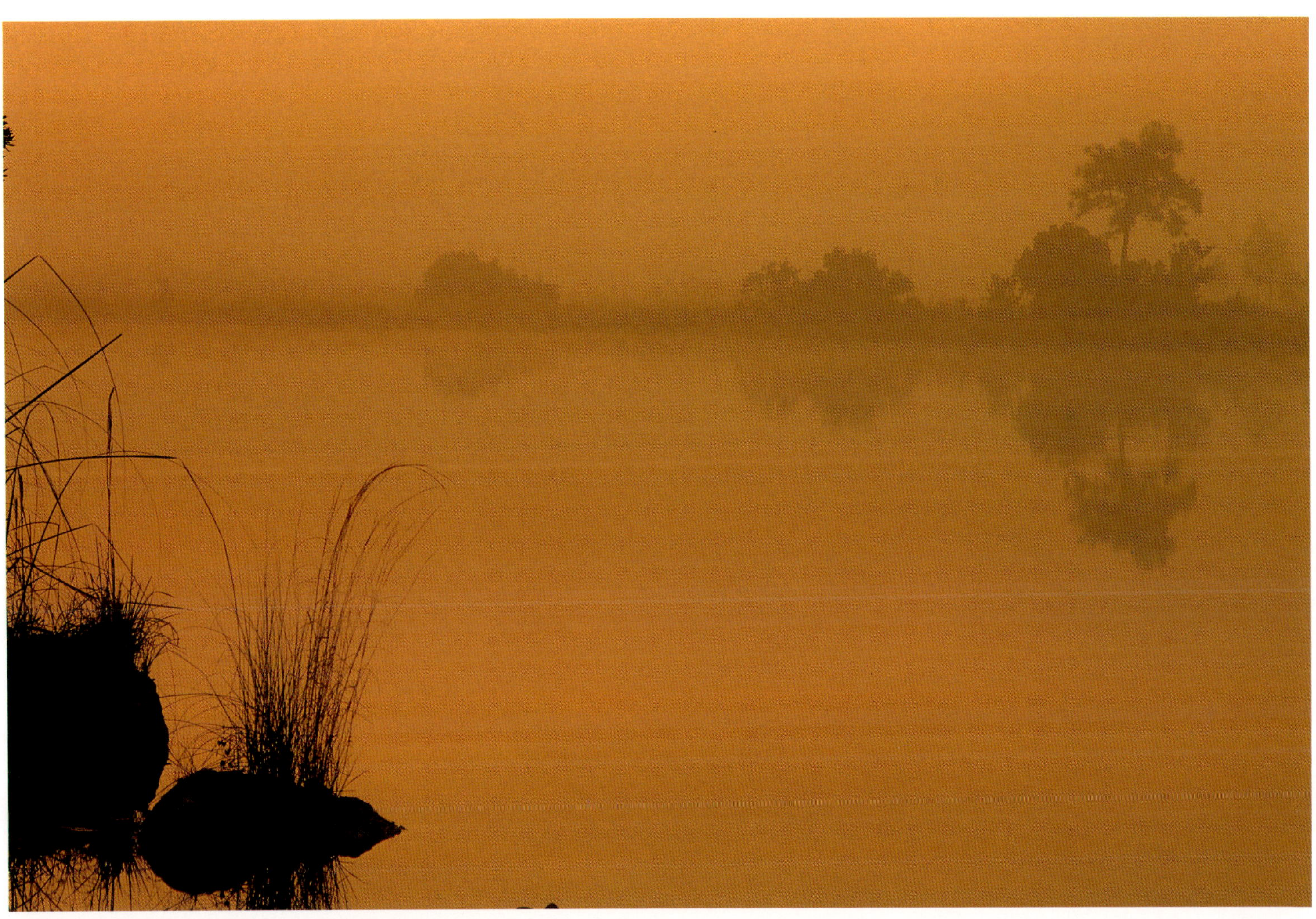

Pond, Everglades, 800-200mm lens, 3 seconds at f/22

This book has been prepared with several goals in mind. First, it is a guide to the best places to visit in Florida's national parks, wildlife refuges, reserves and forests and what to expect to find there. Next, it offers a section on Florida wildlife, describing each species in detail and discussing its habits. This section will help the reader not only to identify an animal in the field but also to recognize some of the complex behavior it may exhibit.

The section on photography offers tips for anyone—amateur or professional—to shoot better photographs. The emphasis here is not on equipment but, rather, on how to use it in the field.

And, finally, I hope the accompanying photographs will inspire those of you who own cameras to take pictures of your own, while reminding you of the many wild places and things that Florida has to offer.

I would encourage all visitors to seek out the state's wealth of information centers and knowledgeable rangers and naturalists, who are eager to share information about current happenings of special interest. Do not forget to take advantage of the numerous interpretive programs as well, which offer factual materials and information of an in-depth nature. These programs are usually presented at information centers or at campground facilities in the evenings.

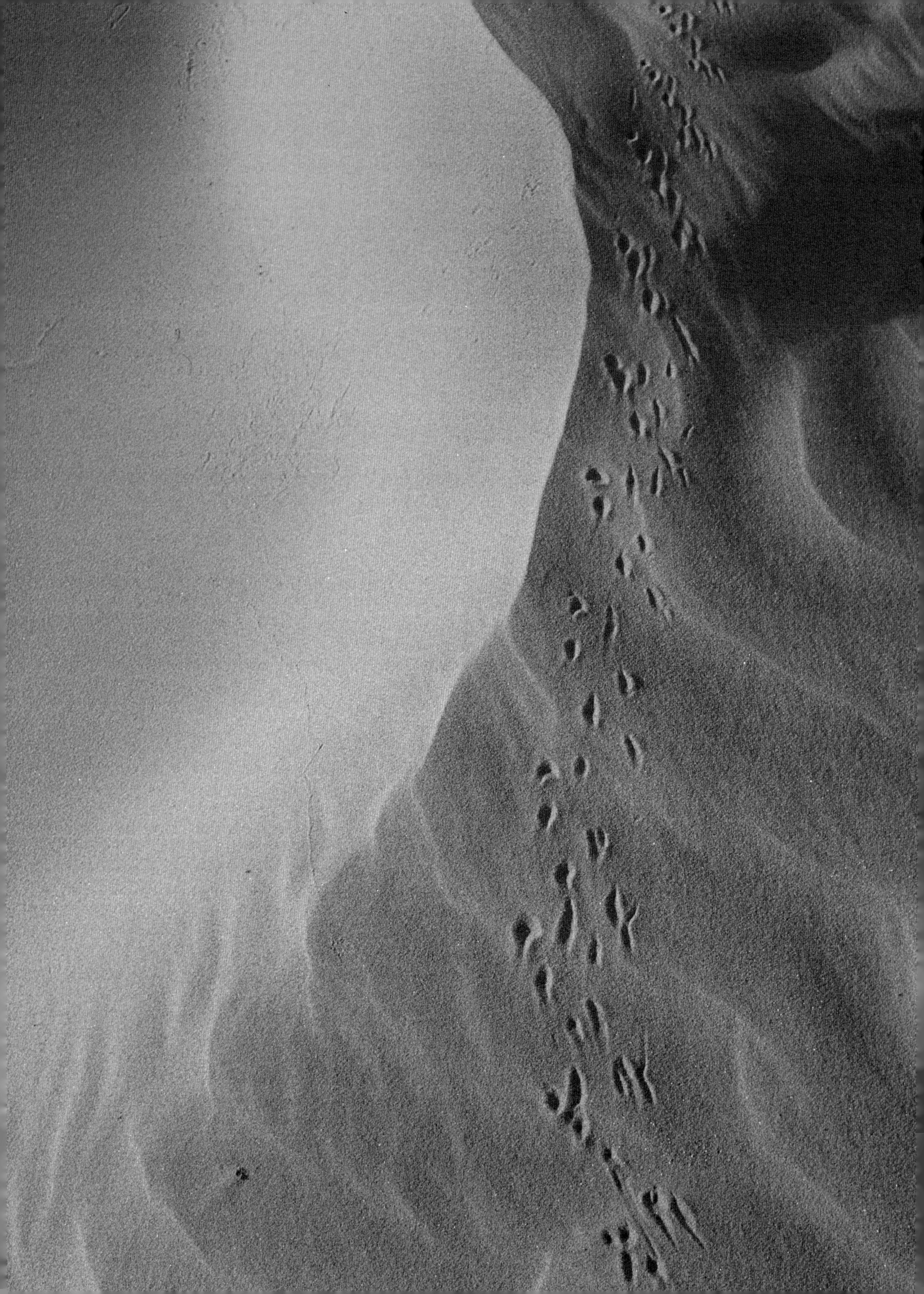

TABLE OF CONTENTS

INTRODUCTION

Florida is a land where sun, water and a subtropical climate combine to provide a home to a variety of plants and animals unique to North America.

No matter where you travel in Florida, you are never more than 80 miles from the ocean. Warm waters that shift barrier islands beat a steady rhythm, spilling shells of every size and color onto the sand. Plumed sea oats hold down rolling dunes and keep them from being blown or washed away, grain by grain.

In the interior of the state are forests of pine and dense undergrowth of palmetto; live oaks line the black waters of the Suwannee River, with ferns and small orchids clinging to their gray bark and Spanish moss hanging from their gnarled limbs. Freshwater flows slowly through the area called the "River of Grass" — the Everglades. There is sawgrass as far as the eye can see, interspersed with the occasional hammock — an elevation of land so thick with tropical hardwoods that you're sure this must be where the elusive Florida panther makes its den.

Freshwater mixes with salt at Florida's southernmost extreme, creating estuaries where millions of birds feed on small crustaceans and fish.

Within this 447-mile-long peninsula are three national forests, two national parks, two national seashores, over a dozen national wildlife refuges and 90 state parks. But the wildlife is not confined exclusively to the boundaries of these preserves, for there are well over 30,000 lakes, 1,700 streams and 8,426 miles of tidal shoreline.

Together, these rich and fascinating elements combine to make the state of Florida.

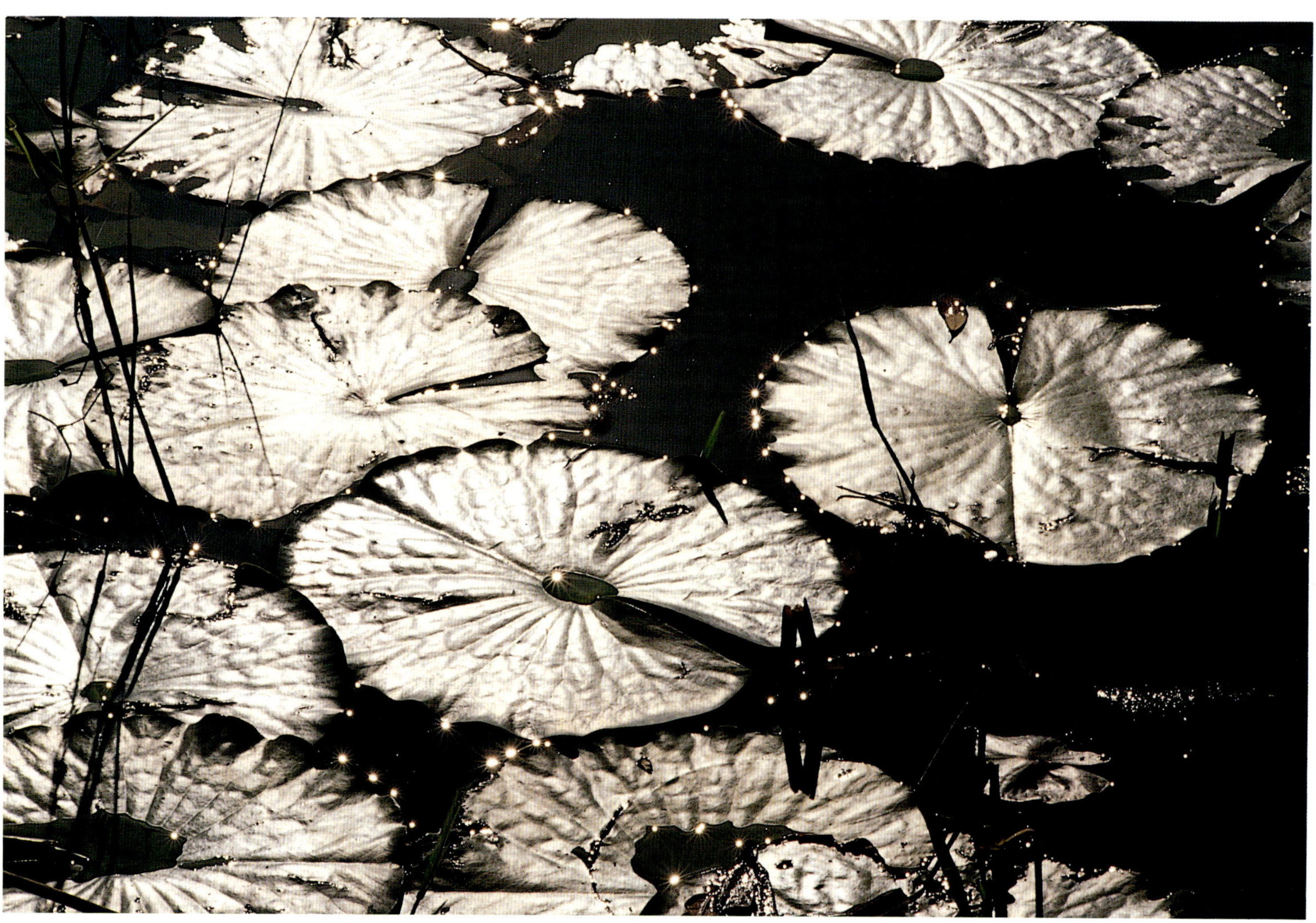

Lily pads, Ocala, 300mm lens, 1/8 second at f/22

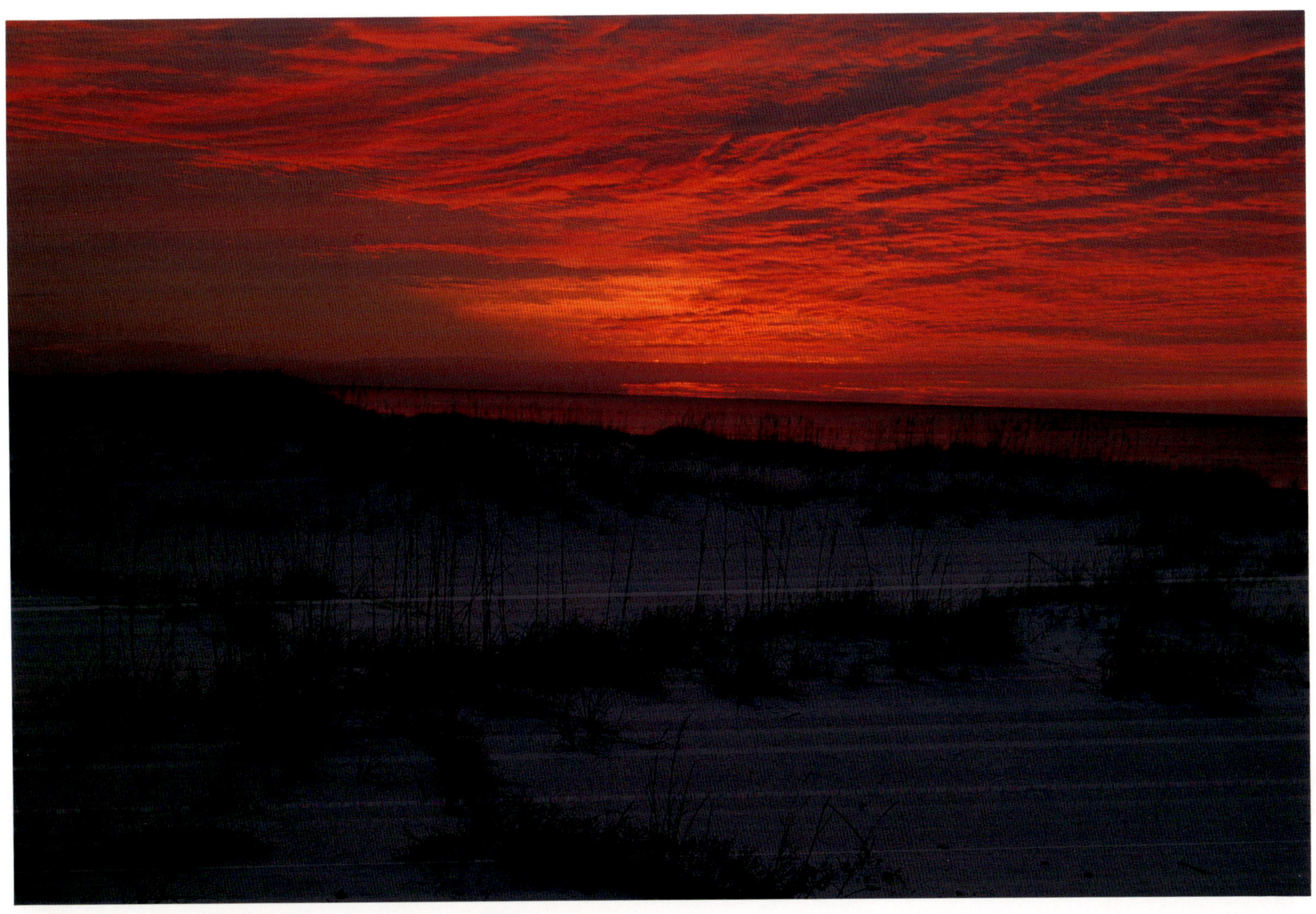

Beach at sunrise, Gulf Islands, 55mm lens, 1 second at f/16

It is Florida's landscape and wildlife that lured me winter after winter to watch, listen and photograph like so many millions of others.

We all have a responsibility, however, to learn the regulations of each area we visit, as well as to find out where we may not pursue or set up close to an endangered species' nest or den without a special permit.

Whether photographing or just observing, we should never interfere with an animal's natural behavior, nor should we remove any vegetation to obtain a better photograph or to take home with us. The natural beauty of Florida must remain unaltered so as to be available for future generations yet to come.

The old saying "Take only pictures, leave only footprints" has found us treading a dangerous path. Some, but not all, put the photograph or the sighting before the safety of wildlife.

Recently, researchers at the J.N. "Ding" Darling National Wildlife Refuge began studying whether to restrict photographers from leaving their cars, thus requiring them to shoot wildlife from automobile windows. So far, their studies have shown that wildlife retreats from photographers 1.8 times as often as from the casual visitor, principally because photographers attempt to get too close.

Please learn the habits of the wildlife before you make your approach. If you are in a boat, be aware that many islands are off limits due to their importance to birds for roosting and nesting.

We have now entered a new decade that promises to be more environmentally aware. Let us all enjoy and experience "the tonic of wildness" that Florida sets before us.

APALACHICOLA NATIONAL FOREST

The Apalachicola National Forest comprises approximately 560,000 acres, which extend at the north into the city limits of Tallahassee. Areas in the northern section, like Silver Lake, Lost Lake and Trout Pond, are more heavily used than other sections, especially the western regions.

Bradwell Bay Wilderness off Highway 13, with 24,600 acres, is the largest wilderness area in any national forest east of the Mississippi River. The national forest also contains 15 major lakes and many smaller ones.

Apalachicola is home to the largest colony of red-cockaded woodpeckers post-Hurricane Hugo. These small woodpeckers make a squeaking sound not unlike that of a rubber duck. They can be found just about anywhere in the pine forests, even though they are an endangered species. Look for white paint on cavity trees to locate them.

In the southeastern section, near the town of Sopchoppy, there is a great scenic river: the Sopchoppy.

Trout Pond is one of the very few 100 percent handicapped-access areas anywhere. It is for day-use only and offers swimming, picnic areas, interpretive trails, showers and rest rooms.

Silver Lake and Wright Lake, two of the major recreation areas here, both offer camping. Silver Lake, the main campground and picnic area, is located on a 23-acre spring-fed lake. Wright Lake, less frequently used, is more of a wooded setting around a tranquil lake. Hiking and canoeing are allowed.

A number of sinkholes are found in the forest, and Leon Sinks is the largest underwater cavern (1.5 miles long).

The Florida Trail goes through Apalachicola, and the Vinzant Riding Trail boasts 37 miles of horse trails with three different routes. An all-terrain bike trail, approximately 5 miles long, is also provided — but you must obtain a permit first.

Wading birds are plentiful in the southern areas of Apalachicola National Forest, especially in the early spring.

Wakulla Ranger District U.S. Highway 319 Route 6, Box 575, Tallahassee, FL 32304 904/926-3561

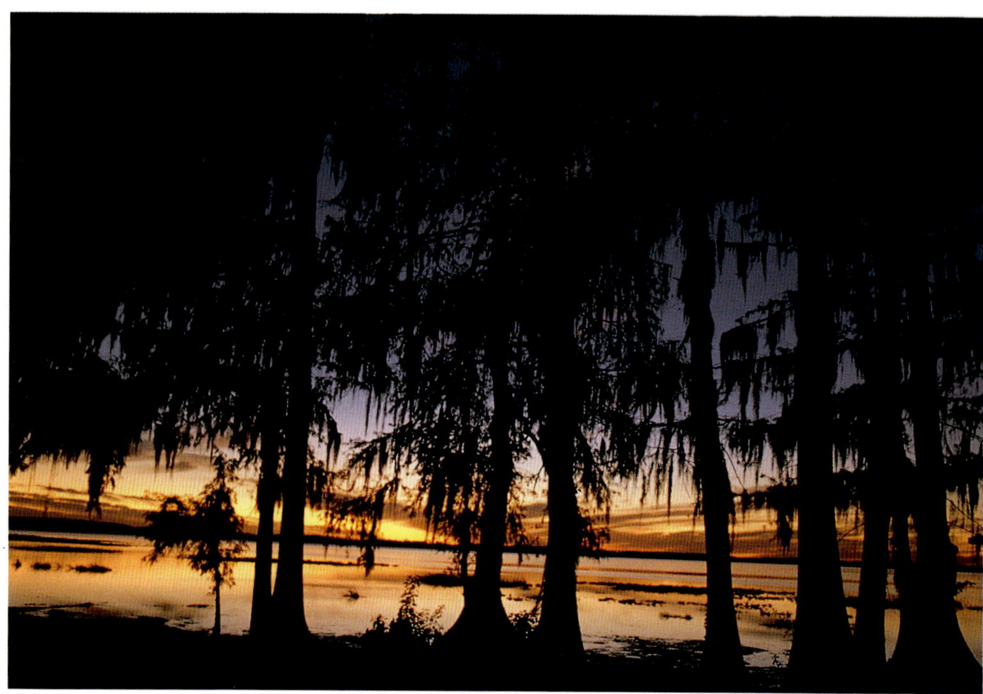

Spanish moss in trees, Apalachicola, 28mm lens, 3 seconds at f/11

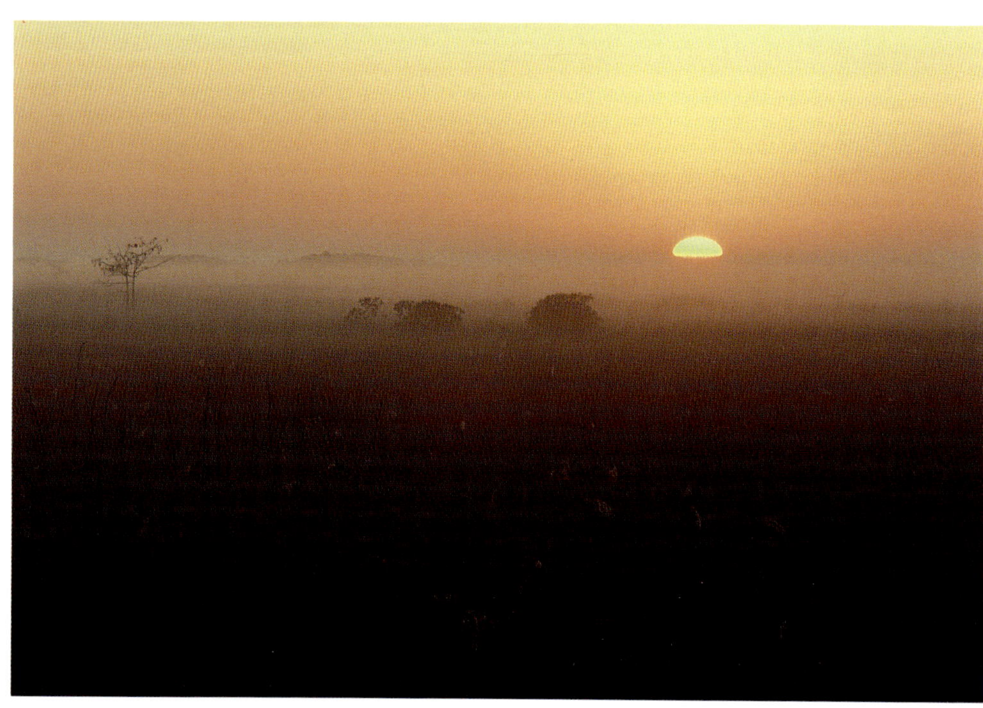

Sunrise over sawgrass, Big Cypress, 80-200mm lens, 1 second at f/16

BIG CYPRESS NATIONAL PRESERVE

With 716,000 acres, Big Cypress is a subtropical paradise consisting of marshes, wet and dry prairies, slash pines, mixed hardwood hammocks — and cypress trees that cover fully one-third of the preserve. Most of the old cypresses were cut down years ago, but a few still stand in the back country.

Big Cypress National Preserve is still relatively new in the system; unlike the Everglades National Park, it has not been developed with numerous interpretive stations and programs.

Instead, there are some unexpected services here not permitted in most other national park systems. Hunting, for example, is allowed during the specified season, as well as off-road vehicles (with permits), swamp buggies, ATV's and the airboat many people mistakenly believe is used in the Everglades National Park.

The Florida Trail begins at the Oasis Visitor Center, where a ranger is on duty and interpretive books and a short film about the area are available.

Two major highways cross the preserve: Alligator Alley (U.S. 41) and, to the west, Route 29. Both highways afford views of large expanses of sawgrass and cypress. The loop road (Route 94) from 40-Mile Bend to Monroe Station is paved for only 8 miles; the remaining roadway is rough and unimproved.

Big Cypress is one of the last strongholds of the endangered Florida panther. During hunting season, the panther usually moves north out of the preserve until it is safe to return to its habitat.

Since the preserve is not developed, more effort is required to get further into the back country. But once you do, you may see some of the largest concentrations of wading birds in southern Florida. If you are traveling alone, be sure to let the rangers know before you set off into the wilderness.

Several campgrounds can be found within a few miles of Big Cypress. A semi-developed campground on Dona Drive offers 10 slots and no hookups. Everglades City has lodging, meals and campgrounds, as well as gasoline and a boat ramp. Many people launch their boats here to go into the Ten Thousand Islands area.

If black bears are to be seen in southern Florida, then the northern section of Big Cypress is probably the best area to look.

Panther crossing signs are posted all along Route 29. Speed limits here should be obeyed, since only an estimated 30 of these big cats are left in the wilds. Also seen in this area — particularly in the water-filled ditches — are woodstorks, egrets, herons, anhingas and alligators feeding out in the open. The still waters will reflect the animals, oftentimes creating beautiful images. If you want to take photographs, try shooting from your car, since most birds in this area fly off as soon as you climb out of your vehicle.

Big Cypress ends just a few miles from the Everglades Shark Valley Information Center and entrance.

Big Cypress National Preserve Star Route Box 110 Ochopee, FL 33943 Oasis Ranger Station 813/695-4111

BISCAYNE NATIONAL PARK

Two things make Biscayne unique. First of all, it is one of the newest national parks in the system. Originally set aside in 1968 as a national monument, it became a national park in 1980.

Secondly, it includes some 181,500 acres, 95 percent of which is water in Biscayne Bay and the Atlantic. Included are numerous reefs and more than 200 different species of fish.

The keys located within the park can claim at one time or another at least 179 different species of birds, though the major emphasis of this park is its vast waters.

Convoy Point is the only area that can be reached by automobile; the remaining areas require a boat for access. Convoy Point offers the main visitors center and the park's headquarters, open seven days a week year-round. An interpretive slide program is available upon request, as are brochures.

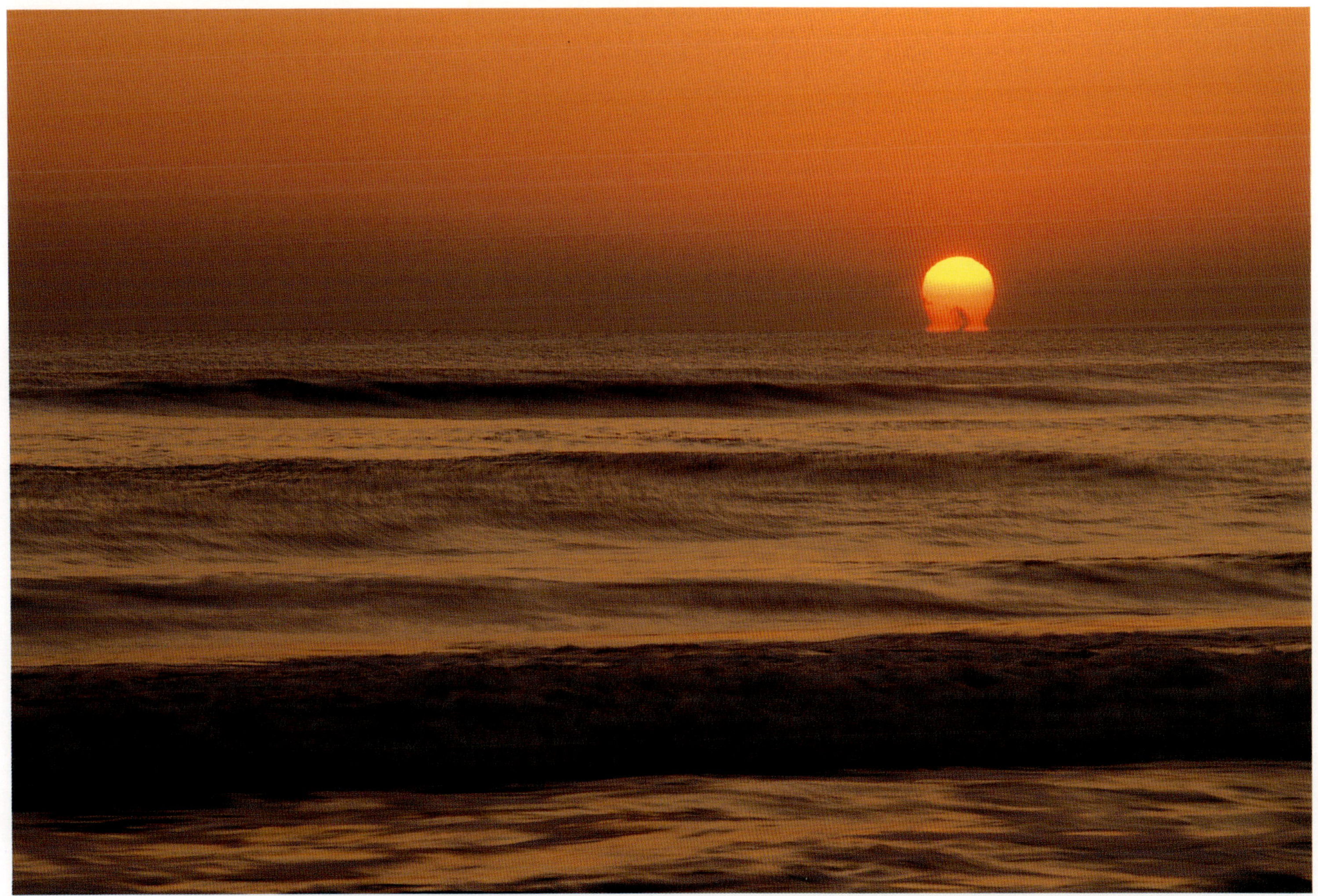

Sunrise and ocean, Biscayne, 80-200mm lens, 1/30 second at f/11

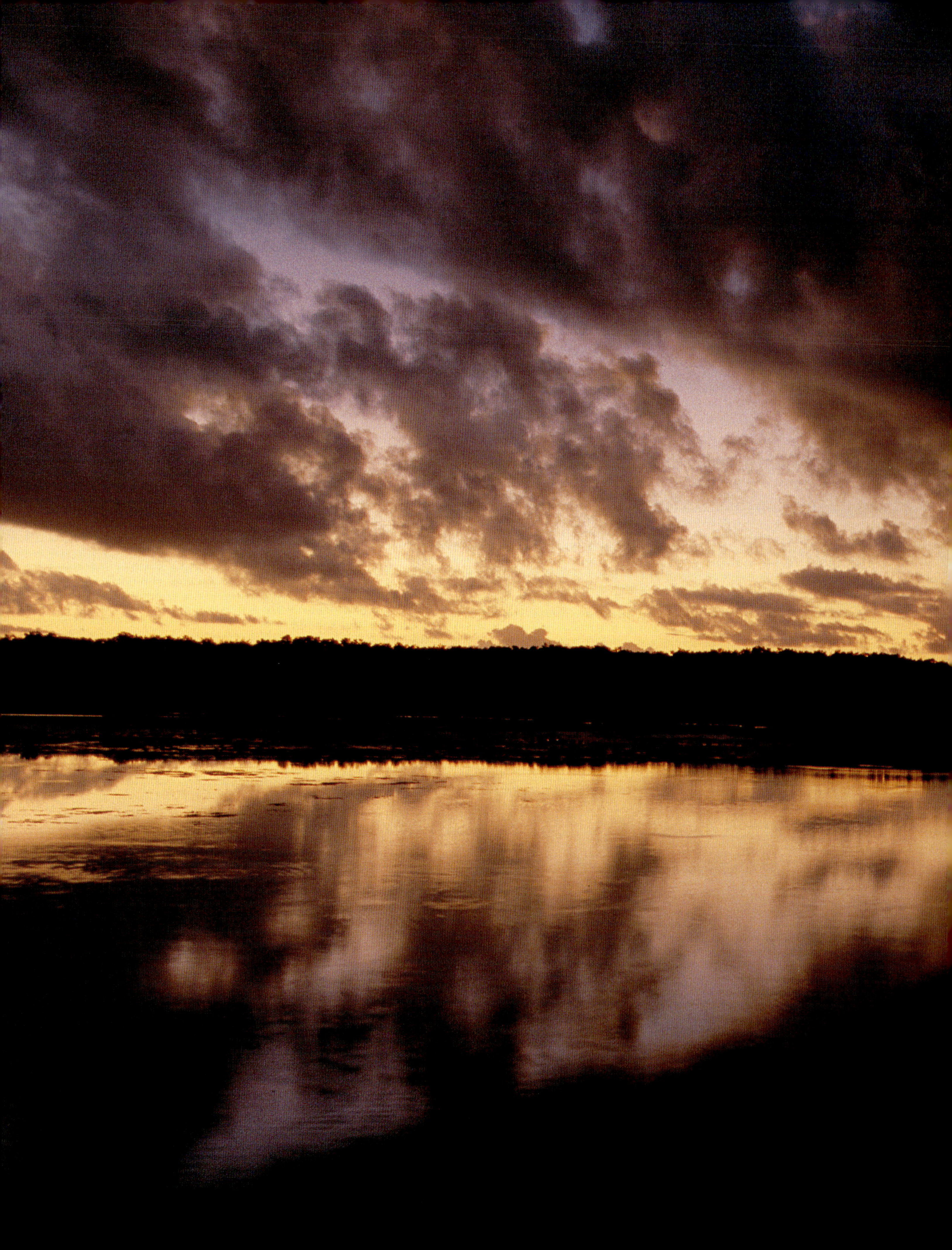

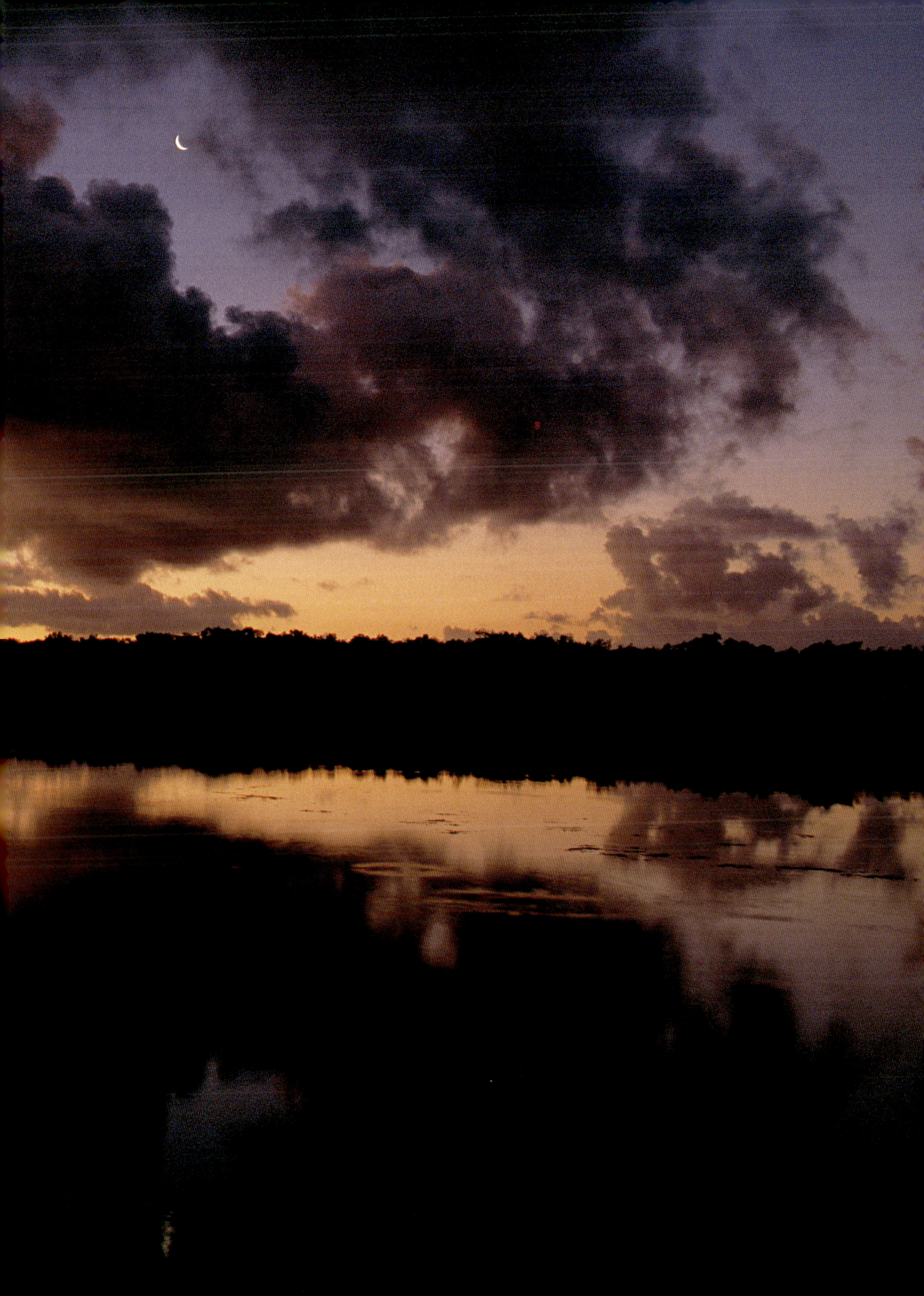

Convoy Point Jetty Trail, which begins and ends behind the visitors center, is 1/2 mile long.

There are concessionaire-operated facilities here, including a gift shop, glass-bottom boat rides and snorkeling and diving tours. The tours are run by the Biscayne Aqua Center; reservations are strongly recommended, since the tours may be full on weekends or may not have enough customers during the week.

If you have your own boat, there is a launch right next to the national park: Homestead Bay Front. Plenty of parking is available at Convoy Point, but absolutely no camping is allowed except on several keys within the park.

Elliott Key is probably the most heavily used, with a visitors center that is open on weekends when staff is available.

Some 64 slips are provided for boats, and picnicking facilities are available. While there are at least 30 sites in the campground, signups are first-come, first-served (though usually the campground is not that full).

There is also a small beach—but not the kind you will find around Miami (it's a little rough on bare feet). Elliott Key Self-Guiding Nature Trail is a popular boardwalk winding through subtropical foliage. Spite Highway Trail is almost 7 miles long, but it is no longer maintained, making it harder to venture into—especially with the swarms of insects.

Boca Chita Key has camping, picnic facilities and restrooms like Elliott Key, but, unlike Elliott, it has no freshwater.

Adams Key offers picnic facilities and restrooms but no camping. It is a day-use area only, except for scheduled environmental groups. There is no information center here, but rangers do live on the key and will assist in an emergency. The half-mile Adams Key trail winds through a tropical hammock.

Sands Key allows backpacking and has a small beach.

Biscayne National Park also includes a number of other keys, some of which are important nesting and roosting areas for birds and are restricted to close approach. Atlantic bottlenosed dolphins and manatees swim in these waters, the latter usually glimpsed near Black Point Marina.

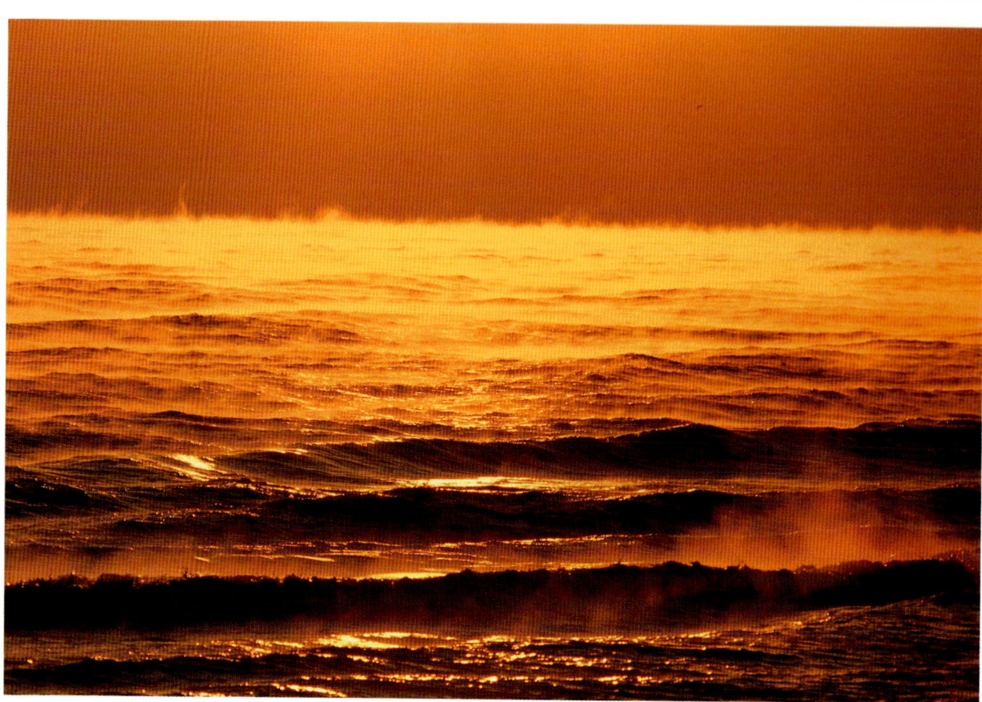

Fog on ocean waves, Canaveral, 300mm lens, 1/125 second at f/16

Mooring buoys are provided on some patch reefs. Always watch where you drop anchor and where you run your boat, since many of these coral reefs are in shallow water and can be destroyed by scraping propellers or the touch of a diver. These reefs are alive and are quite fragile.

Guide books to the reefs are available, and many diving groups conduct orientations, so you will know what is touchable and what is not. It is illegal to take anything from the park but trash—which must be removed, even off the keys, since there is no litter pickup.

Biscayne is only 9 miles from Homestead, where there are numerous motels, restaurants and campgrounds.

Biscayne National Park P.O. Box 1369 Homestead, FL 33090 305/247-7275

CANAVERAL NATIONAL SEASHORE

Canaveral has two points of access: New Smyrna Beach from the north and near Titusville and Merritt Island National Wildlife Refuge from the south. When there is activity on the nearby launch pad, Playalinda Beach at Canaveral's extreme southern point is closed.

The Canaveral National Seashore is made up of 24 miles of unspoiled beaches, with dunes that rise as high as 20 feet. Since there is no way to drive to a mid-point on the beach, a mile's walk from either end will find you all alone on a magnificent beach — something quite rare in Florida.

There is no freshwater available here, however, and when the beach is covered by high tide there is little land left to walk on. At low tide, scallop and cockle shells litter the beach, and ghost crabs, usually more active at night, scurry back to their burrows.

The seashore is an important nesting area for loggerhead and green sea turtles on summer nights. These turtles and their nests should not be harassed, as human scent might attract raccoons that dig up the eggs and devour them. Ridley and leatherback sea turtles also swim off the beaches here.

Shorebirds run along the water's edge, grabbing their prey as the waves retreat, then dashing back further as another wave surges forward.

Since the Atlantic flyway is overhead, many migratory shorebirds pass this way. But I would not recommend that you try to follow them. Because you are out in the open, there are no good places to hide; instead, plant yourself near the waterline and wait for the birds to approach you.

Although this area appears quite barren, the tops of the dunes are covered with sea oats, saw palmetto and sea grapes. In the fall, the sea grapes bear a red fruit eagerly eaten by raccoons and other mammals. Humans, however, should not attempt to traverse these dunes, for the often fragile

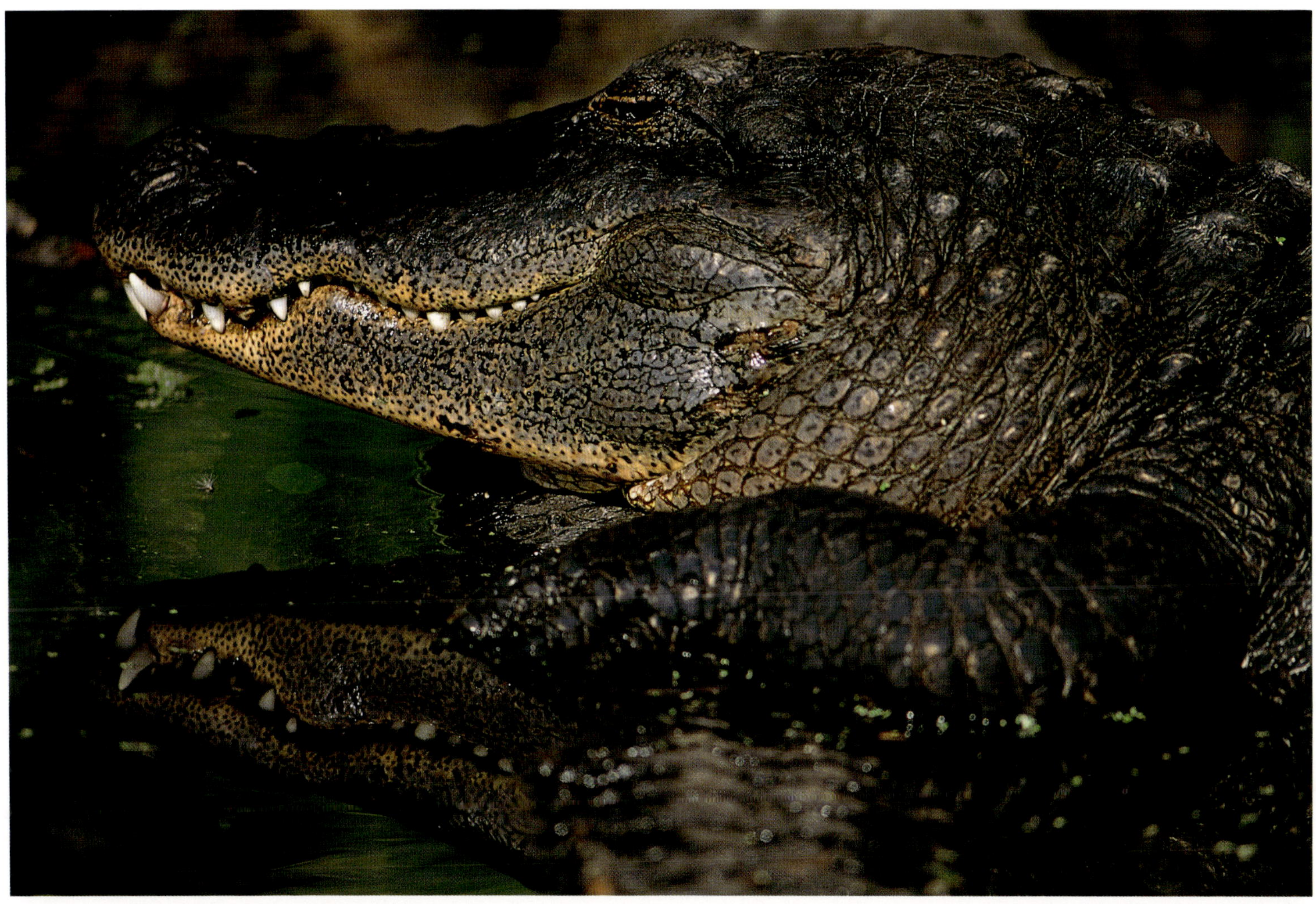

Alligator, Corkscrew, 500mm lens, 1/125 second at f/4

plants not only stabilize the sand and prevent erosion, they also protect the many animals requiring shelter (such as the threatened Eastern indigo snake and gopher tortoise).

In all, there are over 700 species of plants on the seashore, of which perhaps the most striking is the prickly pear cactus, which stands out when in bloom with its bright yellow flowers.

Visitors may wish to take advantage of the Apollo Beach Visitors Center at the northern entrance, which has short films and interpretive materials, as well as several knowledgeable naturalists.

The southern point is served by the Merritt Island National Wildlife Refuge Visitor Center, which also has interesting exhibits and useful information.

Canaveral National Seashore P.O. Box 6447 Titusville, FL 32782 407/867-0667

CORKSCREW SWAMP SANCTUARY

Florida's Corkscrew Swamp Sanctuary, owned and operated by the National Audubon Society, fits most people's preconception of what the Everglades should look like.

Located near Immokolee, Fla. (and little else), these 11,000 acres contain the last and largest stand of bald cypress in the United States. Some of the largest trees are as old as 600 years, and at the right time their tops are filled with the largest nesting colony of woodstorks in existence.

Normally, the storks' nesting occurs between January and March, though the water level, which fluctuates as much as two feet depending on the rainfall, affects nesting more than the season. At nesting time, a portion of the mile-long boardwalk may be sectioned off to prevent disturbing the birds.

Adjacent to the parking lot is a building where you pay admission and where guidebooks and other nature items can be purchased.

From this building, you follow a path through pine trees and cabbage palms, where shrikes and warblers are plentiful.

The first part of the boardwalk extends over a wet prairie, where you can view sawgrasses and glimpse the edge of a cypress grove you will soon enter.

If you inspect the bark of a cypress, you may see reddish lichens, along with stiff-leafed wildpine (an epiphyte) and hanging bromeliads. Where water covers the ground, knobby cypress knees emerge, and duckweed — Florida's smallest flowering plant — conceals some of the 12 species of frogs reported here. Occasionally the plaintive cry of a frog can be heard as it is seized by a hungry egret.

The farther you walk, the more this swamp fits the stereotype. Pond apple trees are draped in Spanish moss, and ferns grow on fallen trees and overhanging limbs. Some of these ferns attain enormous size — especially the leather fern, which has leaves that can reach 12 feet.

Early morning finds the greatest amount of activity. Once a whole family of raccoons walked toward me on the boardwalk, only to climb down when they were within 10 feet, wade past, then climb back onto the walkway and continue on. Deer also wade here, sometimes within inches of submerged alligators with only their snouts and eyes showing. Baby alligators are often visible sunning themselves on logs. The coloring of the youngsters is yellow or creme with black splotches — differing from their completely dark mothers lurking nearby.

Several "lettuce lakes" are found here, where water lettuce blankets the surface of the water. (Due to extreme droughts, however, lettuce may not always be in abundance.) The floating vegetation appears quite stable, even when little blue herons walk across the leaves to feed on insects and crustaceans around the plants. During extremely dry periods, lettuce lakes, like gator holes, are important sources of water and food.

I recommend walking the boardwalk, which loops back to the visitors building, once slowly, then returning to take pictures in areas where the swamp is more active. On the second round, wait and listen. Barred owls and red-shouldered hawks may cry out, although the limpkins and bellowing alligators generally produce the most distinct sounds.

If you study the water lettuce closely, you will likely see turtles pushing their way through the thick plants and frogs hopping from one plant to another. White ibis commonly stand on overhanging limbs to preen, and they wade in groups through pickerelweed and arrowhead, catching crustaceans and small gambusia minnows.

Since the swamp's dense canopy cuts down on the amount of entering light, be careful when photographing at slow shutter speeds, since passersby may cause the boardwalk to vibrate.

Late February is normally a good time to take photographs, although, as mentioned earlier, the water level is a greater factor here than in most other areas. I have seen this area contain almost no visible wildlife one week, and the next week so full you couldn't decide where to point a camera. I recommend calling the visitors center for current information before arrival.

Since there are no major cities near Corkscrew, Ft. Myers (only about one hour away by interstate) is probably best for motel accommodations. Corkscrew Swamp Sanctuary Box 1875, RD 6 Sanctuary Road Naples, FL 33940
813/657-3771

EVERGLADES NATIONAL PARK

The Everglades National Park is close to 1.6 million acres of sawgrass, pine forest, hammocks and mangrove estuaries. This reserve — a biosphere of international significance — contains the largest sawgrass marsh in the world.

At first glance, the Everglades look much like the savannas of Africa; one step off the 38-mile paved road that ends at Flamingo, however, and you're ankle deep in primal muck.

During the wet season (May through November), these saw-toothed plants become a green "river of grass." A sheet of water flows 50 miles wide and a few inches deep, slowly emptying into Florida Bay, a body of water that makes up one-third of the park's acreage.

Few people brave the Everglades during the summer months, due to the heat, humidity, wide dispersal of birds — and the salt-marsh mosquito. A small park pamphlet says it best: "Don't roll down your car windows, avoid grassy areas, do apply insect repellent, do avoid shady areas, do have your car keys in hand as you approach your vehicle."

Winter is the season when visitors arrive en masse. The best time to appreciate the Everglades is from January through March, although if I were to select the ideal month it would be February. This is the height of the dry season, when birds congregate around the diminishing ponds and gator holes.

Hundreds of egrets, herons, spoonbills and ibises can be seen in the early-morning hours feeding frantically in their favorite shallows. In late February, the birds are customarily draped in their colorful courtship plumage, exhibiting their mating rituals.

The national park has built trails to allow visitors access to a variety of prime areas in this uniquely complex subtropical region.

To see most of the park's exquisite wildlife, the visitor must rise before sunrise and transport himself to the area of greatest interest. Birds begin to arrive in large numbers before sunrise and feed for about two hours, depending on the intensity of the sun. Most birds then leave, but a few stay or return off and on for the rest of the day.

Most areas of the park have something to offer all day long, although the wildlife will likely appear in smaller numbers. The main Park Visitor Center at the start of the park stocks and sells a variety of interpretive materials, including books, maps and tapes. There are also naturalists here to answer questions.

Campgrounds are located in the pinelands and in Flamingo along Florida Bay. The one-time fishing settlement of Flamingo also has a ranger station, visitors center, marina, motel, cabins, restaurant and food service.

Visitors who stay in Flamingo and drive out to a favorite location in early morning should exercise caution: Bobcats frequent the roadside while it is still dark, and the endangered Florida panther is returning from a night of hunting. In addition, traffic is heavier in the direction of Flamingo's marina, as fishermen descend on the area to put in their boats for the day.

The sections that follow describe the park's hiking trails and ponds, but there are also canoe trails for the more adventurous. Canoes can be rented at locations just outside the park's entrance, or visitors may bring their own. Books and other literature about the waterway courses are available from the Park Visitor Center.

ANHINGA TRAIL

The first several hundred feet of the Anhinga Trail — which begins only a few yards from the Royal Palm Gift Shop and rest rooms at Taylor Slough — are paved. Taylor Slough, which resembles a pond, encompasses nearly an acre; here great blue herons feed and alligators lie for hours at a time along the banks.

A stone wall separates visitors from the wildlife for approximately 150 feet or so, then gives way to a wooden rail. The rail enables alligators to move freely from one side of the trail to the other.

One of the best locations for photographing anhingas is right where the wooden railings begin. At this point, Taylor Slough is approximately 30 feet wide. Consequently, the fishing birds are all within range of a medium telephoto lens.

The near bank is covered with grass, and anhingas and cormorants favor this site as a place to swallow fish whole and dry their

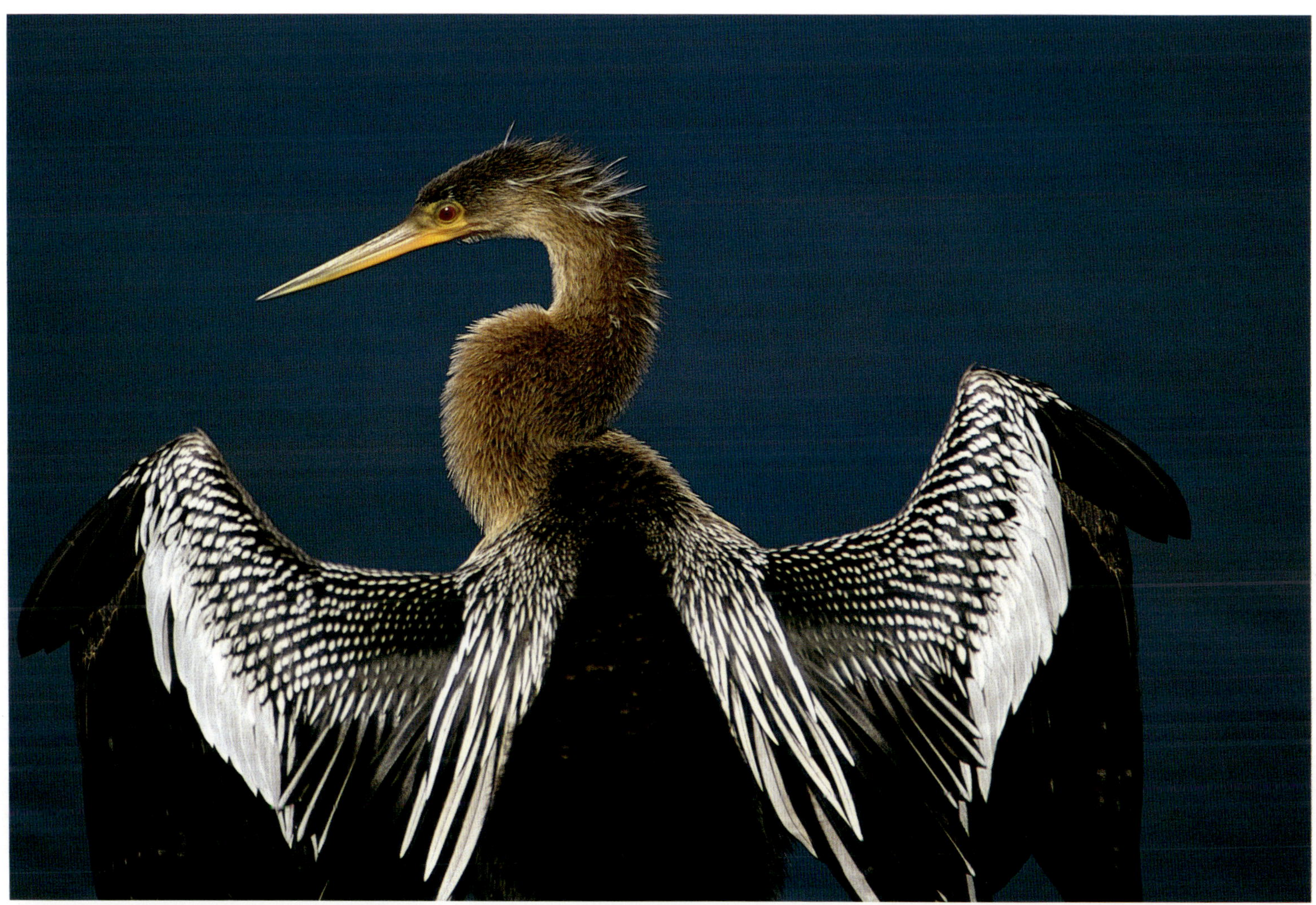

Anhinga, Anhinga Trail, 300mm lens, 1/250 second at f/5.6

wings in the sun. Purple gallinules often feed along the grassy edge; when they reach the spatterdock, they like to climb up onto the large floating pads and eat. Smooth-billed anis are also seen along the canal in the tall grasses. Other birds found along this first portion of the trail include the green-backed heron, tri-colored heron, great egret and least bittern.

A short bridge along the paved area allows water to flow into a small area just to the trail's right. Here, white ibis and egrets often stand on the large rocks, leaning over to catch fish or to preen.

As the trail continues on, the waterway becomes narrower and is covered with spatterdock leaves. Green-backed herons and warblers are numerous here, along with the occasional least bittern.

At this point the wooden boardwalk begins, elevated above the water and leading toward a covered "interpretive area." Directly across from this area, anhingas begin nesting in the pond apple trees in mid-February. These trees are

approximately 100 feet from the wooden platform, making it necessary to use a telephoto lens in the range of 400mm to 800mm to fill the frame with the birds. This area opens up into a larger expanse of water, where alligators glide effortlessly back and forth under the boardwalk.

Shooting photographs from the wooden boardwalk has its disadvantages. First, the walkway is only about four feet wide, so care must be taken to avoid blocking the passageway if a tripod is set up. Then there's the vibration from visitors. Since this is the most popular trail in the national park, there is so much movement that only the fastest shutter speeds can be used.

Eventually, the boardwalk loops back to the paved area, but off to the right the boardwalk leads to a dead end where sora rails have been observed. The birds here are active all day long, but most activity takes place in the early morning and evening.

GUMBO-LIMBO TRAIL

The Gumbo-Limbo Trail is a circular half-mile paved trail that winds through a tropical hardwood forest. Its name comes from the tropical gumbo-limbo tree, which can be identified by its rust-colored bark that flakes off like paper.

At approximately the midway point, the trail passes by an old roadbed that was once the Ingraham Highway. If you take this path to the left and follow the abandoned road, you will probably find more tree snails and zebra butterflies than in any other place in the park.

Each year these colorful tree snails are harder to find, because many park visitors mistakenly assume that carrying out a few "dead" snails won't hurt anything. The snails, however, are far from dead. Instead, they have fastened themselves to the sides of trees and sealed themselves in during the winter dry season to avoid losing moisture.

A large number of bromeliads grow on the ground to the right and just beneath the royal palms.

These bromeliads are not readily visible without walking back into the trees some

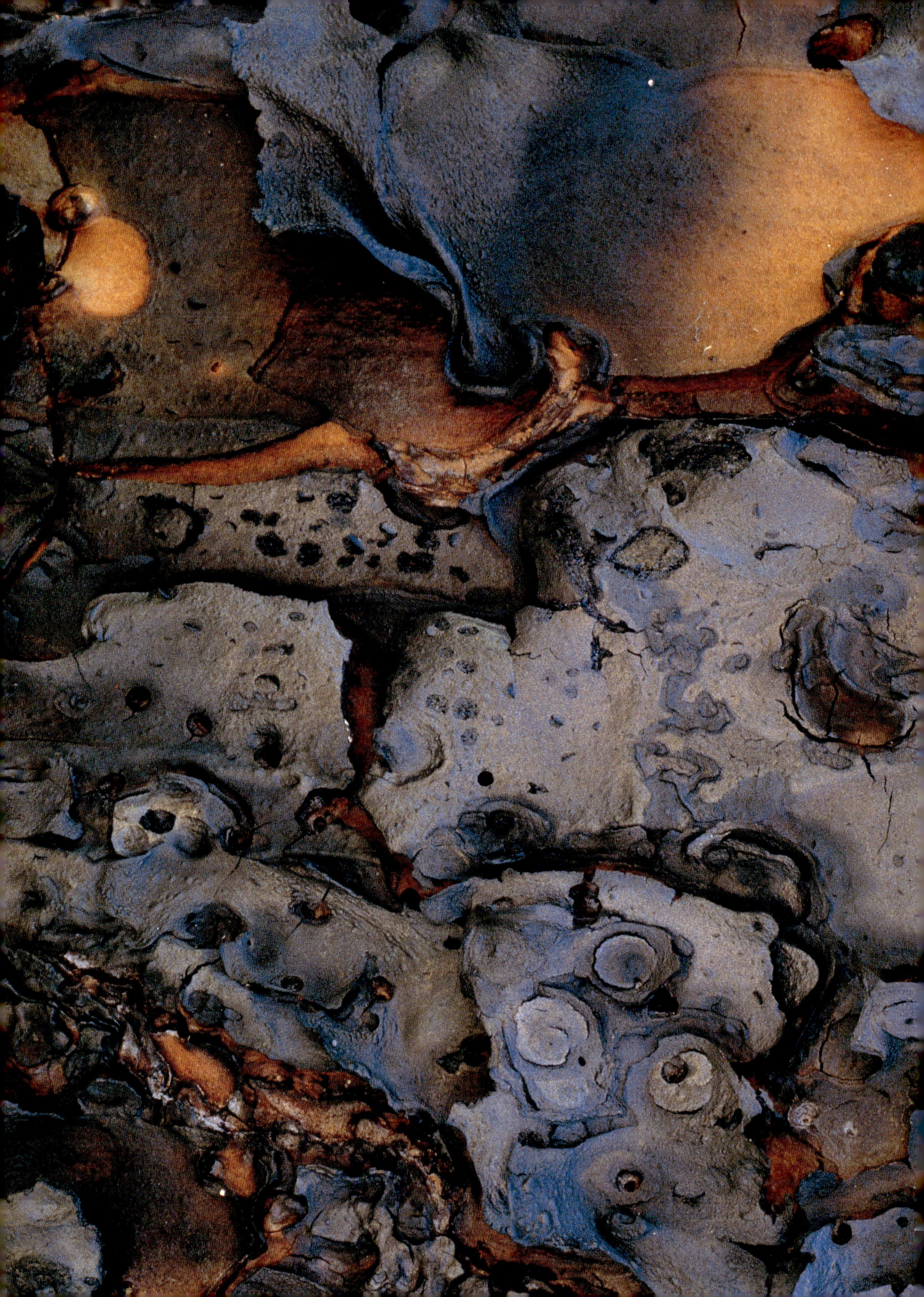

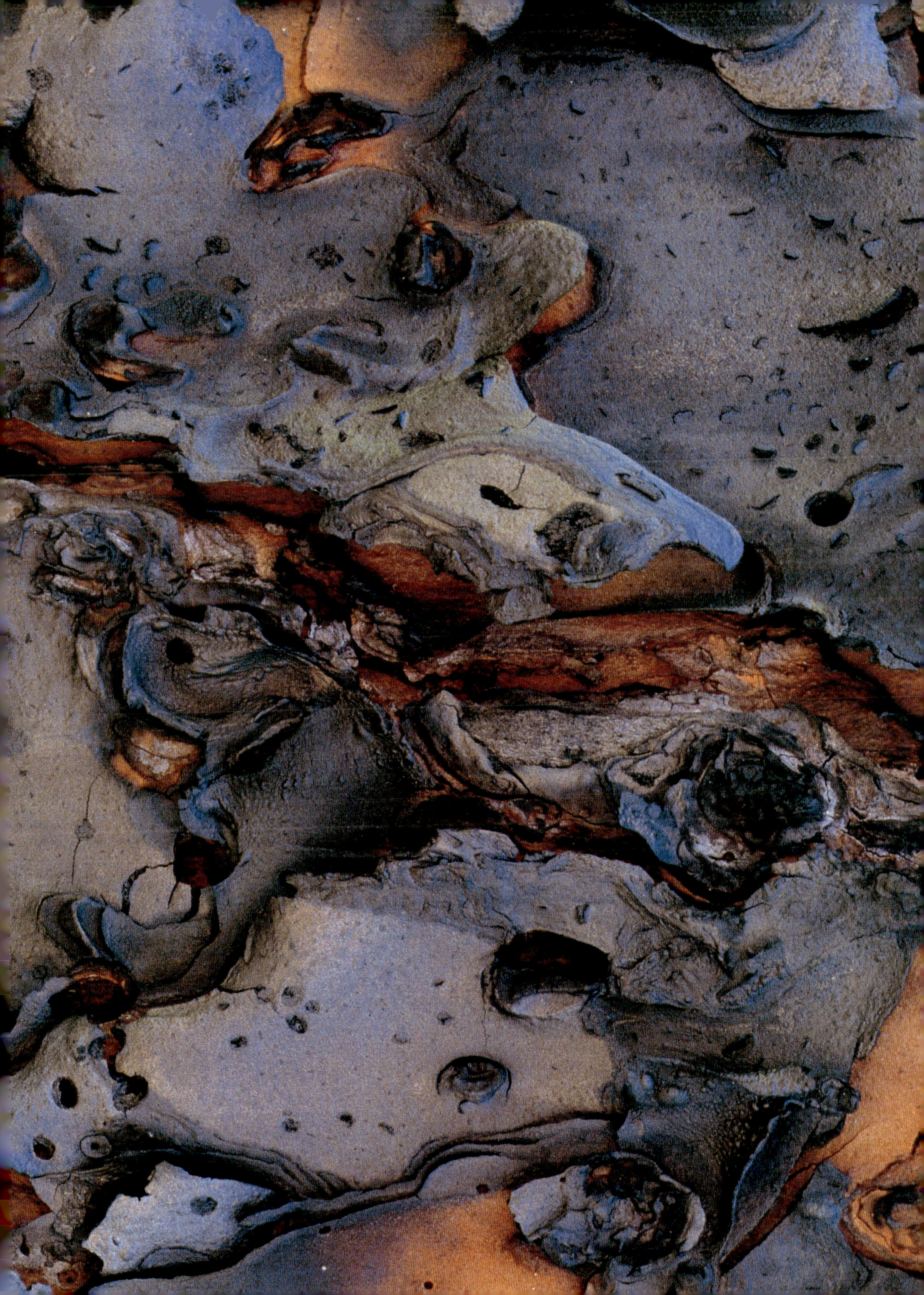

15 or 20 feet. Anoles and frogs like to crawl in and out of these water receptacles. The bromeliads and lush ferns cover some large overhanging tree limbs. Occasionally red-shouldered and short-tailed hawks can be glimpsed flying overhead.

To return to the paved Gumbo-Limbo Trail, hikers must remember to double back on the roadbed.

LONG PINE KEY

The Long Pine Key area is covered with pine forest. The forest floor here is sharp limestone with thick growths of palmettos, ferns and wildflowers. These palmettos, when backlit by the sun, create some truly striking patterns of symmetry.

Warblers frequent the picnic area, as do red-shouldered hawks. Barred owls also nest in this area, but visitors should exercise care to not harass these birds. Their young have been known to fall from the nest when there is increased activity under the nesting tree.

Butterflies visit the wildflowers here in great numbers, and tree frogs hide themselves until nightfall. Squirrel tree frogs have been observed in and around the rest rooms.

A number of fire roads serve as trails where tree snails may be found, but it takes persistence to find them. During or after a thunderstorm, these snails may move about briefly. The park system control-burns in this area to insure the continued existence of the pinelands. The burned bark of the fire-resistant slash pines exhibits some fascinating patterns for close-up abstract photography. The area is also a prime habitat for white-tailed deer.

PA-HAY-OKEE

The one-mile road that ends in the Pa-Hay-Okee parking lot leads through a dwarf cypress forest. During the winter months, the trees here appear to be dead, like bleached skeletons.

At its start, the boardwalk leads into vast expanses of sawgrass. Sometimes animal tracks can be seen here in the soft oolite, and red-shouldered hawks can be heard calling in the distance.

After a short distance, steps lead up to a 20-foot observation tower that commands a view of a large cypress dome to the northeast. Foliage that has grown up here now partially obscures the view.

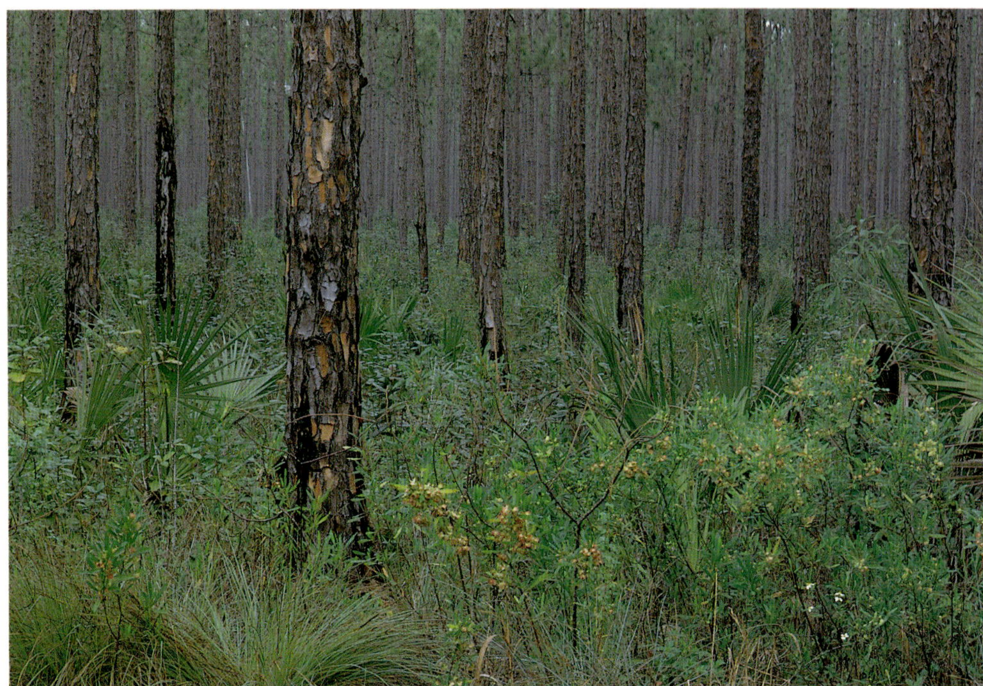

Pine forest, Long Pine Key, 80-200mm lens, 1 second at f/16

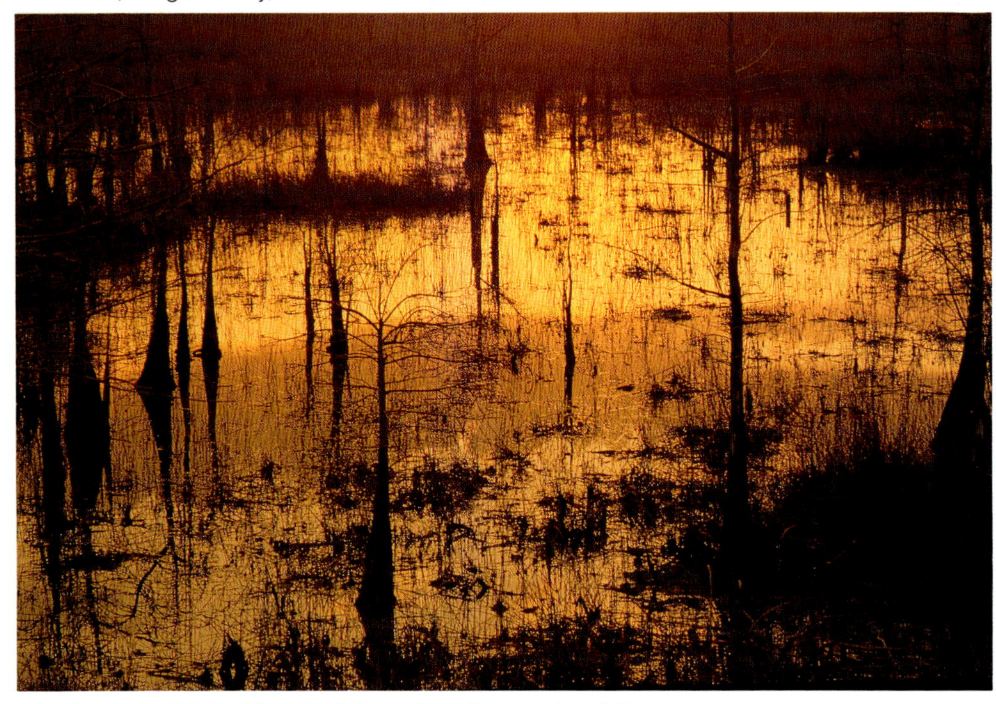

Dwarf cypress, Pa-Hay-Okee, 80-200mm lens, 3 seconds at f/16

The Pa-Hay-Okee Trail boardwalk is one of the shortest in the park. Invariably, the best photographs are to be had from the road's edge at sunrise, where the warm light gives color to the otherwise nearly silver trees and where a darker sky offers contrast. To emphasize the small stature of the dwarf cypress, shoot pictures from a higher angle (such as the observation tower).

At midday, the grasses are usually hard to photograph due to the constant wind. Vultures and hawks frequent the cypress trees along the roadside in search of carcasses or small prey.

MAHOGANY HAMMOCK

The Mahogany Hammock boardwalk winds through a classic example of a lush, jungle-like forest, with gumbo-limbo, satin leaf, strangler fig and the largest known mahogany tree in the United States. The boardwalk starts off on lower ground, then ascends to about 10 feet, where it offers a unique view of the hammock.

Periphyton, a colorful mix of different types of algae, can be seen near the start of the boardwalk. Tall, spiny-edged sawgrasses grow in the soil here, which holds moisture during periods of drought. Near the exhibit area, a large strangler fig has wrapped itself around a host tree.

The boardwalk winds through some darkly shaded areas, where only a few bright spots of sunlight penetrate the dense canopy. Here, cabbage palms with fan-shaped leaves are usually backlit strikingly, creating interesting visual patterns.

Myriads of spiderwebs, attached to fallen, rotting trees and to six-foot ferns, sway in the breezes. A number of air plants and orchids also can be seen here.

White-crowned pigeons are found here during the winter months. Unfortunately, the delicately colored tree snails are usually pilfered when they come within arm's reach of the boardwalk.

Visitors who listen closely may be rewarded by the call of nearby barred owls, which sometimes call to one another during the day.

PAUROTIS POND

Paurotis Pond (named for the rare, clump-growing paurotis palm) is indisputably one of the best areas in the park for viewing and photographing sunsets.

The paved parking area here is only 30 feet from the pond's edge. A number of trees, however, have grown sufficiently tall to obscure the view; as a result, the old boat-launch area is the ideal spot for sunset watchers.

A variety of grasses grow at water's edge, and nearby are several small mangroves that are ideal for silhouetting against the orange reflections in the water as the sun sets behind a large mangrove island. The finest array of colors materializes here about 20 to 30 minutes after the sun sinks behind the horizon. Of course, not every sunset is necessarily intense, but most offer new and different patterns.

Just before sunset, large flocks of white ibis and egrets fly overhead to roost on the distant islands for the night. This impressive sight continues for as long as 30 minutes as lines of birds are silhouetted against the evening sky.

Watch for a couple of alligators that often glide in quite close and can be framed in silhouette at the water's edge. But be very careful: These alligators make it a habit to return because they have been fed by tourists contrary to law. These gators are not tame; they provide a potentially dangerous scenario for humans of all ages.

When the birds soaring overhead begin

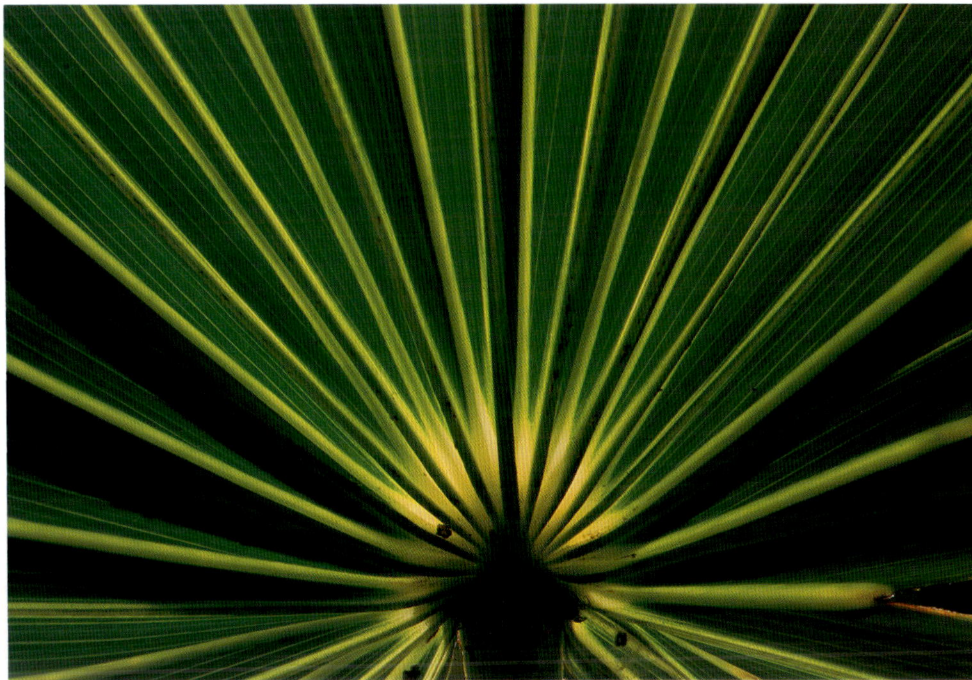

Palmetto, Mahogany Hammock, 55mm micro lens, 1/15 second at f/11

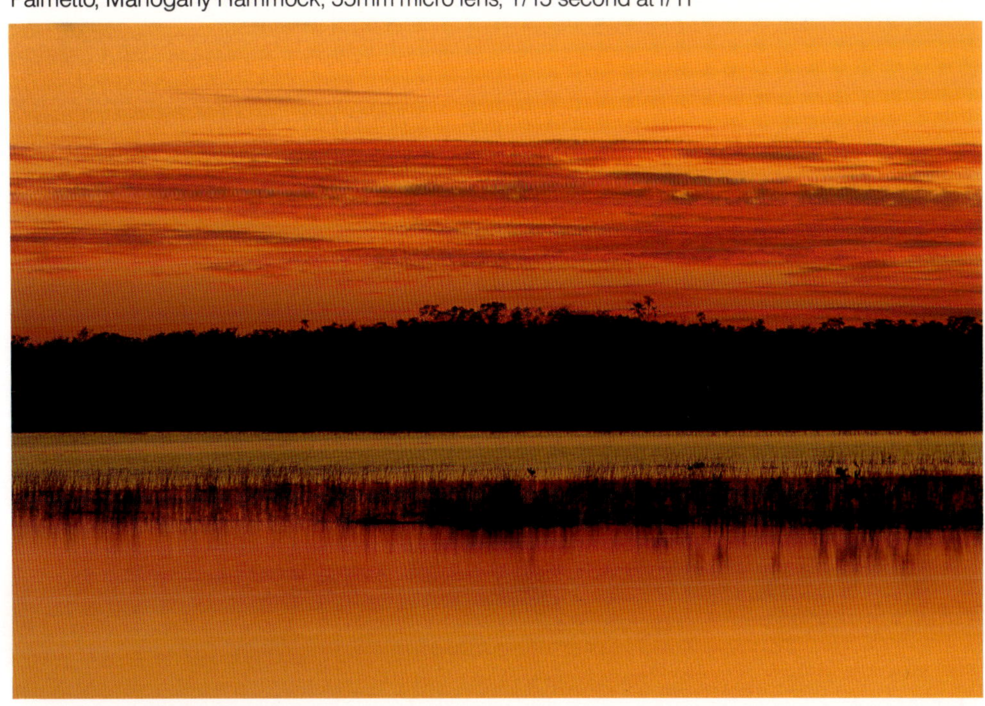

Sunset, Paurotis Pond, 300mm lens, 1/2 second at f/16

to settle in and roost for the evening, another far less welcome creature begins to move about in great numbers: the mosquito. These insects can be absolutely horrendous at sunset. Visitors should apply bug repellent and wear layered clothing, since the night air is frequently quite cool.

One of the best views of red mangroves can be had just before sunset on the opposite side of the main road. Photographers should take note of the lengthening shadows here and be careful to avoid appearing in their own pictures. One sug-

gestion for averting this problem is to stand on the top of a vehicle if it is designed to withstand a person's weight.

NINE-MILE POND

Nine-Mile Pond is a large brackish pond that can be attractively photographed at sunrise, though its size and openness make it prone to choppy waters and less ideal for photography than West Lake.

Grasses grow at the pond's edge, and, in the winter, caspian terns, cormorants, wading birds and alligators may be glimpsed.

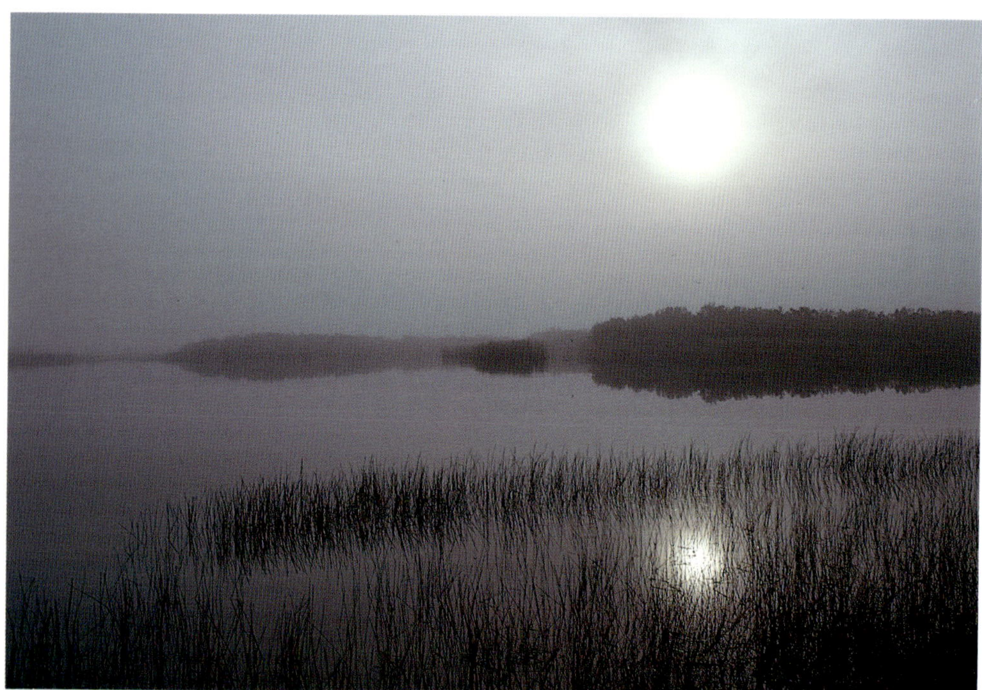

Fog and pond, Nine-Mile Pond, 28mm lens, 1/4 second at f/16

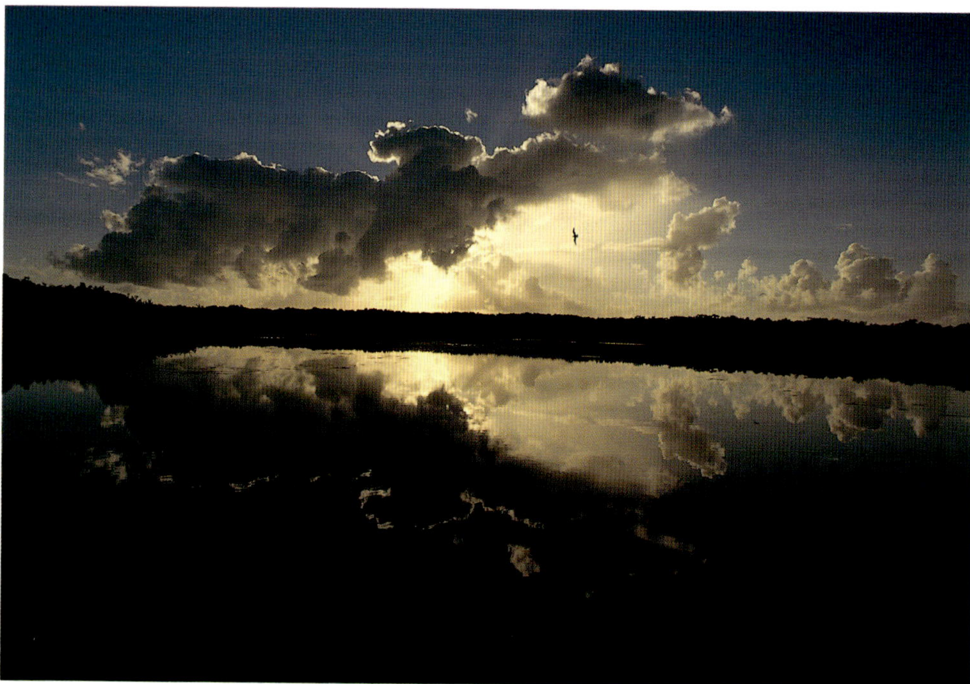

Sunrise, West Lake, 20mm lens, 1/30 second at f/16

water level drops (unless there are unseasonal rains). When the level reaches a certain point, birds flock here from all over. In fact, it is not uncommon to see several hundred birds feeding here at the same time. Unfortunately, this phenomenon sometimes makes it impossible to photograph a single bird, so it may be necessary to try to balance the composition with several birds.

Certainly early morning is the best time to arrive, right at sunrise. A grassy area in front of the pond provides a workable location to set up and take pictures. The sun comes up at an angle that offers strong backlighting for the birds. Fill-in flash can be used to bring out the texture of the birds' feathers.

When sitting or standing motionless, I have had roseate spoonbills walk over to within inches of me, and once a spoonbill even brushed its wings across my head as it flew by.

Visitors should be alerted that just a few hours after sunrise the birds here usually abandon the pond for the day.

COOT BAY POND

Coot Bay Pond is the only wild area in the continental United States where I have ever seen an American crocodile — and that was but once. More commonly viewed are the red-shouldered hawks, which perch back in the dense trees, and the night herons.

On two separate occasions, while returning from a late-night visit with a friend who lives in Homestead, I glimpsed the rare Florida panther near the side of the road in the Coot Bay Pond area.

FLAMINGO

Flamingo is where the road ends at the very tip of Florida's peninsula. Once a small fishing village, Flamingo now is host to a marina with a general store, fuel station, restaurant, gift shop, park visitor center, lodge, cottages and campground.

Black skimmers, brown pelicans, black vultures and laughing gulls can be seen in the vicinity of the marina — often in abundance during the evening hours. At night, yellow-crowned night herons frequent the piers.

Sunset cruises sail from the marina, and small boats can be rented to permit close-up viewing of wading and shorebirds on the mud flats.

WEST LAKE

West Lake provides a fine opportunity for the "classic" lake shot at sunrise. This lake is surrounded by mangroves, which block the wind and create a mirror-like surface for clouds lit by the early-morning sun to reflect in. Several piers here next to the boat ramp and rest room/exhibit area offer a fine vantage from which to shoot. To take in a large portion of West Lake, use a wide-angle 20mm or 28mm lens.

Invariably, one or more alligators will show up here and provide a nice contrast to the hundreds of black, duck-like coots that move together like a mass of seaweed.

A quarter-mile boardwalk leads to the edge of an estuary, winding through black and red mangroves. Buttonwood and white mangrove trees can be glimpsed in areas where the tide does not reach.

MRAZEK POND

Located along the roadside approximately 2½ miles from Flamingo, small Mrazek Pond can be host, at the right time, to one of the most magnificent displays of birds accessible to the general visitor.

During the winter months, the pond's

For a number of years now, a pair of bald eagles have nested on a nearby mangrove island visible through telescopes mounted on the second-level walkway to the left of the restaurant. Be warned, however: It is illegal to step off onto any island and disturb wildlife.

Osprey nest in trees in front of the lodge, and red-shouldered hawks nest in the campground area. In addition, raccoons can be seen (or heard) running around the lodge and cabin areas at night. Marsh rabbits and an occasional bobcat may also be glimpsed.

Eco Pond, located on the right side of the road between the cabins and campground, has been grown over in parts with a tremendous stand of cattails. The National Park Service has built an elevated observation platform here so that visitors may more easily view the small island and its host of roseate spoonbills, white ibis, great egrets, snowy egrets and other birds. I have even seen bald eagles and osprey soar overhead at about 25 feet.

At sunrise and sunset, Florida Bay is especially magnificent. The amphitheater adjacent to the campground at the water's edge is the best location for viewing the sunrise. Several palms can be silhouetted here against the early-morning sky, with the bay reflecting the oranges of the rising sun.

About 50 yards away, visitors may glimpse a large mangrove that has appeared in probably more photographs of the Everglades than any other single tree.

Cormorants stand with outstretched wings on old pilings, joined by the occasional great white heron. Pelicans glide just inches over the water and dive for fish, their wings folded before they plummet into the bay. To photograph early-morning colors reflected in the bay's waters, visitors will be at the mercy of the variable winds here.

SHARK VALLEY

Shark Valley is approximately one and a half hours from the main entrance to the Everglades National Park. It is located 40 miles west of Miami, just off the Tamiami Trail.

There is a large parking area here with rest rooms and a gift shop. In addition, concession-operated trams take visitors on two-hour trips along the 15-mile paved

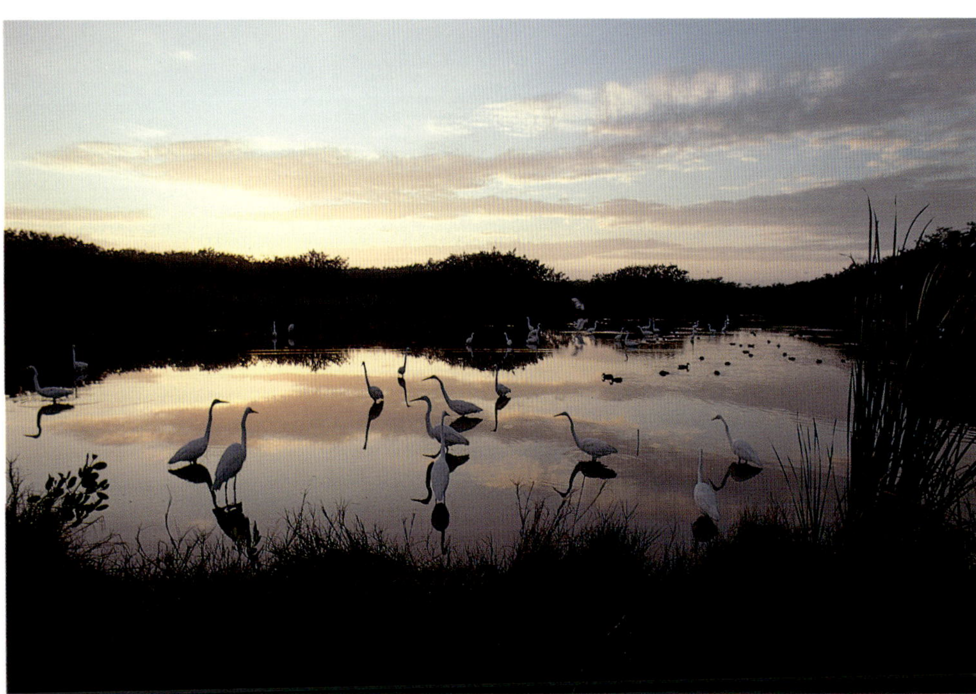

Egrets at sunrise, Mrazek Pond, 20mm lens, 1 second at f/11

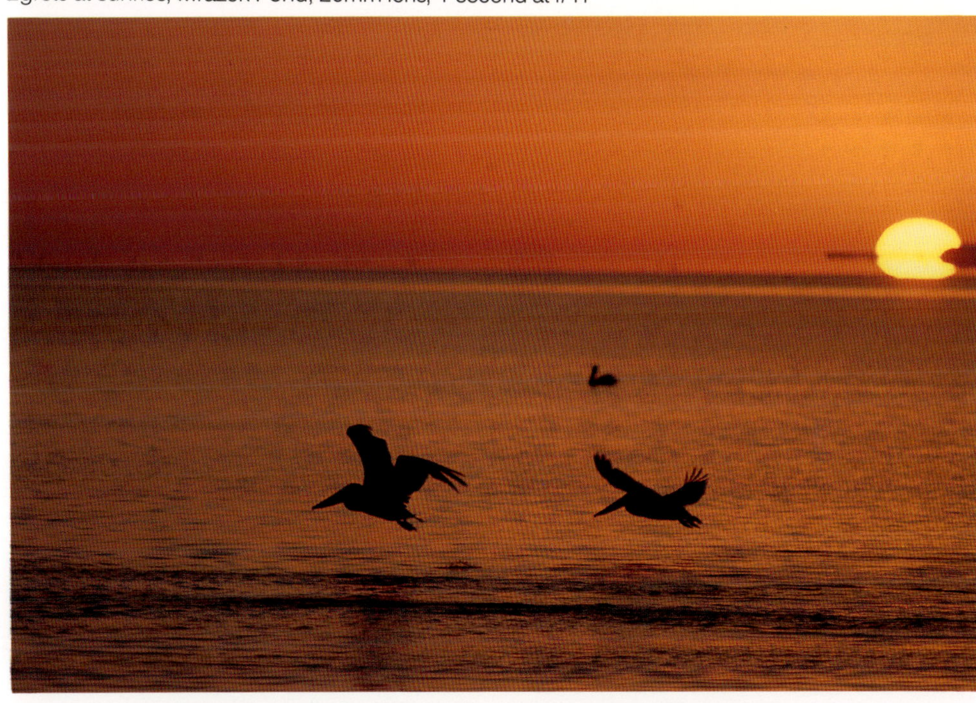

Pelicans at sunrise, Flamingo-Florida Bay, 300mm lens, 1/500 second at f/4

loop road. Bicycles can be rented, and foot travel is permitted on the loop.

The tram offers experienced personnel who interpret the area as the open-air cars move along. I prefer riding the tram in the late morning for an introduction to and overview of anything new or of particular interest in the area.

Early morning is the best time to take photographs along the canal on the right side of the parking area. This area is host to limpkins, which feed on the apple snails, and also the Everglade kite.

In addition, purple gallinules, night herons, tricolored herons, river otters and more alligators than anywhere else in the park have been seen here. Curiously, these alligators appear to be larger than those seen in other areas of the park.

Visitors should consider climbing the 65-foot observation tower, where the tram makes a brief stop. The tower provides an aerial view of the glades and gators below.

Watch for small eyes protruding from the water along the canal, where pickerel weed and arrowhead grow. Baby alligators are plentiful here, gliding quietly in search of food.

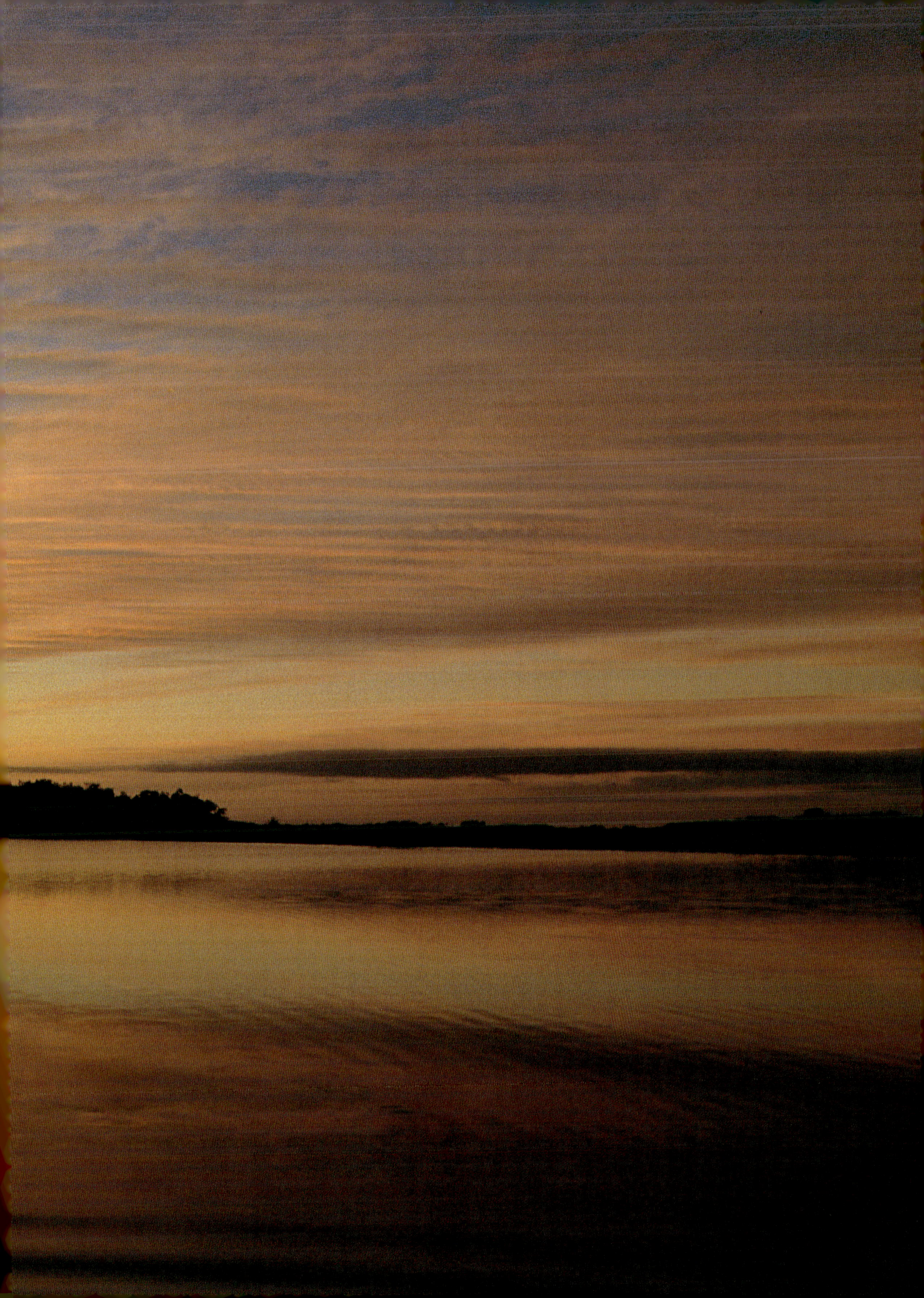

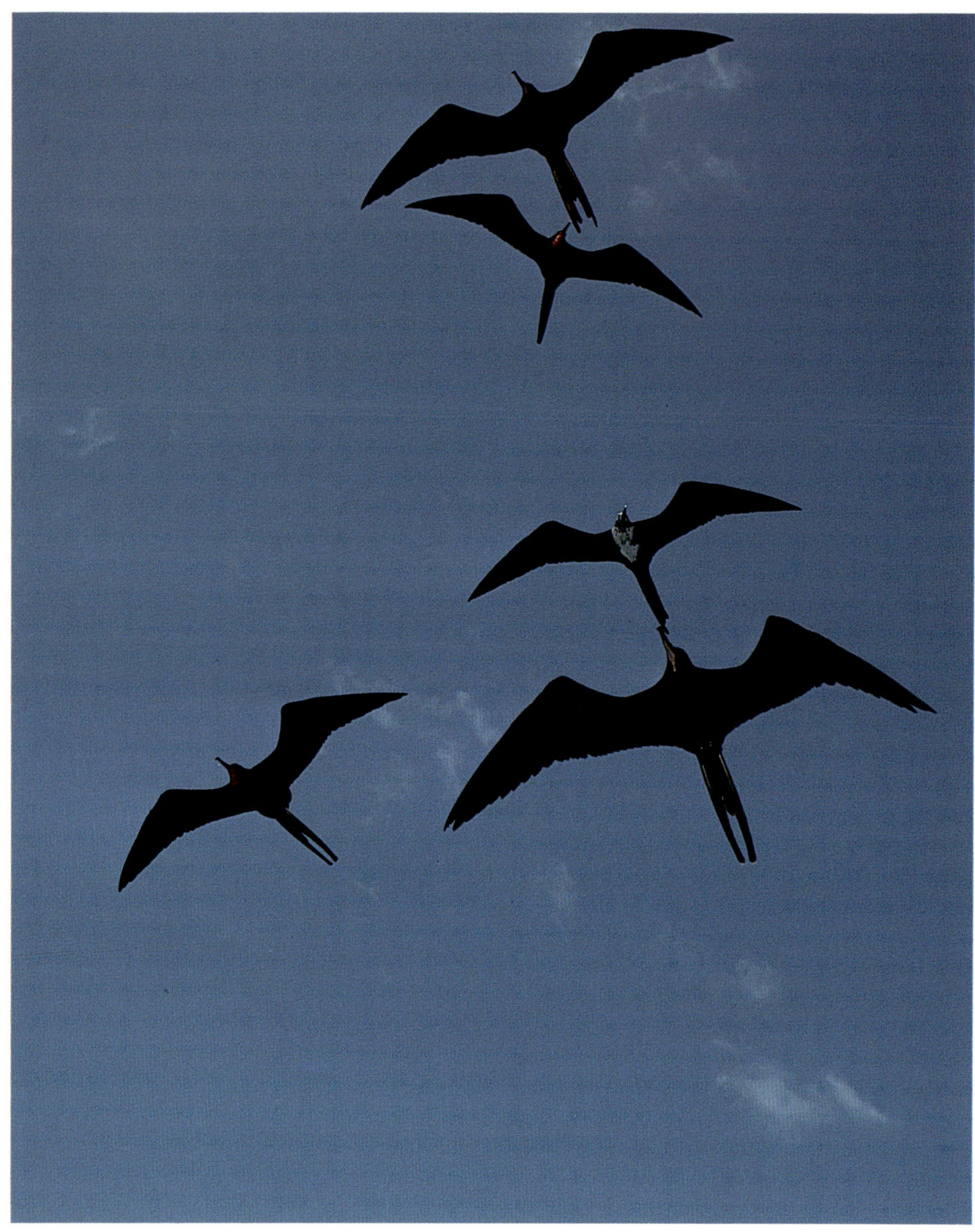

Frigatebirds, Ft. Jefferson, 80-200mm lens, 1/500 second at f/11

To the left of the parking area is the loop road that leads out toward large expanses of sawgrass. The evening twilight casts a warm glow on the grasses and on white-tailed deer that wander the marshes.

A foot trail known as the Bobcat Boardwalk cuts through the dense tropical vegetation here, and deer, bobcat, alligators, raccoons and marsh rabbits are often present.

Superintendent of Everglades National Park Box 279 Homestead, FL 33030

FORT JEFFERSON NATIONAL MONUMENT

Seven coral islands lie 70 miles west of Key West and are known as the Dry Tortugas. Here, on 16-acre Garden Key, stands massive Fort Jefferson, the largest of all the 19th-century coastal forts. With walls 50 feet tall and 8 feet thick, this now-obsolete fortification is open to visitors, many of whom come to see the Civil War prison that housed Dr. Samuel Mudd, who treated John Wilkes Booth's leg after the assassination of President Lincoln.

Garden Key is the only island that has facilities for visitors. A campground, picnic area and restrooms are available, as well as a boat pier, anchorage and helicopter pad.

Summer birds are the main draw, especially the 100,000 sooty terns and 2,500 brown noddies that nest on Bush Key from March to September. Since Bush Key is closed from March to September to protect these birds, visitors must observe them through binoculars from nearby Garden Key or from boats. Roseate terns also nest on Bush, Hospital and Long Keys from May through September.

All the Keys, except for Loggerhead and Garden, are closed from May through September for turtle nesting season. Hawksbill, green and loggerhead turtles can be found swimming near the coral reefs, and the moat around Fort Jefferson may be filled with young turtles. (The U.S. Park Service collects and releases these babies after one year to enhance their chance of survival.) Frigate birds can be seen flying overhead during the summer. A lighthouse on Loggerhead Key is another attraction.

Fewer than 50 species of plants grow on the Dry Tortugas, since they must all be salt- and drought-resistant.

The Dry Tortugas may be reached by boat or seaplane. Figure on about eight hours by boat or approximately 45 minutes by plane. Rentals are available out of Key West and Marathon.

There is no place to obtain freshwater or food, however, so all supplies must be brought in and taken out.

The many coral reefs here are excellent for snorkeling and scuba diving. Sea anemones, lobsters, staghorn coral, sponges and many species of colorful fish can be seen in great abundance.

A national monument map has marked the best areas for diving and fishing.

Superintendent of Everglades National Park Box 279 Homestead, FL 33030 305-247-6211

GULF ISLANDS NATIONAL SEASHORE

When most people think of Florida, they envision white sandy beaches that stretch for miles on end. Nowadays, most of the white sand beaches on the Gulf Coast are developed, but one large expanse of seashore is still protected: Gulf Islands National Seashore, a 150-mile strip from West Ship Island in Mississippi to Santa Rosa Island in Florida.

Most of this seashore is located on barrier island dunes of white sand held together by sea oats and other vegetation. The seashore is broken into several different areas, with development in between.

The first area you approach from the east side is Naval Live Oaks, on U.S. 98, where the visitors center and administrative headquarters are located. Various interpretive exhibits, audiovisuals and brochures are available here.

As its name implies, this area is covered with live oaks. Since these trees are resistant to salt spray, they have become the dominant species around the marshes.

Although this is not an area of white sand beaches, there are several trails worth exploring. The Beaver Pond Trail in the northeast corner of Naval Live Oaks extends for a little over 1 mile through sandhill forest and marshland border. Visitor Center Trail winds three-quarters of a mile through mainland forest.

If you're looking for white sand beaches, travel south on the Highway 399 bridge that crosses Santa Rosa Sound. Fort Pickens and Santa Rosa offer two fine areas to visit on Santa Rosa Island.

Fort Pickens is located at the west end of Santa Rosa Island. Visitors may wander through the historical fort, constructed between 1829 and 1834, and there is a 200-site campground and small general store. The unspoiled beaches here can be explored at will — often to best advantage at sunrise, when there are fewer people about.

Two nature trails are found here. Blackbird Marsh Trail loops from Campground A to E for one-half mile through marshes and a maritime forest; Dune Nature Trail begins across from Campground A and winds through the dunes.

Condominiums and motels edge the seashore boundaries, but if you plan to camp in the Fort Pickens area, reserve a campsite at the ranger station before exploring the area to insure a place to stay.

Raccoons can sometimes be heard quarreling around the campgrounds late at night. Sunrises and sunsets are both rather spectacular in this area.

The popular Santa Rosa facility at the eastern end off County Highway 399 is open only during the day, from 8 a.m. to sunset. It offers restrooms, showers and a visitor contact station.

Boardwalks have been built across the fragile sand dunes and should be used. Except for a few shorebirds, such as gulls, sanderlings, willets and the occasional great blue heron, little wildlife is seen on

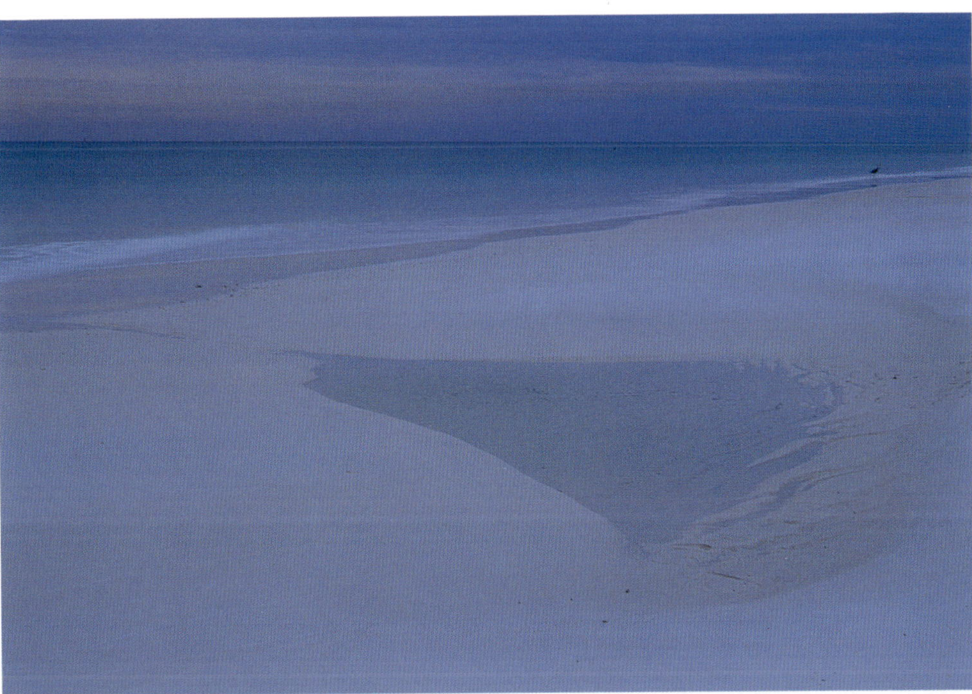

Beach pool, Gulf Islands, 28mm lens, 1 second at f/16

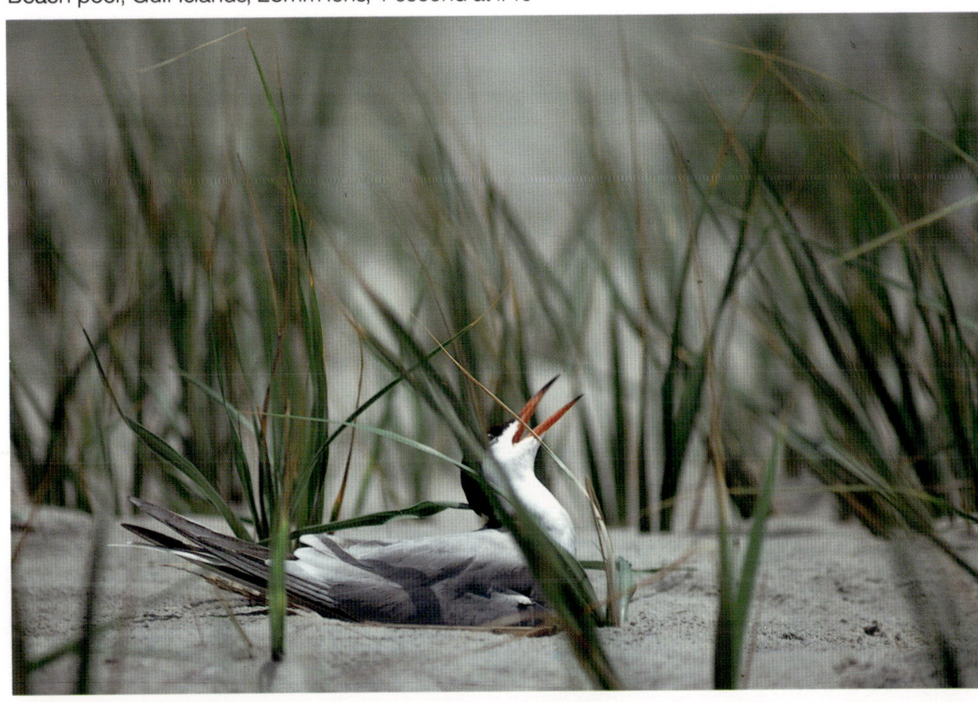

Nesting tern, Gulf Islands, 300mm lens, 1/1000 second at f/5.6

these sand beaches; there are also fewer trees than in other areas. But with over 140,000 acres, there are plenty of coastal plants and flowers, such as sea pink, rockrose, St. John's wort and many hundreds of other floral species.

Superintendent 1801 Gulf Breeze Parkway Gulf Breeze, FL 32561
904-932-0703

THE KEYS

U.S. 1 extends southwest of Miami well over 100 miles, connecting island after island popularly referred to as the Keys.

While wildlife may not be abundant at first glance, side trips off U.S. 1 often reveal wildlife seldom seen anywhere else in Florida (or, in the case of the endangered key deer, anywhere else in the world).

Plantlife includes some interesting cactus on Big Pine Key and birds like the Wurdemann's heron (a rare hybrid between the great blue and great white heron) that stays near the bridge of No Name Key.

Brown pelicans soar with you as you cross Seven-Mile Bridge, where just offshore thousands of wading and diving birds roost in the Great White Heron National Wildlife Refuge. Key West National Wildlife Refuge offers the only known nesting area in the United States of the magnificent frigatebird. The National Audubon Society's research station is located in Tavernier at 115 Indian Mound Trail for the latest birding information.

Many visitors descend on the Keys in the winter, but local residents say the summer, even if warmer, offers clearer and calmer waters.

KEY LARGO

Approximately 6,000 reefs are found between Key Biscayne and the Dry Tortugas. The best — and most frequently visited — are located within the boundaries of John Pennekamp Coral Reef State Park and the Key Largo Coral Reef National Marine Sanctuary. This area contains nearly 178 nautical square miles of coral reefs, seagrasses and mangrove swamps. More than 50,000 people visit this underwater state park each year.

Facilities include 47 campsites, a concession building, visitors center, bath house, restrooms, boat docks and marina. The emphasis here is on snorkeling, scuba diving and viewing the reefs through glass-bottom boats. Rangers offer special snorkeling programs to instruct visitors in the proper way to observe a coral reef without damaging it.

Large numbers of migrating warblers can often be seen along the hardwood hammock nature trail here.

Since this is one of Florida's most popular state parks, reservations should be made well in advance. Boat rentals are also available. Particular caution should be taken to avoid touching or dropping anchor on any coral, for these reefs are still active living organisms.

John Pennekamp Coral Reef State Park
P.O. Box 487 Key Largo, FL 33037

MARATHON KEY

Marathon Key is one of the largest and most populated keys. The main wildlife attraction here is the burrowing owl, which can be located in several areas. If you travel south on U.S. Highway 1, you will see a small airport located on the right; several burrows of the owl can be found just in front of the airport. On the left there is one particular burrow with an entrance frequently littered with shredded paper.

A little farther south, and to the left, Marathon's golf course is home to several owls. The owls here can be seen in the early

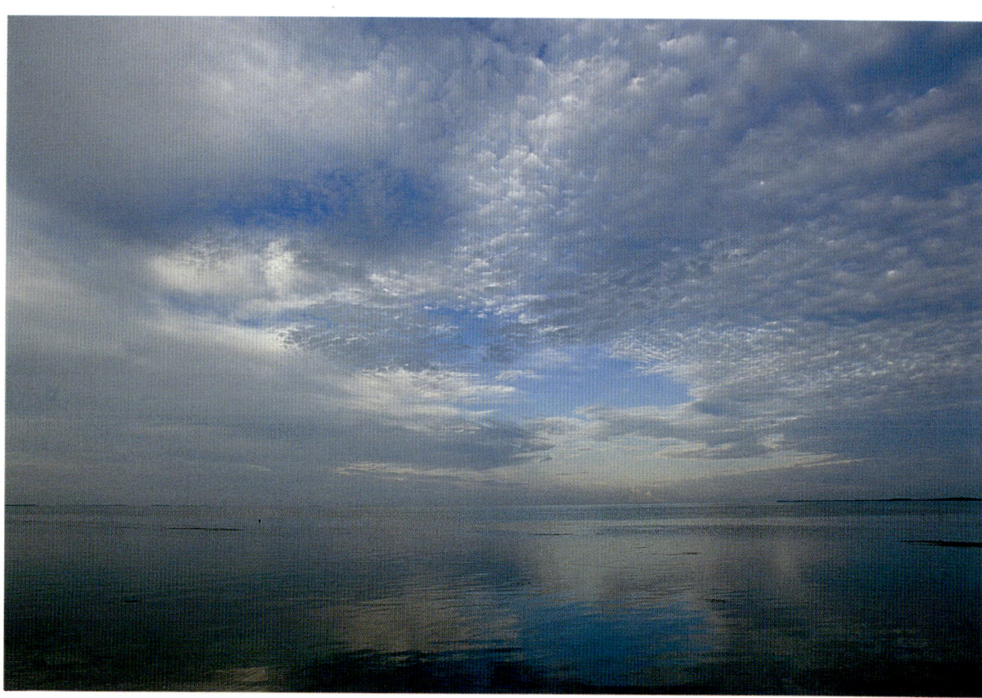

Clouds over water, Keys, 55mm lens, 1/4 second at f/16

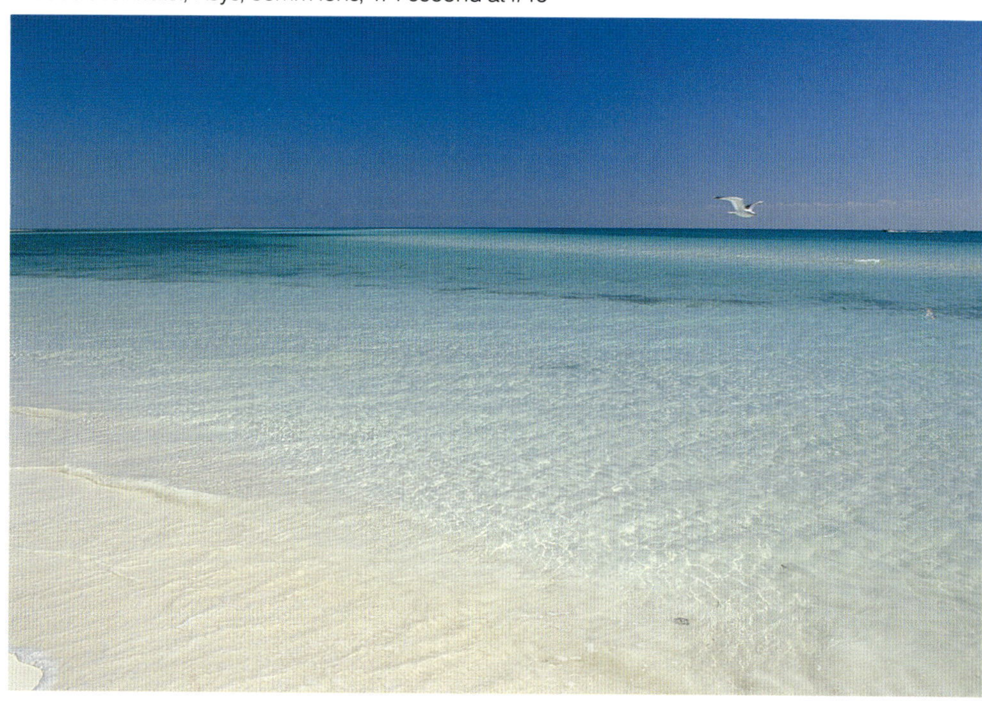

Turquoise waters, Bahia Honda, 28mm lens, 1/60 second at f/16

evening sitting on fences or at the entrances to their burrows. These burrowing owls will tolerate human approach, since they are accustomed to golfers playing through. Use a long lens so as to disturb them as little as possible.

Several excursions may be taken from Marathon Key. Seaplanes and charter boats to the Dry Tortugas can be boarded here. This is also a good location to rent a boat to see the Great White Heron National Wildlife Refuge.

This refuge—nearly 7,000 acres of keys in an area 40 miles long and 8 miles wide—is home to the great white heron, which occurs only in south Florida and the Keys. Thousands of brown pelicans, and double-crested cormorants frequent the mangrove-covered islands.

There are numerous restrictions on approaching this area, and no landing is permitted. Fortunately, many of these birds stand on sandbars and can be photographed easily.

BAHIA HONDA KEY

Bahia Honda Key has one of the few — and one of the best — sand beaches in the Florida Keys. Located in the Bahia Honda State Park, the key boasts handsome white sands and turquoise waters. The entrance, located immediately off U.S. Highway 1, is on the Atlantic side.

Least terns, royal terns, black skimmers and a variety of gulls are some of the many shorebirds that frequent the area. A few frigatebirds have been spotted soaring overhead in summer, but they are much more common around Key West and the Dry Tortugas.

Various tropical hammocks here play host to satinwood, spiny catestaea and dwarf morning glories.

A nature trail at the far end of Sandspur Beach follows the shore of a tidal lagoon through a coastal strand hammock and back to the beach.

The park opens at 8 a.m. and closes at sunset year-round. Cabins and campgrounds are available.

Bahia Honda State Recreation Area
Route 1, Box 782 Big Pine Key, FL 33043

BIG PINE KEY

Big Pine Key is home to the smallest deer in North America: the key deer. A subspecies of the larger Virginia white-tailed deer, the key deer now numbers fewer than 300 animals. The National Key Deer Refuge is headquartered on Big Pine Key, with more than 4,000 acres of slash pine, thatch palms with red and black mangroves extending into saltwater estuaries.

It is hard to determine where the refuge begins and ends, but the whole island is populated by the tiny deer. Watch for refuge boundary signs and obey all posted speed limits, since most deaths of the deer are attributed to cars. By all means, don't feed the deer.

To reach the refuge, turn onto Key Deer Boulevard from U.S. Highway 1. A variety of paths are provided for viewing the deer, although most deer are usually seen crossing back roads. If you turn left onto Watson Boulevard, you will find the refuge headquarters at the end; more information can be obtained here, and personnel are available to answer questions.

Further down Key Deer Boulevard and to the left is the Blue Hole area, where a water-filled quarry holds ducks and alligators and serves as an important source of freshwater for the deer.

Even further down Key Deer Boulevard, and again on the left, is a nature trail that

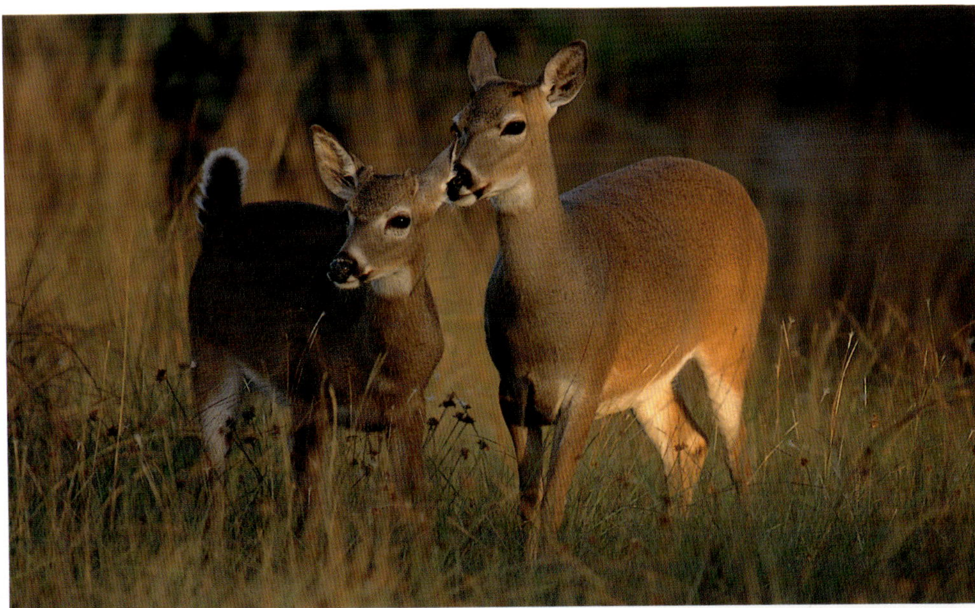

Key deer, Big Pine Key, 500mm lens, 1/60 second at f/4

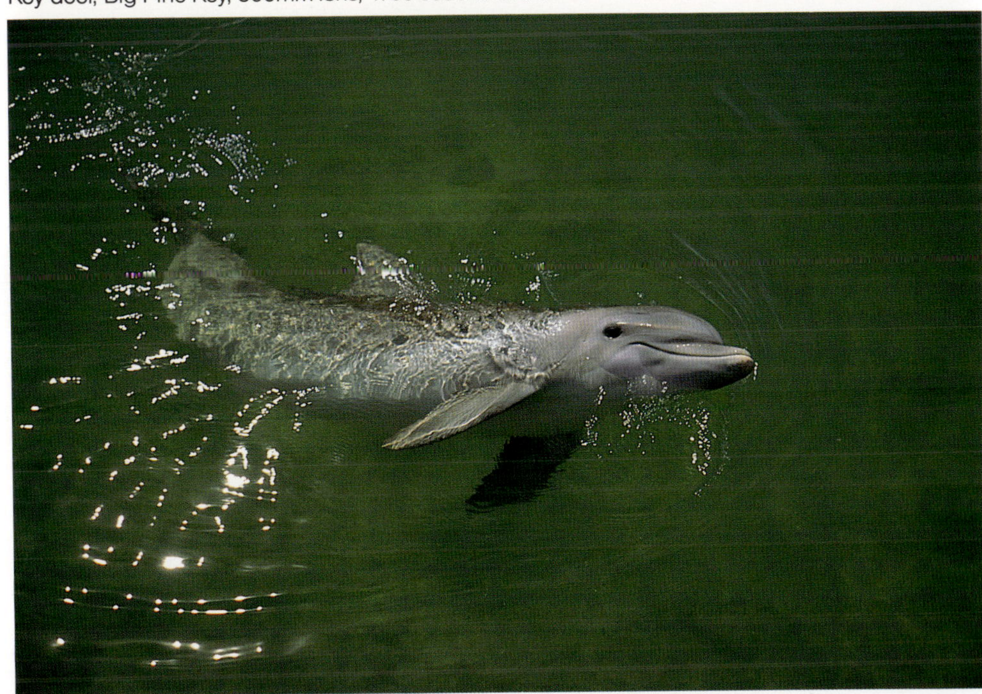

Dolphin, Grassy Key, 55mm lens, 1/60 second at f/8

winds through slash pine and palms. This trail is covered with pea gravel and is surprisingly noisy, so walk as quietly as possible. (If there is any breeze, however, the rustling of palm leaves will usually cover the noise.)

Locals will tell you how common the sightings of key deer are, but remember these people live here and are more likely to glimpse animals because they travel these roads every day — especially since the residential area and the refuge seem to intermingle.

At the very end of Key Deer Boulevard is an open grassy area with trees scattered about. For me, this has proven the most productive area for viewing the deer. Deer seem reluctant to approach closely, however, since there is less cover without the thatch palms. This area is infested with mosquitoes, so dress in layers. The best times to view the key deer are early morning and late evening.

While you're in the area, I would suggest you drive on over to No Name Key. At the end of the key, a lighter-colored race of raccoons lives in the mangroves and can be seen fairly easily. Despite restrictions, people still come to feed these unusual-looking raccoons.

Refuge Manager P.O. Box 510 Big Pine Key, FL 33043

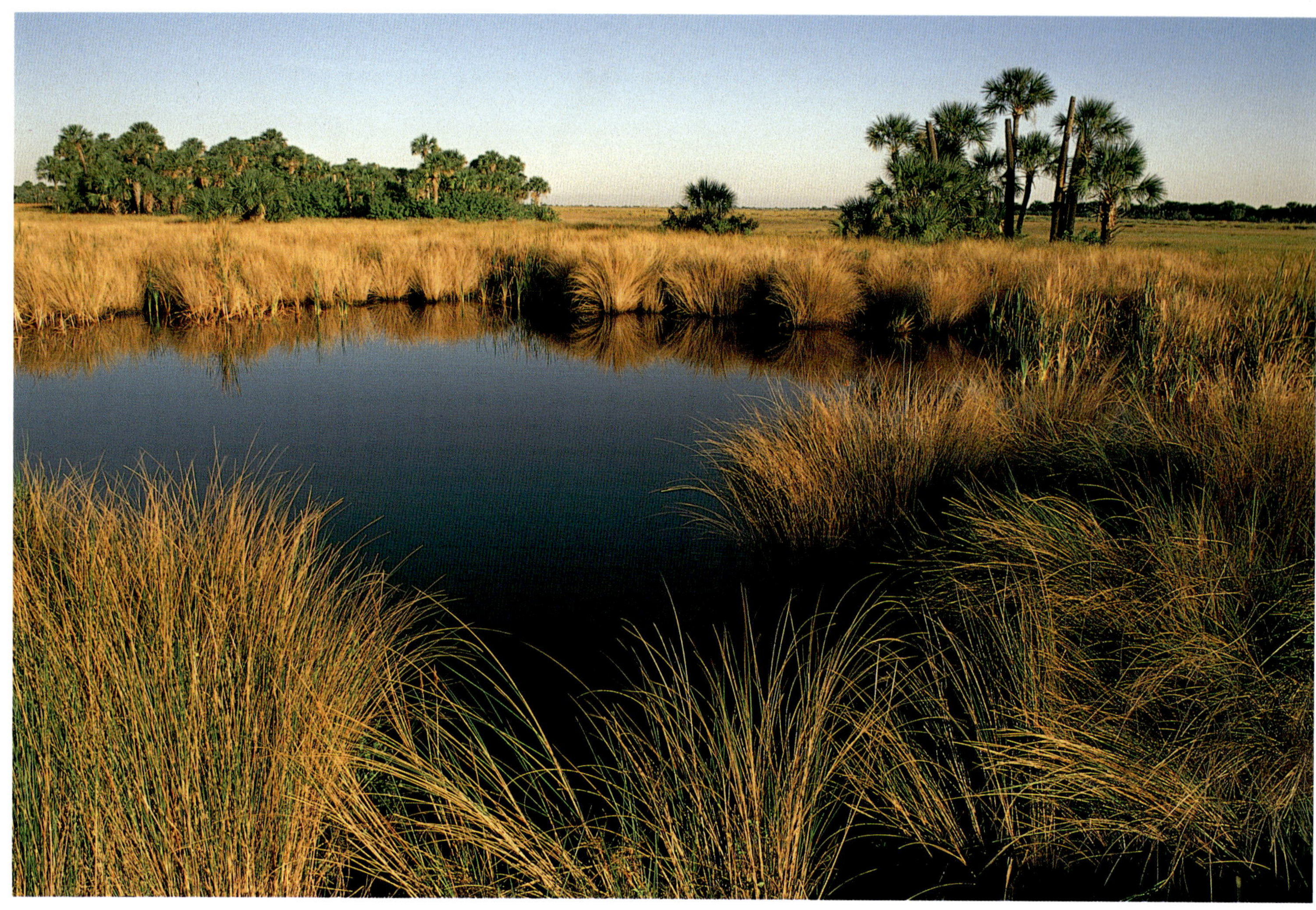

Marsh, Merritt Island, 28mm lens, 1/15 second at f/16

GRASSY KEY

The Dolphin Research Center is located on Grassy Key. This research facility offers a walking tour and a swimming program with dolphins.

The "dolphin encounters" here begin at 9:30 a.m. This facility may get you closer to a dolphin than you're likely to ever be again, and at the same time educate you to this magnificent mammal's habits and needs.

KEY WEST

Key West is probably best known for its celebrated bars, shops and lively nightlife. The usual coastal birds, such as the brown pelican, herons and sandpipers, are seen here, as well as the more unusual white-crowned pigeon, visible in trees near Eisenhower Drive.

Where else can you find a crowd that gathers to watch the sunset and applaud as the sun sinks into the water?

MERRITT ISLAND NATIONAL WILDLIFE REFUGE

Located midway down Florida's Atlantic coast is the 140,393-acre Merritt Island National Wildlife Refuge. This refuge consists chiefly of marshes that are brackish, both salt- and freshwater, with hammocks of palm, oak and pine flatwoods.

Numerous ponds and lagoons abound, the best known of which is named Mosquito Lagoon (with good reason). On calm, windless days, the mosquitoes here are fierce.

More than 280 different species of birds have been recorded here, and it is estimated that as many as 70,000 ducks and 100,000 coots winter here. (The refuge is located beneath the Atlantic flyway.) At sunset, coots silhouetted in the orange-colored waters look like floating islands moving about in masses of thousands.

A strange dichotomy exists here between the primal marshes and the unmistakable signs of the Space Age, visible when one looks across the expanses of grasses and water toward a shuttle pad looming like an ancient monolith at the John F. Kennedy Space Center. When the space shuttle is on the pad, certain key areas are closed off. Visitors should contact the refuge visitors center for information about launches.

One of the best areas for observing and photographing birds is along the Black Point Wildlife Drive. Here, sandy roads have been built atop dikes that allow area managers to raise and lower the water from 6 to 18 inches, creating ideal conditions for egrets, herons and ibises.

There are a number of roadside ponds and several large expanses of water — all of which are best viewed from a car. Unlike at the J.N. "Ding" Darling National Wildlife Refuge, which is so heavily visited,

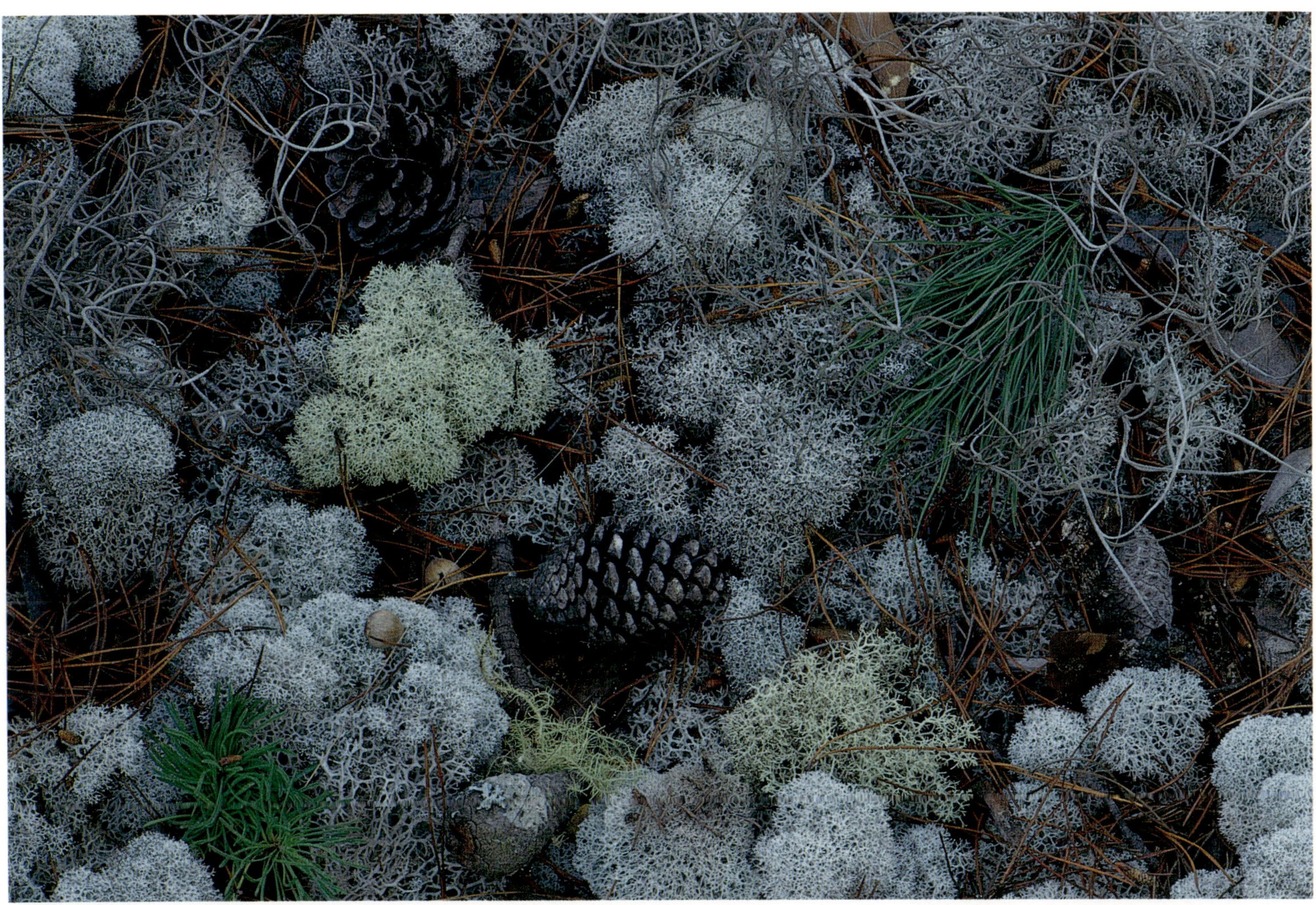

Lichens, Ocala, 55mm micro lens, 1 second at f/32

birds here don't allow you to get out without flying off to some distant feeding area. (See the section entitled ''Photographing from a Car.'')

The speed limit on this 7-mile road is 25 mph, but slower speeds are recommended for locating and viewing wildlife. The road is just wide enough to pull over and allow traffic to pass.

Early morning and late evening are the best times for viewing birds in large numbers — as well as raccoons and bobcats. This is also an area where I have consistently seen large flocks of glossy ibis.

For scenics, you will want to leave your car, for there are several small ponds surrounded by marsh grasses with picturesque palm hammocks in the background. Cruickshank Trail, for example, is a 5-mile foot path leading to a closer view of the marsh.

Occasionally woodstorks and egrets stand in trees near this area and watch the visitors. Ospreys and eagles also nest here, though not in the abundance they used to. It is estimated that Southern bald

eagles have five active nests in the refuge.

Just a few miles past the visitors center is the beginning of Oak Hammock Trail, which winds through dense growths of ferns before crossing railroad tracks into a dense growth of trees, especially oaks. Much of the trail here is a boardwalk, as the low ground is occasionally flooded.

Mosquito Lagoon is not just for mosquitoes. It also hosts a number of white and brown pelicans.

Although armadillos are often encountered flattened on Florida highways, few are actually seen in the wild. The roadsides here at Merritt, however, are prime areas to view these armored mammals as they dig for insects. Terns and gulls also feed in the marsh ponds and on the mudflats.

Since the waters here are contained except on particularly windy days, their surface acts as a mirror and reflects the grasses, palms, birds and sunset colors.

Merritt is less popular than a number of other wildlife refuges in the state (most visitors are interested in the beaches at

nearby Canaveral National Seashore), so you will likely not be bothered here. The visitors center offers some fine books and guides to the area.

Refuge Manager P.O. Box 6504 Titusville, FL 32782-6504
407-867-0667

OCALA NATIONAL FOREST

Ocala is one of the most visited national forests in the entire United States. Located in central Florida, it boasts 430,000 acres of diverse habitat. Ocala's main attraction is its multitude of warm springs, where people can swim or canoe down five canoe runs in the forest system.

Hundreds of campground sites are available throughout the forest. At Alexander Springs, which spouts out some 80 million gallons of water a day, there are 63 campsites; another popular area, Juniper Springs, has 79 sites. During hunting season, deer often retreat into Juniper Springs, where hunting is not permitted.

The Juniper Springs canoe run is a 7-mile

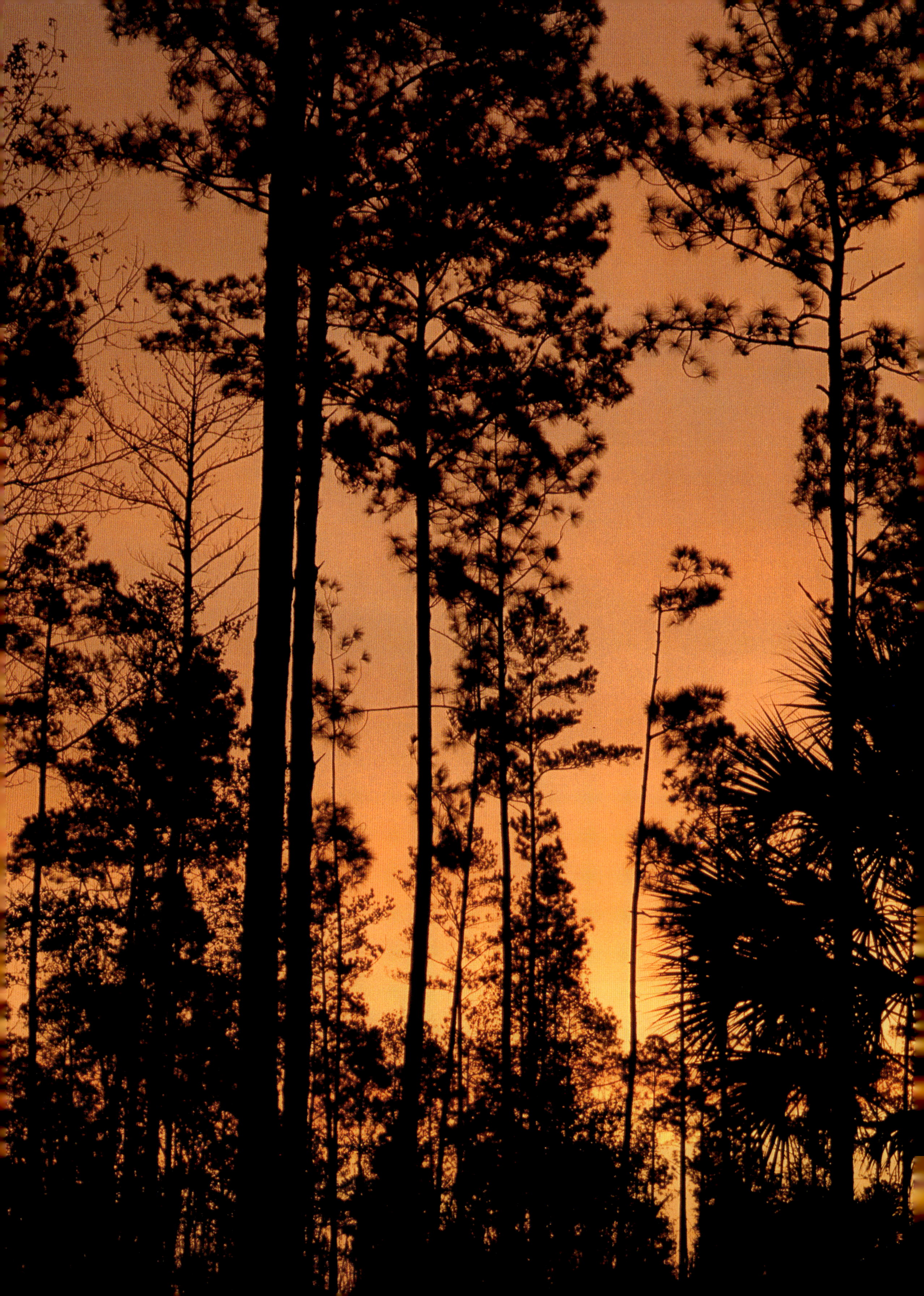

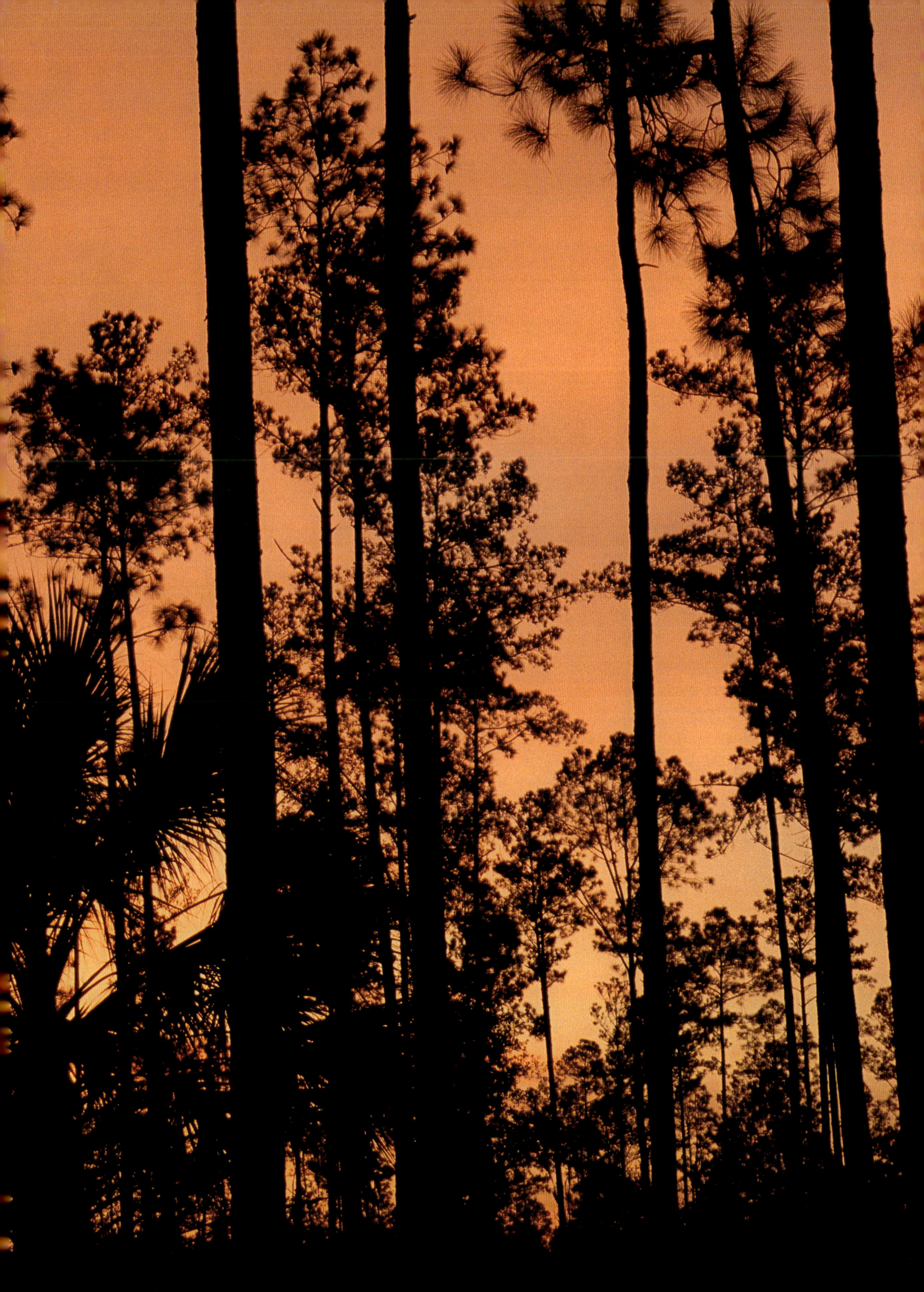

journey that ends at Highway 19; Alexander Springs runs 7 miles to Road 552. Both runs typically require around five hours, though longer and shorter trips are possible. Canoe runs are excellent for viewing wildlife seldom seen in more developed areas.

The largest concentration of big scrub sand pine in the world is found in Ocala — growing in pure sand. The rare gopher tortoise can be found in this area.

At the northern end of the forest, around Pats Island, Norwalk Island and Hughes Island, indigo snakes can also be found.

A recent addition to the forest is Silver Glen, formerly privately held land, which is considered by many to be one of the prettiest areas.

Visitors who swim in the marked area should encounter no problems with alligators.

Many areas in the national forest are developed and have good access roads, but some of them are sandy roads in places like the Big Scrub which require 4-wheel drive.

There are a number of short nature trails for hiking, as well as a 66-mile portion of the Ocala National Recreation Trail, which is part of the Florida National Scenic Trail that will eventually run the length of Florida.

There are also several horseback-riding trails here. The Flatwoods Trail is a 40-mile loop cut through the longleaf pines; the Prairie Trail, also 40 miles, runs through sand pines and grassy prairie. Baptist Lake Trail is 20 miles long and passes by Baptist Lake. All three horse trails are off Highway 19, about two miles north of Altoona.

Lake George is home to nesting bald eagles and many species of wading birds. Eagles, otters and limpkins may be seen along the Oklawaha River, especially in the early morning.

With more than 600 lakes and 23 streams, it is easy to see why Ocala is regarded as such a rich haven for Florida wildlife. Among the more memorable features of Ocala for me are the variety of lichens — often highly photogenic — that flourish in clumps beneath the pines. Since Ocala National Forest is located so close to the city of Silver Springs, there are always accommodations to be found near or in the area.

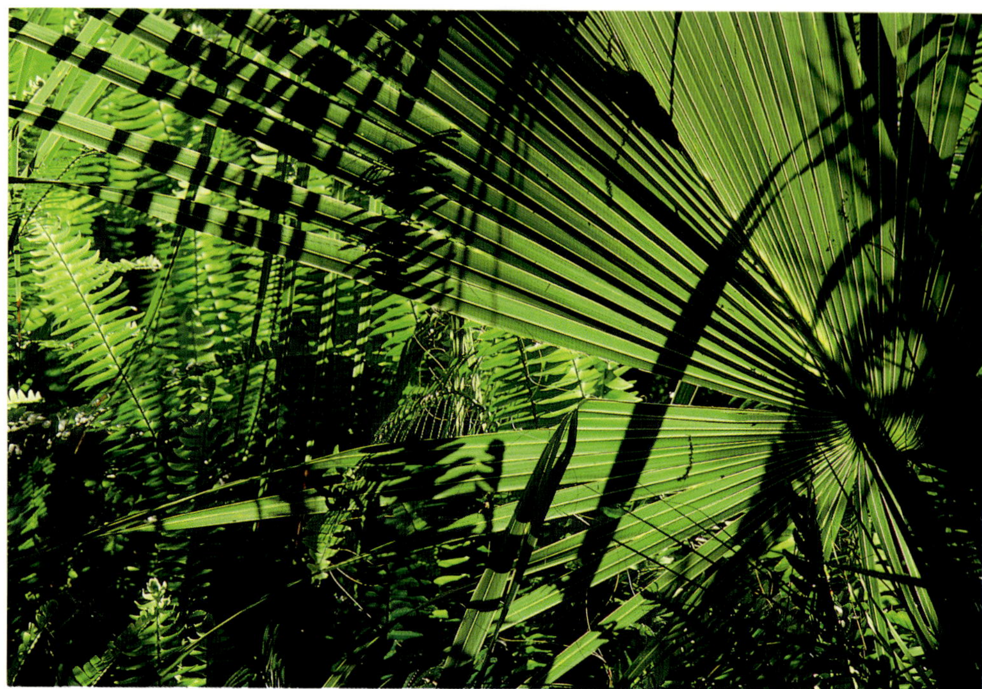

Palms and ferns, Osceola, 80-200mm lens, 1/60 second at f/11

Lake George Ranger District Florida Highway 40 East Route 2, Box 701 Silver Springs, FL 32688 904/625-2520

OSCEOLA NATIONAL FOREST

Osceola is the smallest of Florida's three national forests with 180,000 acres. Roughly one-third of the forest is in swamp or wetlands — something not readily apparent from the large expanses of pines that visibly dominate the forest along the main highways.

Penetrate the interior, however, and you will find a 1,760-acre lake, Ocean Pond, rimmed with cypress trees and bands of maidencrane grass that support small fish and frogs. This lake and several others are relatively infertile and do not support large quantities of fish. In the winter, diving ducks such as ringnecks and scaups can be found on Ocean Pond, but, in general, the lake is host to a rather small number of wildlife species.

Big Gum Swamp Wilderness is 13,600 acres of cypress gum swamps with a perimeter of pine flat woods. It is accessible by foot and by horse on the old tram lines.

Osceola has a higher concentration of black bears than Ocala, but they're harder to find. The national forest also has a sizable population of carnivorous plants, such as sundew and pitcher plants.

Deer are more common here in the summer, though they do show up from time to time in nearby O'leno State Park. Sandhill cranes migrate through the northern section, around Impassable Bay, in mid-November, returning on their way back North in March.

Approximately 50 colonies of red-cockaded woodpeckers are active here, primarily along U.S. 90. The largest colony, however, may be found by taking U.S. 90, turning north on Still Road for 1 1/2 miles, then right on Forest Road 278E, which intersects with Forest Road 215S, then 2 miles back to U.S. 90. This entire area is frequented by the endangered woodpecker.

Sherman's fox squirrel — which is about twice the size of the gray squirrel — can be found in this forest. Lochloosa and Orange Lake to the south are out of the national forest boundaries, but they are particularly good for viewing bald eagles and wading birds.

There are 50 units for camping around Ocean Pond, where the Florida Trail passes through.

To the north, Pinhook Swamp has been added to the national forest. The best access to this area is from the north into Georgia. Alligators, woodstorks and other large wading birds are seen here in large numbers.

Osceola Ranger District U.S. Highway 90 P.O. Box 70 Olustee, FL 32072 904/752-2577

SANIBEL

Sanibel is a subtropical barrier island 12 miles long connected to the mainland by a toll causeway. Though this island is covered with condominiums and shops, it hosts some of the best shelling beaches in the world, as well as several wildlife areas, the best known of which is the J.N. "Ding" Darling Wildlife Refuge.

Approximately 300 different species of birds either migrate through or make Sanibel their permanent residence. There are numerous areas open to public parking, but the best are reserved for holders of special parking permits that can be obtained at City Hall for $30 (the same cost as a parking fine).

Two of Sanibel's finest beaches are Bowman's Beach and Turner Beach. Bowman's — Sanibel's prettiest beach — charges admission fees but offers plenty of parking, restrooms and picnic tables. There is a 4-mile stretch of beach here, which is particularly good for sunset photography. Turner Beach has public parking also, and, like Bowman's, it is covered with shells.

Hundreds of varieties of shells wash up on this island all the time, though the best time for collecting is when low tide coincides with early morning. Fewer people are out early in the morning, but visitors should be advised that the beaches are never devoid of shell hunters.

During the winter months, the best shelling is right after a storm has churned the waters; summertime, however, is still the best season for shelling. The water is clearer and much warmer in summer, thus permitting wading and snorkeling. Hurricanes, of course, are something few people wish to experience, but the period immediately following a tropical storm of this nature is actually one of the very best times for shelling.

Other good shelling is done by hiring a boat and locating sandbars that catch the shells first before they are washed ashore. On North Captiva, which is less accessible, the shells are not as picked over as elsewhere. One of the most prized shells here is the junomia, a cream-colored shell with square chocolate markings. Finding this shell will get your picture into the local paper, although, ironically, these very same shells can be purchased in any shell shop for around $9 apiece.

Some areas have limits on the taking of

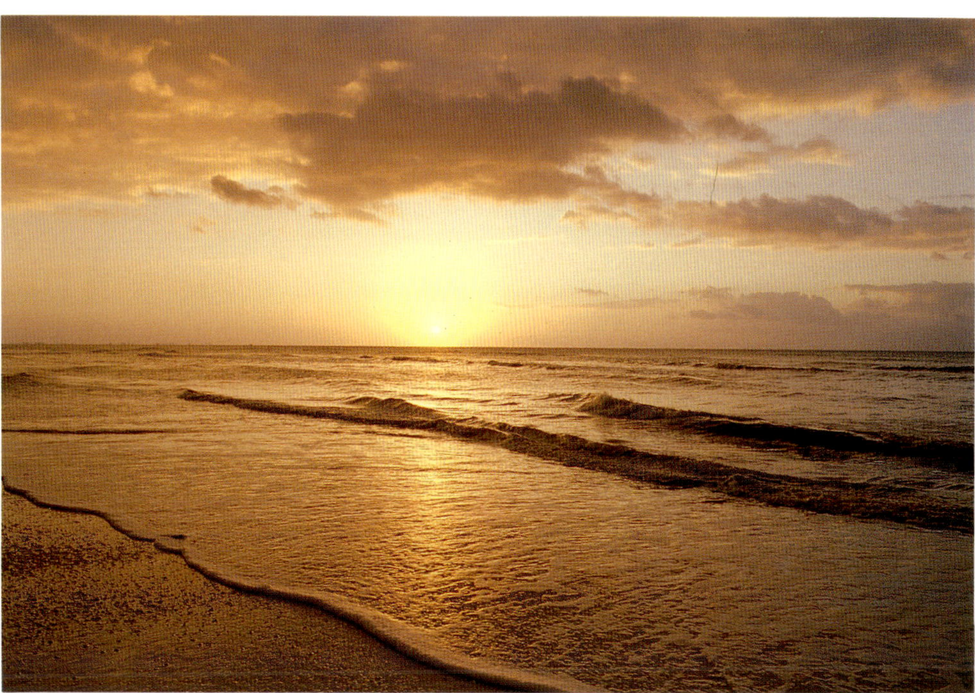

Beach at sunrise, Sanibel, 28mm lens, 1/60 second at f/16

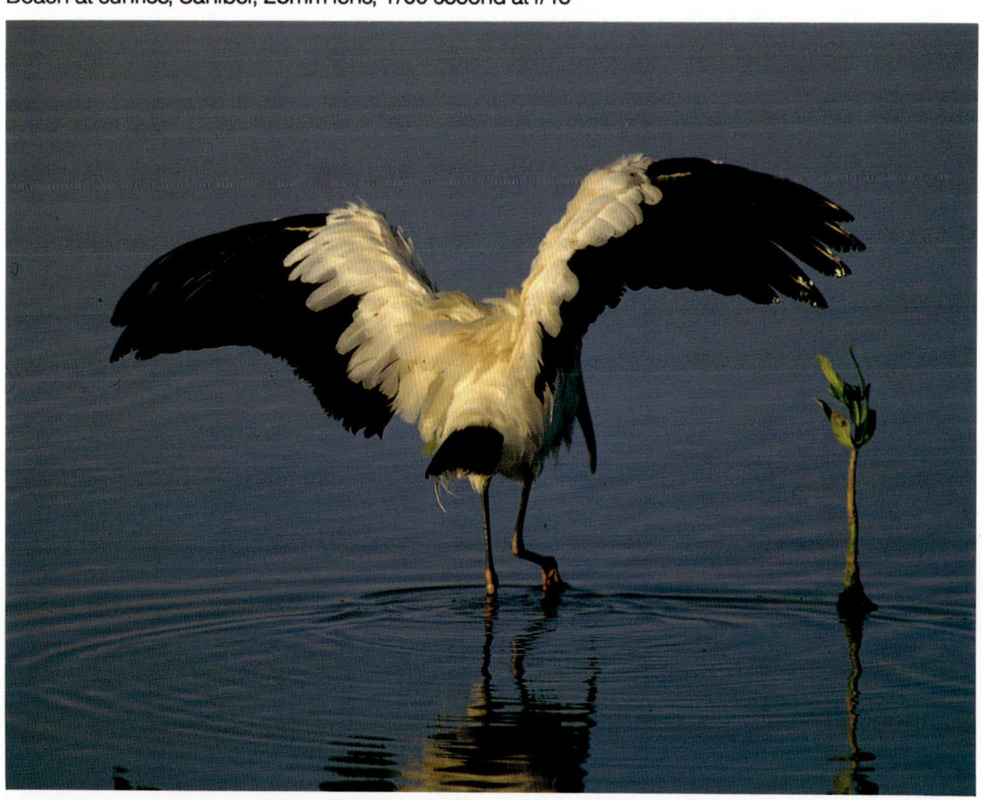

Woodstork, "Ding" Darling, 500mm lens, 1/500 second at f/5.6

live shells; other areas prohibit the taking of any live shells at all. The best shells found by locals have already been long dead.

The J.N. "Ding" Darling Wildlife Refuge — 5,014 acres of water and mangroves — serves as habitat to magnificent displays of virtually every species of Florida wading bird. There is a one-way 5-mile road built on top of dikes originally constructed for mosquito control. To see the most wildlife, visitors should arrive at sunrise just as the

refuge opens its gate. The roadbed is as wide as any other Florida highway, so if you spot an interesting animal, you can pull over without blocking traffic.

The animals — especially the birds — have become accustomed to automobiles and humans, so for the most part they will ignore you. If you decide to get out of your car, exit on the side opposite the animal. Approach your subject slowly; should it show any signs of alarm, stop until it resumes its natural behavior.

The road runs along a canal where anhingas perch in the mangroves, drying their wings. On each side of the road are areas open to wide expanses of water. Great egrets, reddish egrets, spoonbills, white ibis, woodstorks and many other species can be seen wading and feeding. Early morning is the best time for viewing, though in the evening fairly sizable concentrations gather before returning to their night roosts.

With birds on both sides of the road, you can photograph them frontally or backlit as they raise their wings with feathers glowing. When I photograph here in mid to late February, migratory waterfowl and white pelicans are fairly abundant. In April and May, the water level is lower, and birds (especially the spoonbill) converge here in greater numbers.

A number of trails have been opened, as well as a boardwalk, to enable visitors to see the area close up. Osprey feed and nest in this area and often can be glimpsed at close range. Yellow-crowned night herons wade along the road's edge, catching small crustaceans like the young horseshoe crabs so common here. An observation tower affords an excellent view of the surrounding open waters and birds, but if you're trying to take photographs, be aware that any movement can cause severe vibration and ruin pictures taken without a fast shutter speed.

At sunset, the larger wading birds can be photographed in silhouette against the orange reflections in the water. Black skimmers and various species of gulls also frequent the roadside at day's end.

Recently, there have been some seasons or even years when the Everglades were not "productive" photographically, while "Ding" Darling was at its best.

Elsewhere on Sanibel, the Sanibel Conservation Center offers 400 acres and approximately 4 miles of trails. An interpretive center provides more information, and volunteers are constantly out on the trails.

While wildlife abounds all over the island, most areas of Sanibel are actually private property. One of the best locations to photograph osprey is at the end of Dixie Beach Boulevard, an area that requires a sticker permit for parking.

Sanibel boasts numerous places for vacationers to stay — chiefly motels and condominiums — but very few areas for camping. Reservations for campsites are

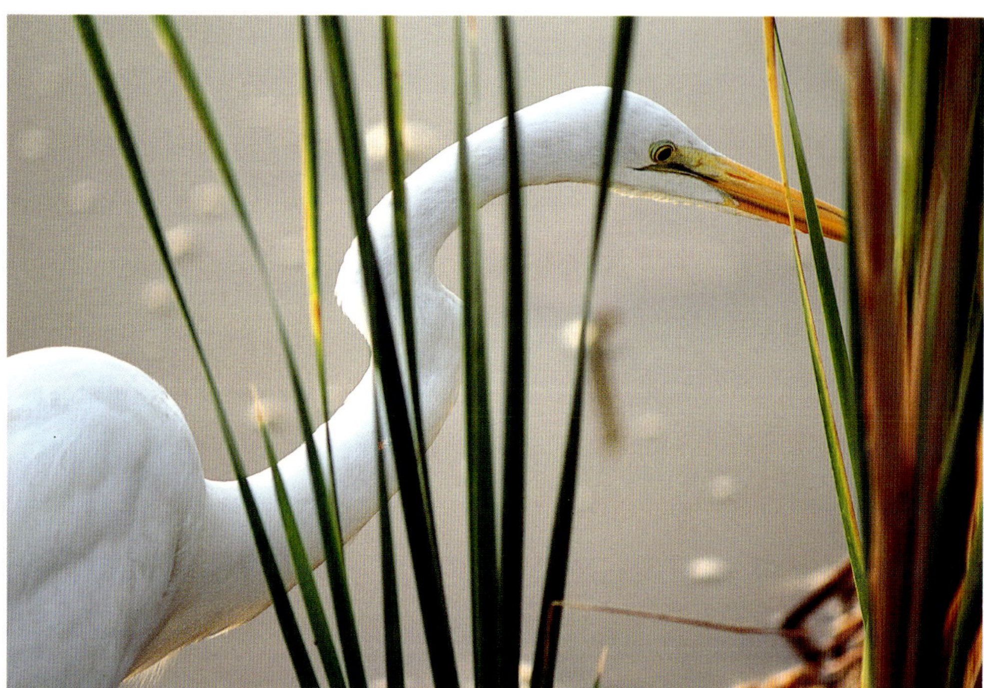

Great egret, St. Marks, 300mm lens, 1/15 second at f/4.5

recommended, although Ft. Myers is only 15 minutes away by car, so accommodations there are another option.

Sanibel has an active shell club, a chapter of the Audubon Society and a care and rehabilitation center for wildlife where current information can be obtained.

J.N. "Ding" Darling National Wildlife Refuge 1 Wildlife Drive Sanibel, FL 33957 813/472-1100

Sanibel-Captiva Conservation Foundation 3333 Sanibel-Captiva Road Sanibel, FL 33957

ST. MARKS NATIONAL WILDLIFE REFUGE

One of the oldest wildlife refuges in the system, St. Marks consists of 65,000 acres of land and an additional 31,700 protected acres of Apalachee Bay.

Freshwater impoundments, salt marshes, tidal flats, hardwood swamps and pinelands provide some of the diversity of habitat so attractive to the more than 300 species of birds here (of which roughly one-third also nest in the refuge). Two of the rarer nesting species are the bald eagle and red-cockaded woodpecker.

Hunting is allowed here in season, as in many of the other national wildlife refuges. At this time of year, however, it is much harder to sight deer, bear and waterfowl.

The best location for observing wildlife is along the seven miles of road (County Road 59) from the visitors center south to the St. Marks lighthouse. Marshes and ponds alongside this road attract hundreds of wading birds. One pond has several picnic tables that command a view of a nesting osprey on the opposite side, visible with the naked eye. Bald eagles also frequent this area, where they land on snags of dead trees.

Numerous trails have been built across the dikes and through the hardwood swamps. Mounds Pool Interpretive Trail winds by a fire tower where warblers are fairly abundant. Farther on through Live Oak in the slash pines there is an observation platform that overlooks a pool of water where waterfowl and wading birds feed. Beyond the tower is a dike built to create freshwater pools for migratory waterfowl.

There are two fairly long walking trails off County Road 59: Stoney Bayou Trail (7.3 miles) and Deep Creek Trail (12.7 miles). The latter trail leads directly under an osprey nest.

Black-crowned night herons migrate into the headquarters' pond area for about one month each year.

Refuge Manager St. Marks National Wildlife Refuge P.O. Box 68 St. Marks, FL 32355 904/925-6121

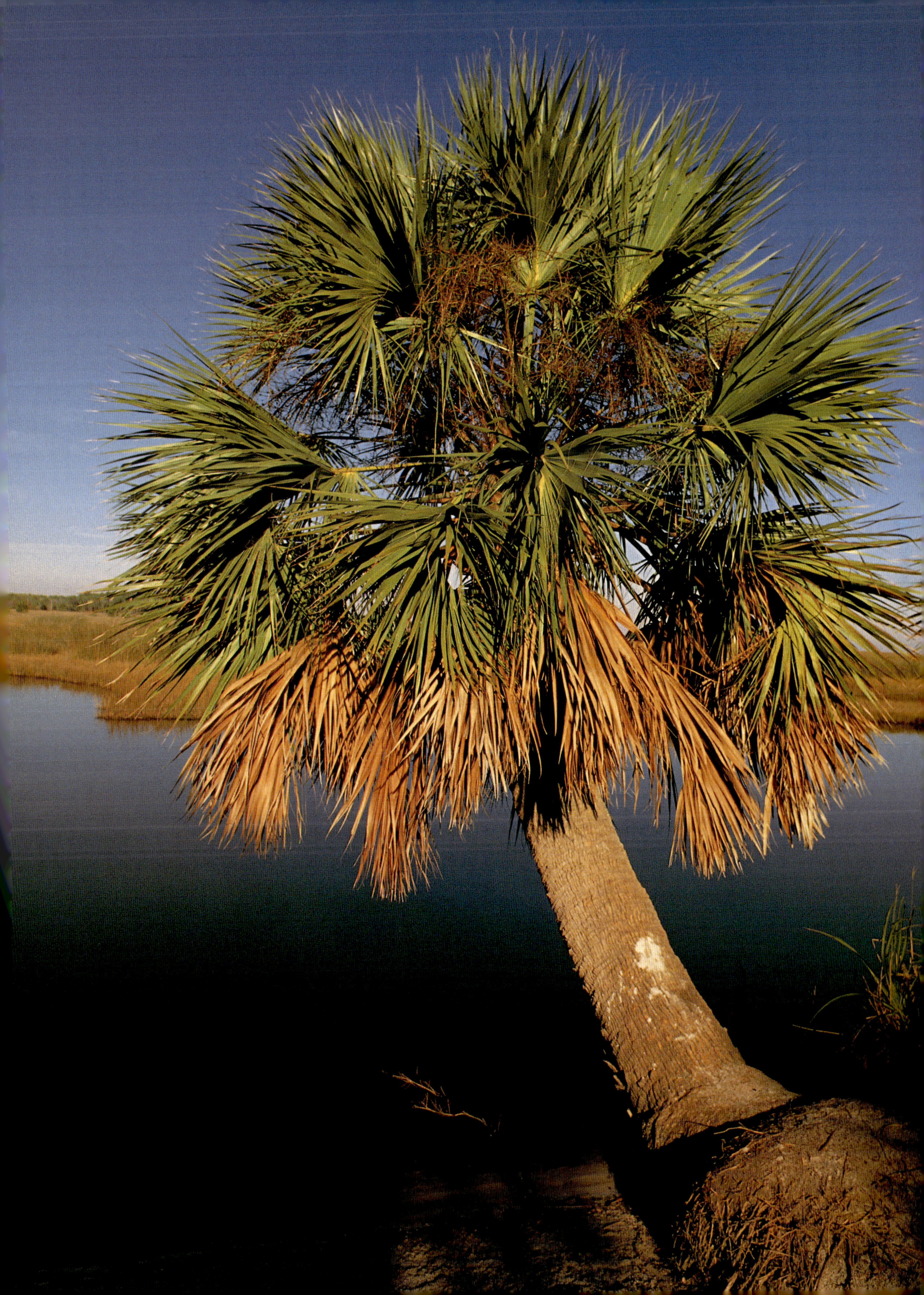

BIRDS

ANHINGA

The anhinga is probably the most interesting, most sought-after and most photographed bird in Florida. The unusual behavioral patterns of this species often permit closer approach by humans and longer periods of observation.

When hunting for food, the anhinga (or "water turkey") enters the water and sinks silently beneath the surface; when it spies a fish, it catches it by spearing it with its sharp beak.

The anhinga must come up for air every few minutes, at which time it characteristically reveals only its head and neck. Because its body remains submerged, the anhinga became known as the "snake bird," creating the appearance of a serpent rising from the water.

After spearing a fish, the anhinga usually remains in the water and flips its prey in the air (if the fish is small), before swallowing it and submerging again in search of bigger prey.

When a larger fish is impaled, the anhinga leaves the water and heads for a low-growing branch or the shore. Often the bird will beat the fish against the ground or limb to prevent its escape. The fish is then flipped, and the anhinga begins to swallow it headfirst. When a fish is so large that it would seem impossible for the thin-necked bird to ingest it, the anhinga's neck simply bulges and stretches to accommodate the fish.

Lacking the waterproof feathers of most other water birds, the anhinga must dry its wings before taking to long-distance flight. It thus remains on shore or perched on the limb of a tree with its wings spread out to dry.

When its wings are outstretched, the anhinga runs its beak through its feathers, offering a fine opportunity to shoot a photograph of the bird's head against its glossy wings engaging in its flamboyant preening behavior.

During the breeding season, the anhinga's eye-rings are a beautiful turquoise color. The wings, when almost dry, appear black and silver. The male of the species can be distinguished by its black neck; the female's neck is brown.

Anhingas may breed throughout the year in Florida, though nesting usually occurs along the Anhinga Trail from February through March. The Anhinga Trail, a half-mile trail with a raised boardwalk in the Royal Palm area, just inside the Everglades National Park, is the best area to photograph these birds.

Anhingas nest in pond apples near the halfway point over Taylor Slough. Photographing the nests from a distance requires a 500mm to 800mm lens to fill the frame. Watch for the male bird as it brings leaf-covered twigs to the female to line her nest. The eggs hatch in roughly three to four weeks; while the young are in the nest, both parents are kept busy feeding their offspring, regurgitating partially digested fish down the babies' throats.

An 80-200mm zoom lens is adequate for photographing anhingas at the start of the Anhinga Trail, where they dry their feathers. Anhingas prefer freshwater, while the cormorant (a bird often confused with the anhinga) usually feeds in saltwater. In recent years, however, cormorants have also fed in Taylor Slough.

ANHINGA TRAIL — EVERGLADES NATIONAL PARK J.N. "DING" DARLING NATIONAL WILDLIFE REFUGE

BALD EAGLE

Few Americans are unable to describe what the bird that is our national symbol looks like. With its large dark-brown body, white head and tail — an indication that it is at least 4 to 6 years old — and its brilliantly colored yellow eyes, beak and feet, the bald eagle is truly a magnificent sight. In fact, its courtship ritual, performed by a male and female locking talons in mid-air and tumbling earthward before swooping skyward again, is utterly breathtaking.

After Alaska, Florida has the most breeding pairs of any state. There are well over 300 nesting pairs here, and more than 50 pairs are found within the boundaries of the Everglades National Park. Since there are numerous storms during the summer and fall, few nests ever reach the enormous size of the Northern bald eagles; most nests here eventually topple from the tops of dead trees. The stick nests are lined with mangrove leaves and grasses and are built several miles apart, since bald eagles are territorial. The young hatch around February and fledge around April and May, when they may migrate to Canada for the summer.

Approximately three-fourths of a bald eagle's diet consists of fish, which it actively catches or steals from the osprey — a bird that resembles the eagle at a distance. Eagles are not above scavenging, and they sometimes consume wading birds and diamondback terrapins.

Their call is not fierce; hearing it for the first time, most people are surprised, for it is a soft, broken whistling sound. This distinctive sound will alert you to the eagle's presence long before you ever see it.

The Everglades eagle population is concentrated around Florida Bay and the western section of the park. Eagles are mostly seen around water, since this is where they nest and feed.

As with other birds, you should never approach a bald eagle's nesting site. Federal law prohibits anyone within a quarter mile of an active nest.

EVERGLADES NATIONAL PARK, ST. MARKS NATIONAL WILDLIFE REFUGE

BLACK AND TURKEY VULTURE

From a distance, most people have a hard time distinguishing these two large black scavengers from one another. In flight, the turkey vulture's wings are V-shaped. The black vulture, on the other hand, holds its wings fairly flat, flapping more than the turkey vulture; its white-tipped wings are also broader, and its tail is shorter. Both have a bald head, though the turkey vulture's is bright red and the black's is the color of its name.

Both vultures can be seen soaring in circles as they ride warm thermals in search of animal carcasses. The majority of their food is provided by road kills.

In the early morning, especially after a cool night, vultures spread their wings to collect the warmth of the sun. After they are sufficiently warmed, the birds will fly from their roost in search of whatever the speeding cars have provided them from the night before. Both species will feed together on the same carrion.

The black vulture is the stronger bird; it can rip flesh open more easily than the turkey, even though the latter has a larger wingspan at 6 feet. Its head is smaller but still has the same characteristic white-tipped hook beak.

Where they have become accustomed to people in areas like Flamingo (located at the extreme southern tip of the Everglades

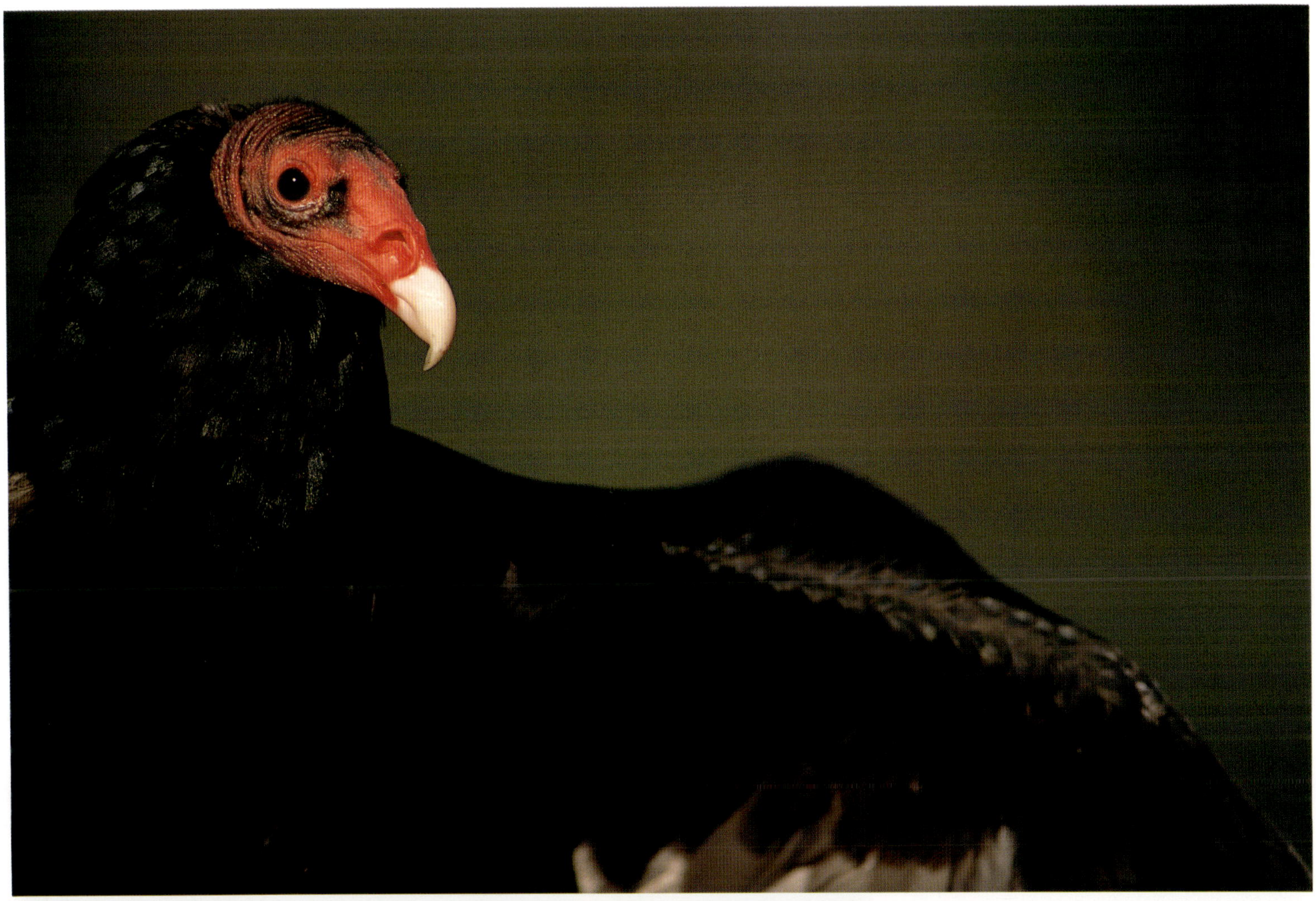

Turkey vulture, Everglades, 500mm lens, 1/500 second at f/4

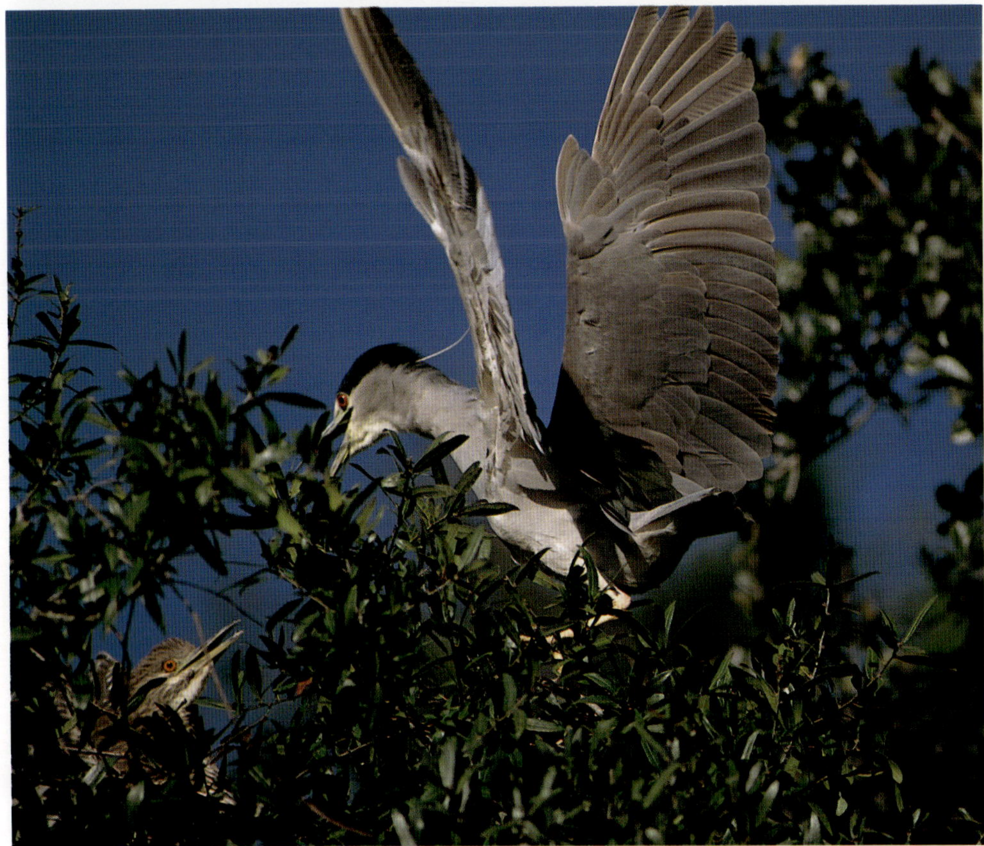

Black-crowned night heron, Alligator Farm, 500mm lens, 1/1000 second at f/4

National Park), vultures will perch on light poles and in trees waiting to see what scraps have been left by picnickers. Once I even witnessed two vultures fly down to an unattended cooler and begin tossing packages of luncheon meats into the air.

If agitated, the black vulture will sometimes make a peculiar barking sound.

Both birds nest on the ground, usually around saw palmetto thickets.

Although most people do not think kindly of birds that eat dead animals on the side of the road, vultures actually provide an invaluable service. Without them, the rotting roadside flesh would pose a serious threat as potential carriers of diseases.

FLAMINGO MARINA, CAMPGROUND — EVERGLADES NATIONAL PARK, ALMOST ANY CITY DUMP

BLACK-CROWNED NIGHT HERON

This heron is active, as its name implies, at night. It is not exclusively nocturnal, however, but it does enjoy far less competition from daytime feeders.

Night herons can be seen around marinas, where the artificial lights attract minnows. When fishing, they prefer standing on rocks or on low overhanging limbs, since their legs are short and their bodies fairly stocky. When at rest, the bird pulls its head in tight, contrasting its black crown against a black back and shoulders. Also notable are the bird's brilliant red eyes.

Serrations on the night heron's sharp beak enable it to hold onto its prey as it shakes it into submission before swallowing it — especially larger fish and frogs. Night herons also eat crayfish, crabs and algae. They are good swimmers when they need to be, and during takeoff they exhibit a faster wingbeat than most herons.

Night herons usually roost in low, bushy trees. A number of these birds can be seen sitting together along the canal at Shark Valley in the Everglades National Park.

ALLIGATOR FARM, ST. AUGUSTINE

BROWN PELICAN

Anywhere you find fishermen cleaning their catch you will likely see brown pelicans nearby. It's hard to believe that just a few years ago the very survival of this pelican was threatened. (The threat came from overuse of pesticides, which caused the bird's eggs to collapse from abnormally thin shells.) Today, however, this pelican can be spotted throughout all coastal areas of Florida.

When they're not scavenging or begging from fishermen, pelicans fish the bay areas, hovering over the water for a few seconds before folding their wings and plunging into the water headfirst. After catching a fish underwater, a pelican bobs back to the surface and tilts its water-filled pouch downward to drain the water before swallowing the fish.

Sunrise is a wonderful time to witness the act of feeding, when pelicans are silhouetted against the glow of the morning sun. Pelicans frequently fly together in a straight line two to seven at a time, gliding just inches above the water and alternating their wing flapping. Pelicans, which can fly at speeds of 15 to 25 mph, and on windy days they often can be seen suspended in one spot before breaking off to fly with the wind instead of against it.

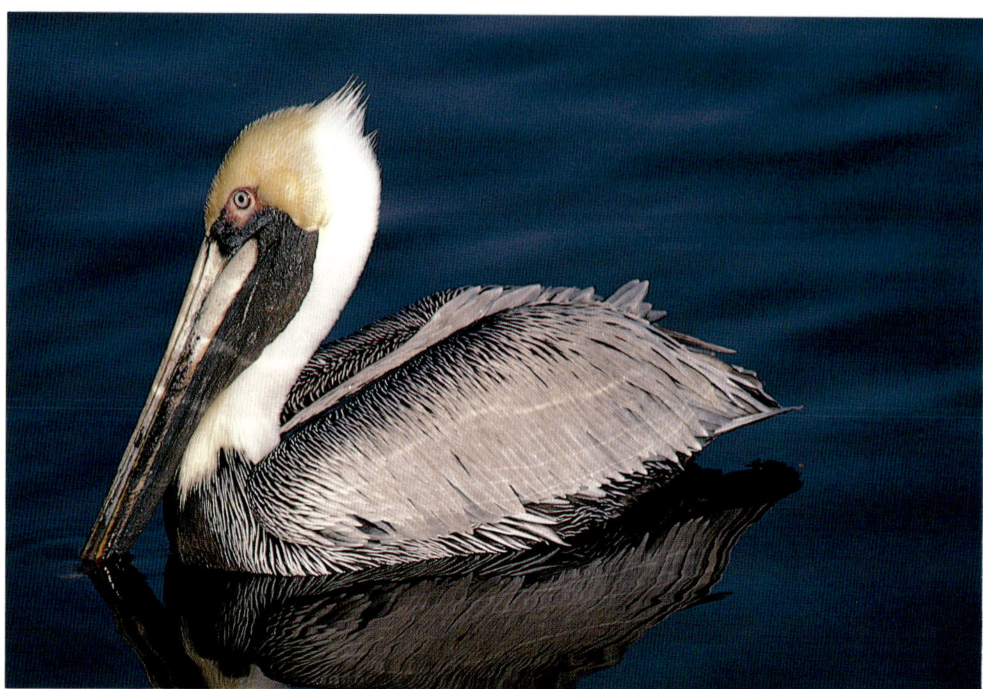

Brown pelican, Florida Bay, 300mm lens, 1/500 second at f/4.5

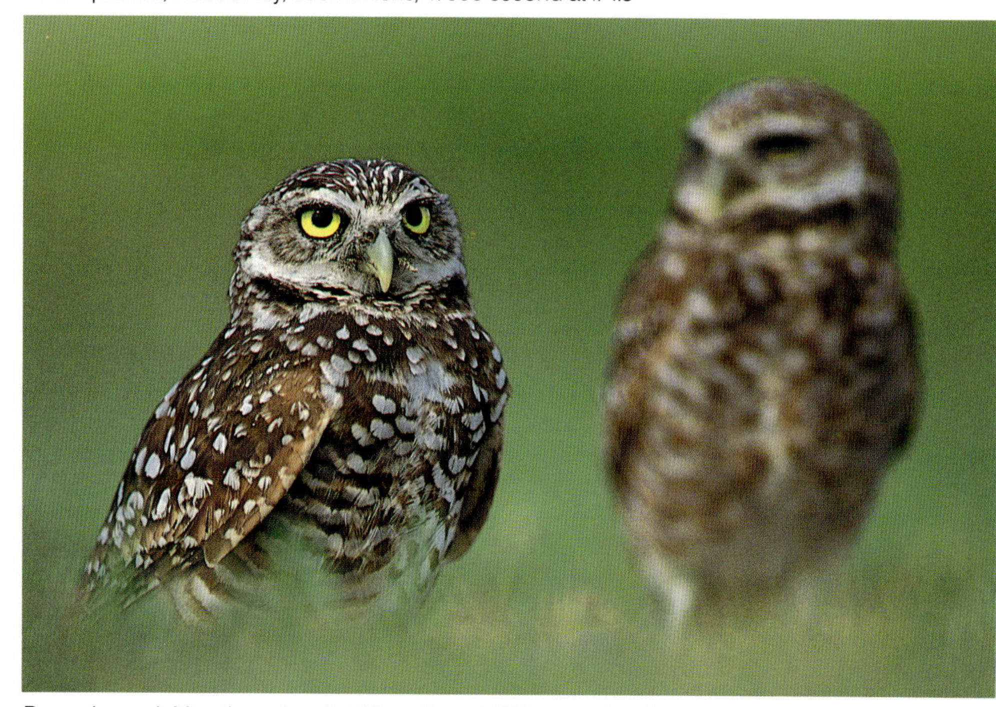

Burrowing owl, Marathon airport, 500mm lens, 1/250 second at f/4

Striking changes in plumage are visible from juveniles to adults and from winter to summer. In fact, many people think they are looking at different species of pelicans when actually they are viewing different phases of brown pelicans huddled together.

Check local marinas for subjects to photograph, as pelicans usually perch there on pilings with their beaks tucked into their back feathers.

ALL ALONG COASTAL AREAS

BURROWING OWL

The burrowing owl is one of the more easily located species, if you know where to look. These owls prefer open fields, such as airports and golf courses. They are usually active in the early evening, when they stand outside their burrows watching for flying insects.

Their average height is 9 inches, with a wingspan of almost 2 feet. The yellow eyes of the burrowing owl stand out in contrast to the tawny brown of the feathers, which blend in well with the short

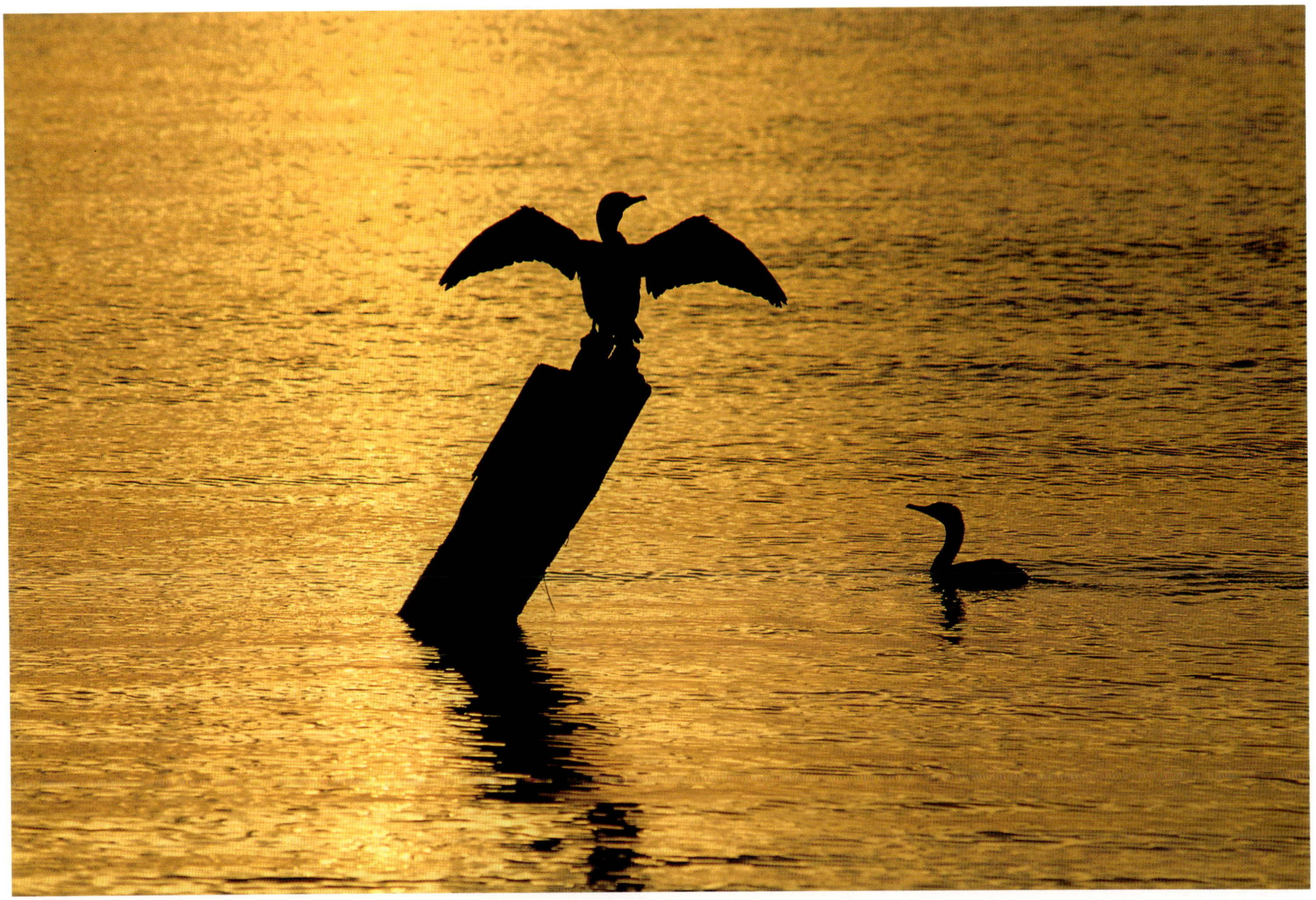

Double-crested cormorant, Florida Bay, 300mm lens, 1/250 second at f/11

grasses. Its legs are considered long for an owl, but when approached it crouches low, bobbing and chattering. If a person draws too close, the owl will usually retreat to its burrow rather than fly away.

The owl's main diet consists of insects, but it will also eat frogs, lizards and rodents. Nesting begins around March, and both sexes incubate the eggs. The young, which hatch in about six weeks, generally wait to emerge from the nest entrance until about the 11th or 12th day. Another month will elapse before the babies take to flight.

If not harassed, owls will nest in the same burrow year after year. Several pairs have nested for years on Marathon Key at the airport and at Sombrero Golf Course. Normally their range is from Orlando to the Keys.

If you're looking for a burrowing owl, watch the ground where they spend most of their time. They may be sighted in trees from time to time, but this is fairly uncommon.

SOMBRERO GOLF COURSE, AIRPORT — MARATHON KEY, MANY COLLEGE CAMPUSES IN SOUTHERN FLORIDA

CATTLE EGRET

This small white bird is usually the first egret seen along the grassy medians of the interstate. Unlike the other egrets, this species does not wade in water to search for fish; instead, it follows cattle, tractors or whatever else scares up insects. It feeds any time of the day — dining exclusively on insects.

The cattle egret is one of the few exotic animals that came to this continent on its own. About 100 years ago, the first cattle egrets arrived in South America; today, this egret is found in every state in the U.S.

During nesting season, the crest of the cattle egret is a bright orange-yellow, setting off the bright yellow eyes. Both sexes incubate their eggs, sitting on nests constructed of loosely woven sticks.

Although the cattle egret does not compete with other egrets for food, it does tend to displace them from their nesting areas.

CATTLE RANGES, INTERSTATE MEDIANS

DOUBLE-CRESTED CORMORANT

The cormorant is easily confused with the anhinga from a distance, since both species spread their wings to dry before diving for more fish. The cormorant's upper bill is hooked, however, so instead of stabbing fish underwater it must grab them.

The cormorant is found mainly around saltwater, but it will fish in freshwater, too, where it can stay underwater for well over a minute before coming up for air. Its neck is much shorter than the anhinga's, and it has distinctive blue eyes.

The cormorant's range is fairly widespread; it can be seen along all Florida bay areas, usually perched on pilings.

The greatest concentration of these birds I have ever seen was on the islands of the

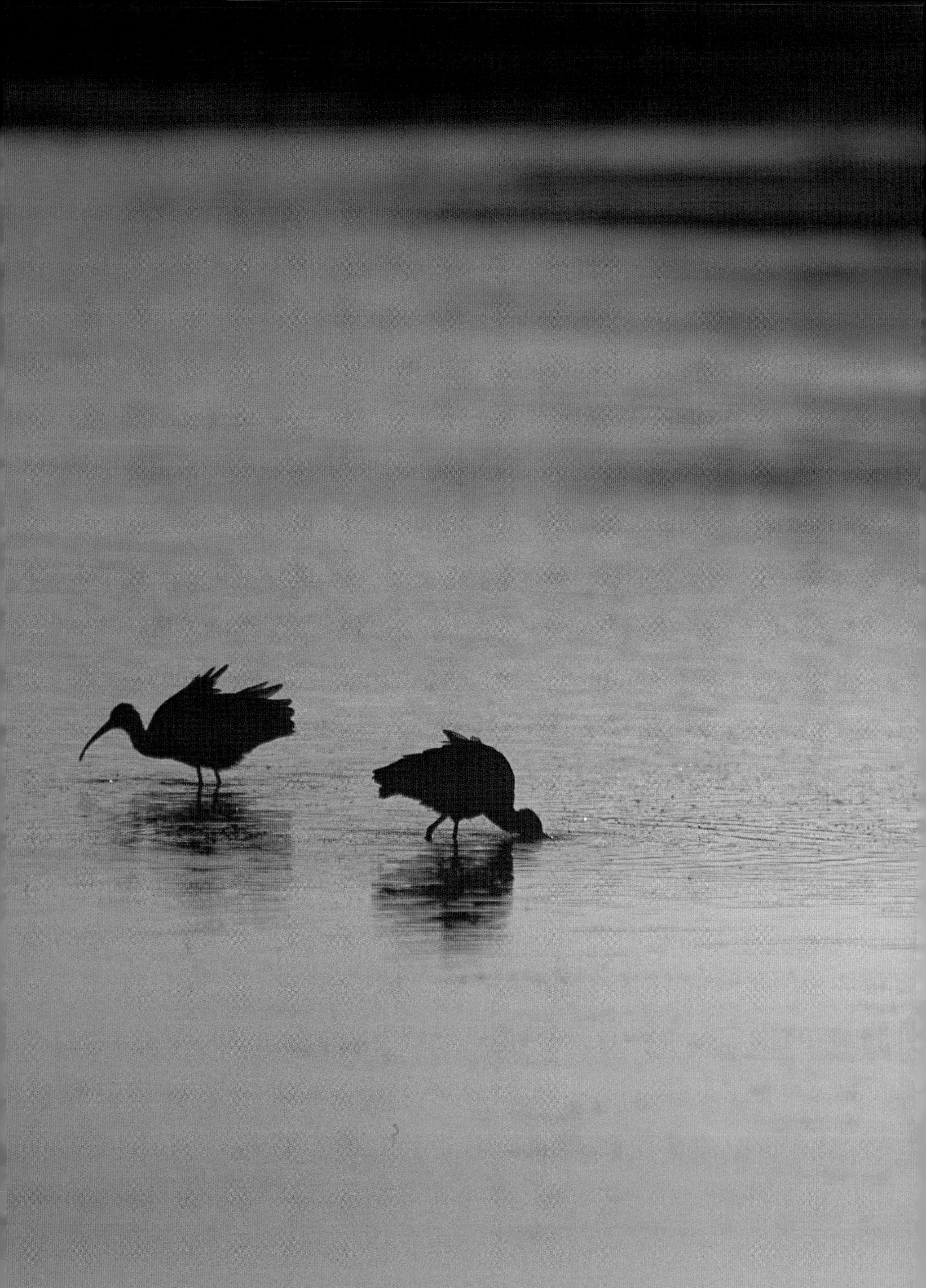

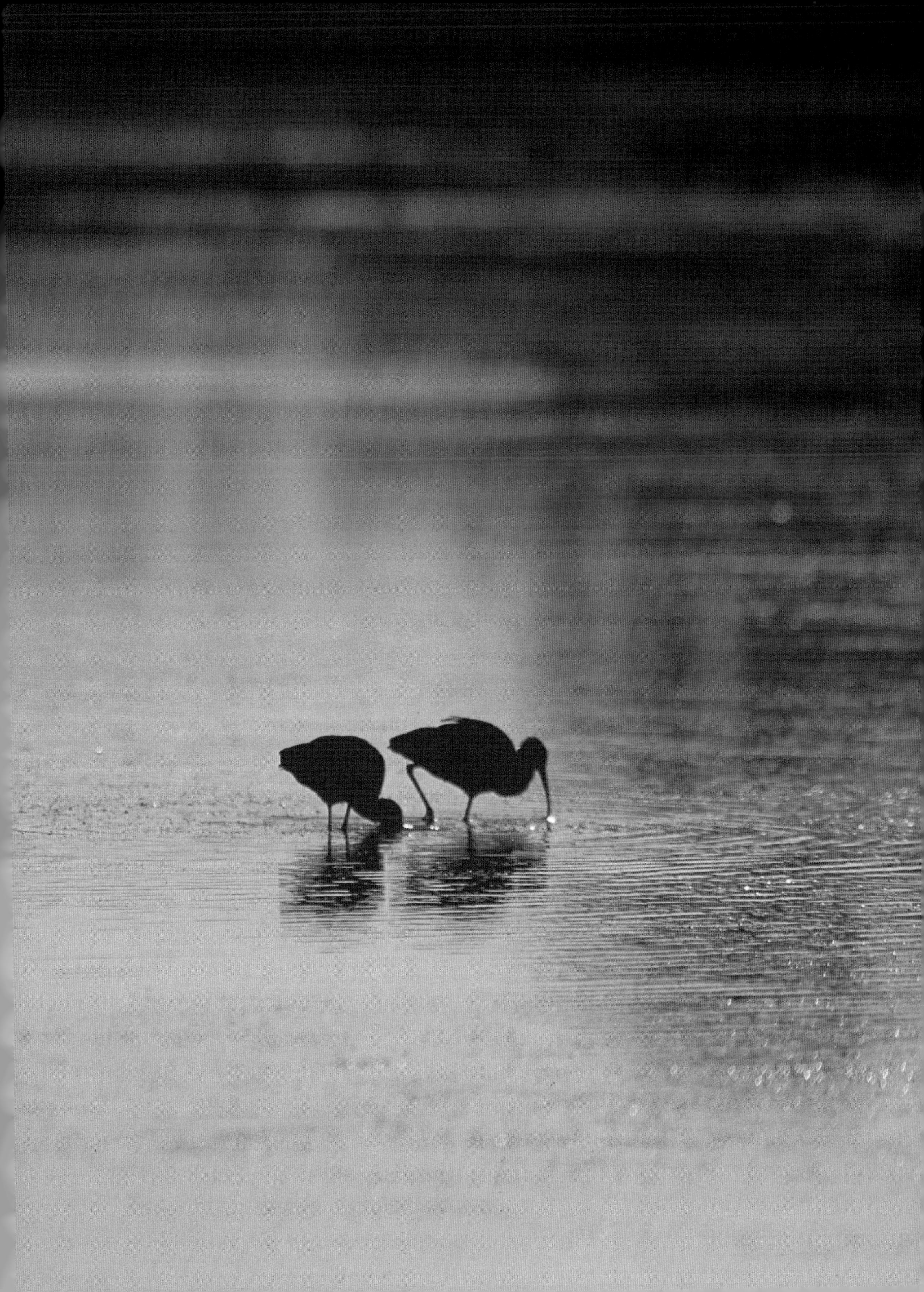

Great White Heron National Wildlife Refuge, where literally thousands of the birds had congregated.

The double-crested cormorant's name comes from two tufts of feathers on display in breeding plumage.

GREAT WHITE HERON NATIONAL WILDLIFE REFUGE

EVERGLADE KITE

The Everglade kite offers a prime example of the detrimental impact of one animal's total dependency on another species for food, especially when there is competition for that same food source. The kite feeds only on the apple snail pomacea. Unfortunately, with people draining the swamps and other animals feasting on this snail, the kite has found itself with a dwindling supply of food. This has put the kite in an alarming ecological position, and many people have concluded this bird is doomed to extinction.

The Loxahatchee National Wildlife Refuge, however, fenced off areas abundant with apple snails and set up nesting platforms for the kites. Over time, their numbers have increased.

The kite, a brown bird with red eyes, has a 45-inch wingspan. Its beak is sharply hooked, enabling it to extract the snail from its shell. When hunting for snails, it flies from 5 to 30 feet off the ground, but when observed by people it is usually soaring at much higher altitudes.

SHARK VALLEY — EVERGLADES NATIONAL PARK, LOXAHATCHEE NATIONAL WILDLIFE REFUGE

GLOSSY IBIS

The glossy ibis looks almost exactly like the white ibis — with curved beak for probing and long legs for wading — except in color. The glossy is dark brown with an iridescence of green, blue and bronze, depending on the angle that sunlight strikes it.

Like the white ibis, the glossy ibis flies low with rapid wingbeats and alternate gliding. It tends to feed in flocks of its own species more than the white, eating fish, frogs and insects and probing crayfish holes in search of morsels. These birds nest along freshwater marshes and, from March through May, along the Shark River.

The glossy ibis is not gregarious in its nesting habits, rarely allowing other birds within range of its nest. Young ibises are never left alone at the nest, and the parent feeds each individual fledgling until it is full before moving on to feed the next.

MERRITT ISLAND NATIONAL WILDLIFE REFUGE

GREAT BLUE HERON

The great blue heron, standing almost 4 feet high, is the largest and most widely distributed of the North American herons. This slate-gray bird is almost impossible to get close to in most Northern states, yet in Florida you may find yourself able to approach within a few feet.

When stalking their prey, great blue herons seem to be the slowest of all the herons, extending their long necks and turning their heads to get a better look through the water's reflecting surface.

Once on the Anhinga Trail a group of photographers set up their equipment to shoot a great blue heron and waited for more than two hours before it flew from the area where it had been preening. Everyone was so startled when it finally flew away without warning that no one got a single shot.

The great blue heron has longer legs than most wading birds and seems inclined to venture out into deeper water, sometimes to such a depth that it resembles a long-necked duck.

When alarmed, this heron makes a grating croak and may even attack other birds, including anhingas, forcing them to abandon their freshly caught fish.

Great blue herons eat fish, frogs, salamanders, snakes and baby alligators. Larger fish are usually speared; smaller fish are caught with the beak partially opened. Like most herons, the great blue heron swallows its prey headfirst.

On takeoff, the great blue heron often appears clumsy, but once airborne it flies with slow, graceful wingbeats and its long neck folded in.

These birds nest in colonies at the tops of tall trees, making observation from the ground through the limbs rather difficult. Some birds have been seen plummeting nearly to their death after losing their footing, since they are sometimes unable to open their large wings because of the tree limbs.

SILVER SPRINGS, ANHINGA TRAIL, BEACHES

GREAT EGRET

The great egret is one of the most common and beautiful of Florida's wading birds. There is nothing more enchanting than watching these graceful birds with their feathers spread and the morning light filtering through. During mating season, which begins in late February, these black-legged birds with yellow beaks develop long white breeding plumage that drags on the ground.

When feeding, the great egret wades slowly through shallow water — at times so slowly that any movement is hard to discern. But when they straighten out their long, folded necks, they do so with lightning speed. Few fish, lizards or frogs can escape the fatal stab of an egret. Great egrets appear to have favorite fishing areas and a definite pecking order within their own species. If another species wanders into their area, it is ignored, but another great egret will be chased out and, with a deep croak, usually fly to a safer feeding ground.

The great egret's range extends all the way into Canada, although during the dry winter it is found concentrated around water. They feed mostly in early morning and late evening but can be observed at midday along the water's edge, stalking their prey. Occasionally one will catch a snake, which may wrap itself around the egret's beak, requiring the bird to use its feet to dislodge the serpent and stab it a few times before swallowing it whole.

These birds are utterly magnificent in flight, their necks folded back and large, distinctively graceful wings flapping.

AROUND ANY WATER (PONDS, RIVERS, STREAMS)

GREAT WHITE HERON

This handsome bird is another species that can only be seen in southern Florida. Actually, it is not considered a species of its own, but, rather, a white-phase race of the great blue heron.

Like the great blue, the great white heron stands approximately 4 feet tall. The great white can be seen along all the Keys, where the largest concentration may be found around the Great White Heron Refuge.

These birds feed along the water's edge and on tidal flats, where they catch the saltwater fish that comprise the majority of their diet.

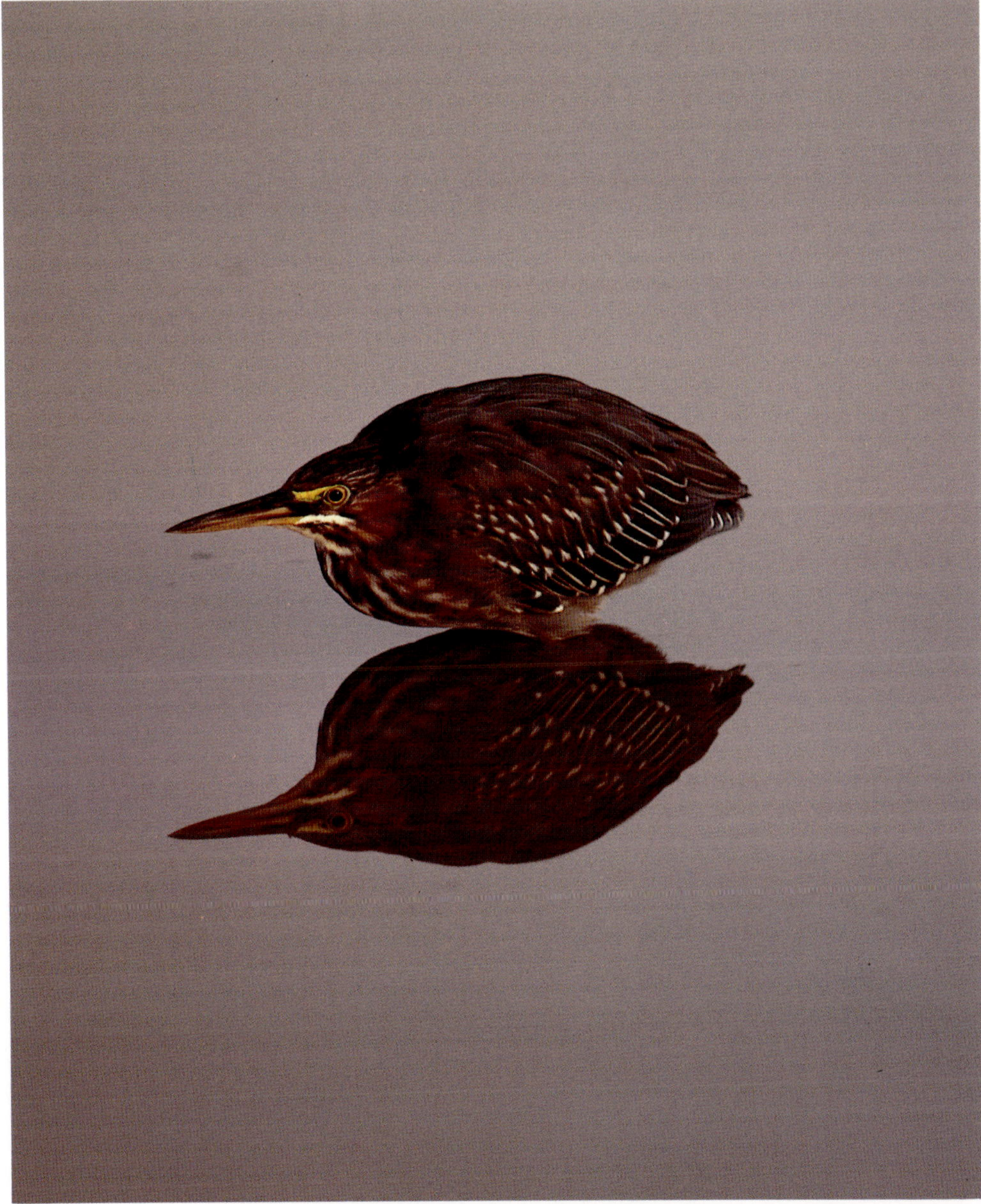

Green-backed heron, Mrazek Pond, 80-200mm lens, 1 second at f/5.6

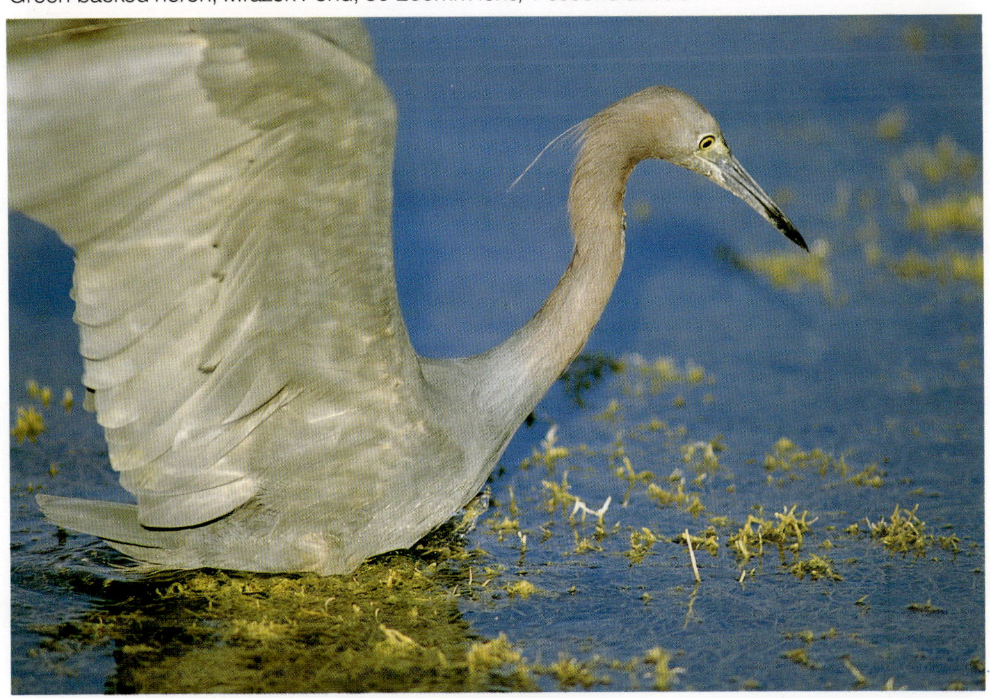

Little blue heron, Anhinga Trail, 500mm lens, 1/500 second at f/4

Great white herons like to watch fishermen cleaning their catch, often coming in close to eat the discarded parts.

FLORIDA KEYS

GREEN-BACKED HERON

This smallest of North American herons is also one of the shyest. It will remain motionless to avoid detection but croak loudly when disturbed, especially just before flying off. It flicks its tail when agitated and raises its crest, especially when approached by one of its own species.

The green-backed heron is a daytime feeder, preferring to feed from logs in the water or low overhanging branches. It typically remains motionless for long periods of time before thrusting its neck forward to grab its prey.

This heron prefers feeding in grown-up areas instead of open waters. Its plumage varies in color; the mix of dominant shades includes rust, blue, green and gray.

ANHINGA TRAIL — EVERGLADES NATIONAL PARK

LIMPKIN

The limpkin resembles the white ibis in size and shape, but its coloring is dark brown with light spots and streaks. It is usually found in marshes and swamps, where the apple snail — its favorite food — dwells. Other foods include frogs and lizards.

The limpkin will seize a snail in its beak and bring it to the shore, where it uses its feet to hold down the snail while extracting the meat with its beak.

One effective way to locate a limpkin is to search the ground for a pile of empty snail shells — a good indicator of a regular feeding area.

Unlike egrets, limpkins prefer roosting in tall grasses rather than in trees. Limpkins are fairly secretive birds, but they can often be located by listening for their loud screams.

CORKSCREW SWAMP, OKLAWAHA RIVER

LITTLE BLUE HERON

This quiet, slate-blue heron does not seem to be as popular as the larger birds with more plumage. It prefers feeding

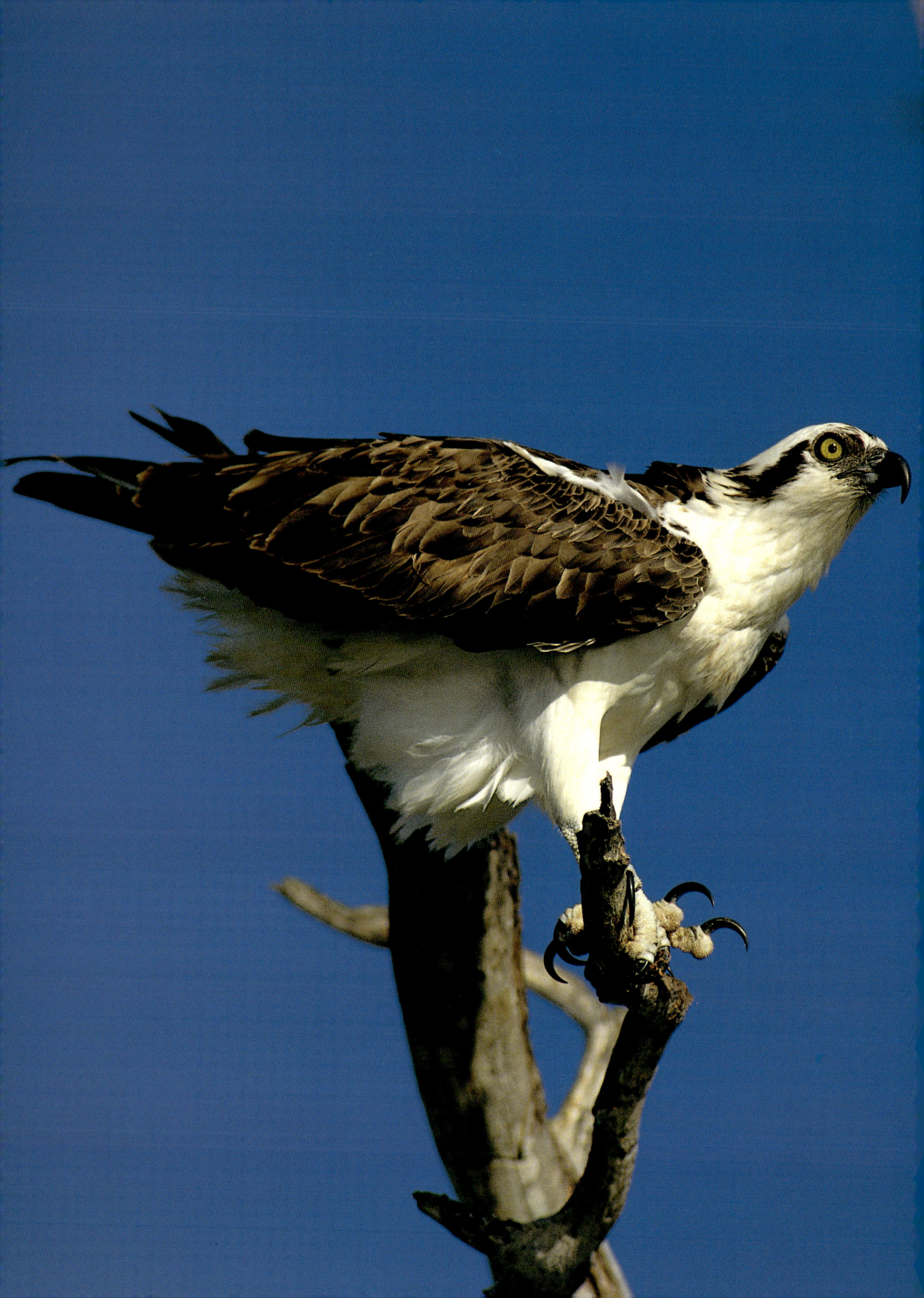

alone during the day, but in the evening the birds gather before returning to roost. Like most other herons, it flies with its head drawn in.

When feeding, the little blue heron may wade or hang over the water's surface, waiting for fish or crustaceans to come within striking range. It then seizes its prey or pierces it with its sharp beak, depending on the size of the prey.

The little blue heron is often seen walking across water lettuce, turning up leaves in search of food clinging to the plants' undersides.

The breeding plumage changes little from the regular plumage, unlike most other wading birds.

This heron prefers a freshwater habitat, but it also feeds regularly in brackish water.

CORKSCREW SWAMP, ANHINGA TRAIL

OSPREY

The osprey, one of our most beautiful birds of prey, is often confused with the bald eagle because of its prominent white head. Unlike the eagle, however, which has a completely dark body, the osprey is predominantly white underneath and has a dark mask across its face.

Ospreys can regularly be seen sitting in dead snags of trees near water. When actively feeding, they soar and hover, then plunge completely underwater, talons first, to catch fish. They then come up flapping their waterlogged feathers. After gaining altitude, the osprey will shake all over, like a dog, to rid itself of the water. Ospreys have been known to drown when unable to let go of fish caught in their talons and unable to rid themselves of water trapped in their feathers.

The osprey positions a fish in its talons headfirst to cut down on wind resistance. The bird then usually lands on a snag, where it eats its catch. The male will furnish a continuous supply of food to a female sitting on eggs or to fledglings.

It is obvious when the male is approaching the nest, for long before the human eye can see the bird the female starts calling excitedly. The female may even leave the nest and land on a snag to devour its food, depending on how far along the nesting is.

The female and her young (especially the latter) flatten themselves in the nest if

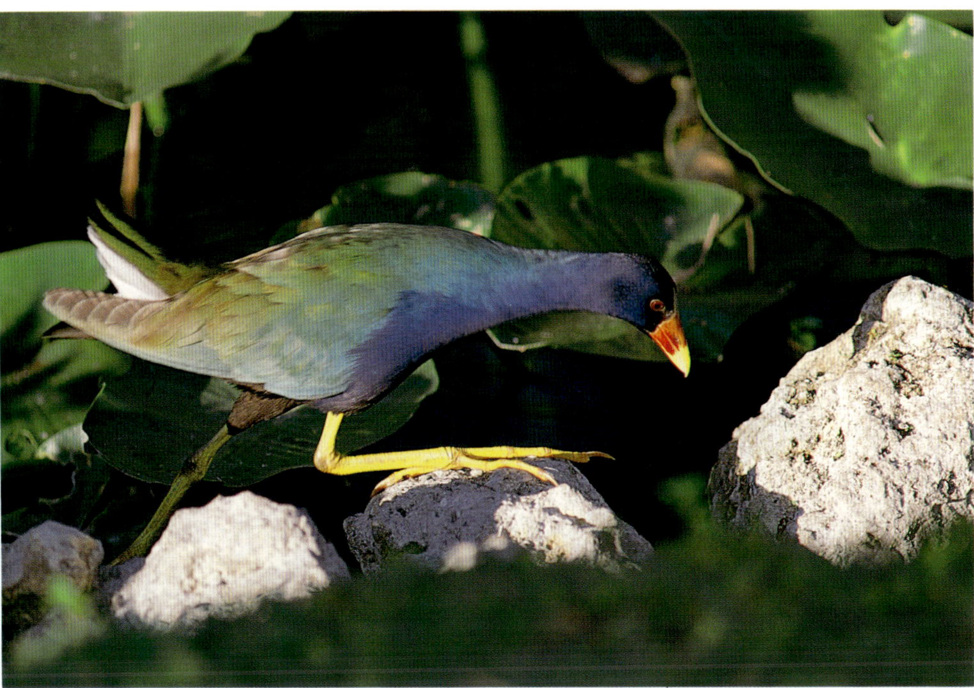

Purple gallinule, Anhinga Trail, 300mm lens, 1/250 second at f/4.5

humans approach too closely. Ospreys are quite vocal, so it should be obvious if you are disturbing them. That's when it is time to abandon your position.

Osprey nests are sometimes seen on utility poles, but many birds have been injured at these nests, so local conservation groups throughout Florida have erected nesting platforms for the birds.

For approximately four and one half weeks the male will bring fish to his mate while she incubates the eggs; another six more weeks are devoted to feeding the young.

Since osprey cultivate favorite perches, it is relatively easy to study the birds once you have located the sites.

MERRITT ISLAND NATIONAL WILDLIFE REFUGE, J.N. ''DING'' DARLING NATIONAL WILDLIFE REFUGE

PURPLE GALLINULE

This little chicken-sized bird is sought after by nearly every photographer on the Anhinga Trail in the Everglades National Park. The feathers of the purple gallinule are iridescent, and, depending on how the sun strikes the bird, its colors vary from deep blue to purple, with tinges of bronze and green. Its beak looks like candy corn with brilliant orange and yellow, and its large feet are bright yellow, contrasting the dark-green spatterdock leaves as it spreads its toes to distribute its weight on the water plants.

The purple gallinule does not remain still

for long; as it eats seeds, flowering buds and the occasional frog, it weaves in and out of tall grasses along the shore's edge. When agitated, it flicks its tail, showing the white feathers underneath, and emits a distinctive clucking noise.

Freshwater ponds are the gallinule's favorite feeding areas. Here, they turn over the floating leaves with their feet in a seemingly endless search for prey. The female can usually be distinguished from the male, for it lacks the male's vivid coloring — sporting instead a dull greenish-bronze color.

Unlike the large wading birds, gallinules prefer to nest in reeds and willows, surrounded by water and out of the view of all but the most persistent.

SHARK VALLEY, ANHINGA TRAIL — EVERGLADES NATIONAL PARK

RED-COCKADED WOODPECKER

The red-cockaded woodpecker is an endangered bird that nests in mature pine forests. The largest colonies since Hurricane Hugo are now located in Apalachicola National Forest.

This woodpecker is a very ''sociable'' species, living in a clan made up of two to nine birds. There are approximately 600 of these colonies in Apalachicola, where cavity trees have a band painted on them. The birds are easily seen in most other areas, too.

The red-cockaded woodpecker is only

slightly larger than a bluebird. The back and top of its head are black, and numerous small white spots arranged in horizontal rows on the back create a ladderback appearance.

The woodpecker spurns dead pines, preferring instead to hollow out cavities in live ones. To locate their holes, look for larger, older trees with pine sap glistening in the sun. Red-cockaded woodpeckers nest between late April and June.

APALACHICOLA NATIONAL FOREST, OSCEOLA NATIONAL FOREST

RED-SHOULDERED HAWK

This common species is one of the loudest of the hawks, especially during breeding season, thus making it an easy bird to locate. Found chiefly in wet woodlands, it feeds on frogs, snakes and rabbits. It is brown in color, with a reddish patch on each shoulder.

The red-shouldered hawk will take over a barred owl's nest, but it builds its own lining of leaves and feathers.

Many palmetto hammocks — especially in the Everglades — host a healthy population of these birds.

I have seen nests in Flamingo Campground as low as 12 feet from the ground, but, on average, they are built 30 to 40 feet high.

These birds perch on road signs and dwarf cypress trees along the road from Homestead to Flamingo.

FLAMINGO, CORKSCREW SWAMP

REDDISH EGRET

The reddish egret, while not one of the more abundant egrets, is certainly one of the strangest in terms of feeding. This bird chases after fish, which seems to explain its different running patterns. Sometimes it runs in a zigzag pattern with its wings outstretched, other times in a straight line with a few mid-air hops while its arched neck wavers from side to side. Its preference is for feeding in coastal areas.

Plumes on the head, neck and breast are long and pinkish in color, and the eyes are white.

J.N. ''DING'' DARLING NATIONAL WILDLIFE REFUGE

ROSEATE SPOONBILL

Seen only from the neck up, the adult spoonbill might be considered one of the

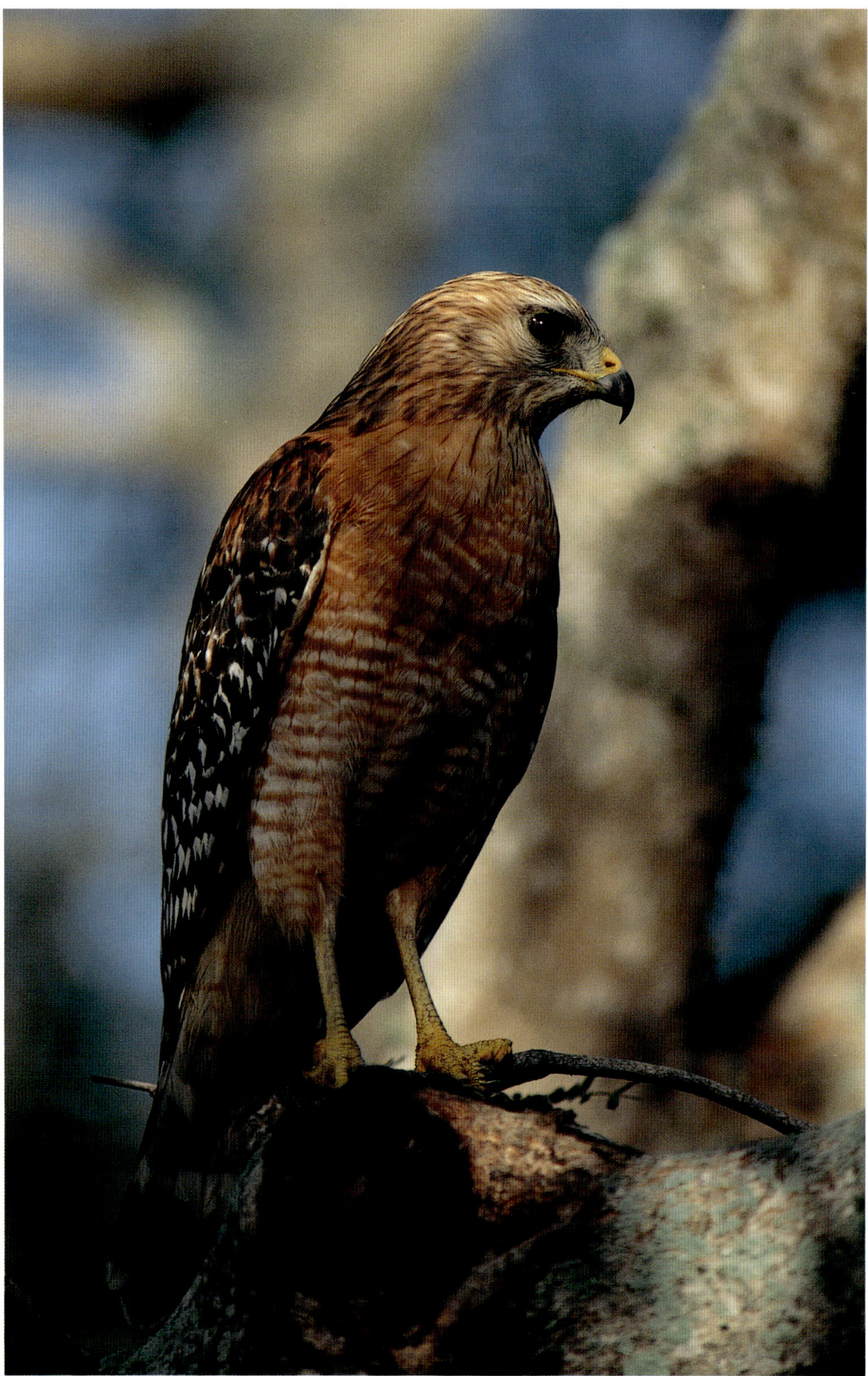

Red-shouldered hawk, Flamingo Campground, 80-200mm lens, 1/125 second at f/4.5

ugliest birds in North America. It has a greenish bald head, red eyes and a spatulate-shaped beak. Its feathered body, however, makes it one of the most popular birds in Florida.

The spoonbill's body and wings are a delicate pink, and its shoulder and tail coverts are a brilliant red — contrasting the white neck, breast and back feathers. Unlike adult birds, the young are almost a solid white, with feathered neck and head.

The roseate spoonbill feeds in shallow water, moving its flat beak through the water in an arc. When small fish or crustaceans are encountered, the bill snaps shut and the bird throws its head back to swallow its meal. These birds prefer salt or brackish water and are most active in the early morning and late evening.

Unlike many egrets, spoonbills prefer congregating with one another and tend to maintain a distance between themselves and people.

The spoonbill is the only large pink bird to be found in the area, unless a flamingo has been blown in by a tropical storm or has escaped from Hialeah Park.

While most birders visit southern Florida during the winter, spoonbills can be found in greater abundance in May and June in Sanibel's J.N. ''Ding'' Darling National Wildlife Refuge. During the month of February, small groups may be found on Sanibel, in the Everglades and in tidal ponds along the upper Keys.

In flight, the spoonbill's neck is outstretched and its wingbeats slow, making the bird easy to identify from a distance.

Courtship and nesting begin in November, and the young hatch in December. After nesting, these birds disperse as far north as the Florida Panhandle. Major nesting areas are in the Everglades; they prefer red mangroves for roosting, especially on Sanibel.

J.N. ''DING'' DARLING NATIONAL WILDLIFE REFUGE, ECO POND, MRAZEK POND — EVERGLADES NATIONAL PARK

SANDHILL CRANE

It's hard to miss sandhill cranes as they migrate to Florida in November: Their call is a loud trumpeting sound, issued as they fly together in large flocks. Many people initially mistake them for geese if they hear them first, but one glance skyward reveals a long-necked, long-legged bird — usually in search of open prairie, marsh or pasture.

These large gray birds with red-capped heads walk slowly, jabbing their sharp beaks into the soft ground to feed on insects and roots. The largest concentration of sandhill cranes is found around Paynes Prairie State Preserve.

An observation platform on U.S. 441 affords a view of these birds in the mornings as they fly over before settling down to feed. Wakahoota Road nearby is an especially fine vantage for observing the birds feeding. When alarmed, sandhill cranes begin to trumpet, departing all at once or a few at a time.

By the month of February, the migratory cranes are usually heading back north. At this time they may stop over in the Pinhook swamp area above Osceola National Forest.

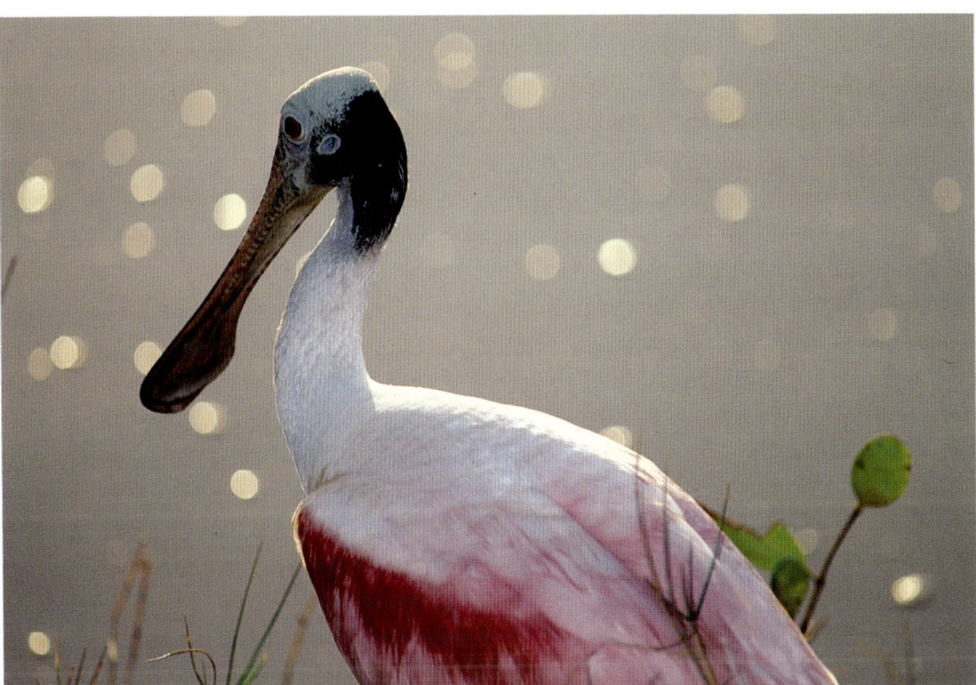

Roseate spoonbill, Mrazek Pond, 80-200mm lens, 1/60 second at f/4.5

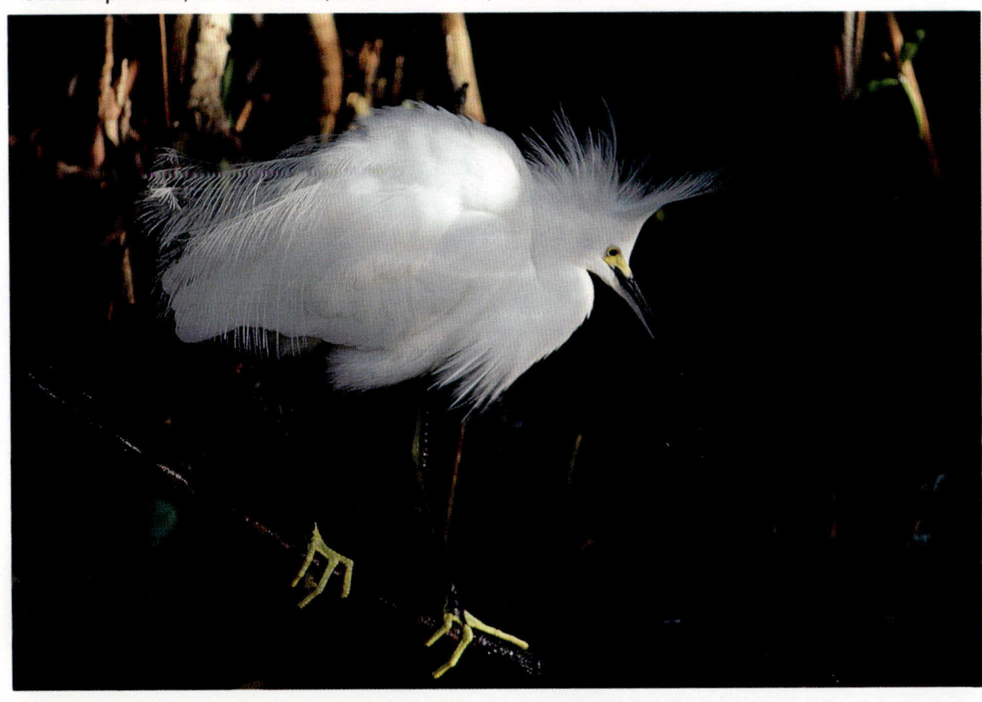

Snowy egret, Mrazek Pond, 300mm lens, 1/30 second at f/4.5

A smaller, nonmigratory sandhill crane has become a permanent resident, but it is harder to locate than the migrant flocks.

PAYNES PRAIRIE STATE PRESERVE

SNOWY EGRET

This is the egret everyone comes to Florida to see, recognized by its black legs and bright yellow feet. During breeding season, its white feathers are more showy, especially on its crest. When agitated or engaged in its courtship ritual, the snowy egret raises its crest; back and tail plumes are raised when birds greet one another at nesting time.

This egret exhibits a broader range of feeding habits than the larger wading birds. Like the great egret, it moves slowly, neck arched, until it spots a fish. It then quickly thrusts its head forward to seize its prey.

This bird will fly low over the water's surface and drag its feet to scare fish into swimming ahead. Extending its neck, it then reaches down and grabs its meal. The snowy egret also stirs muddy and grassy areas beneath the water's surface with its feet, watching for prey to swim within striking range.

Snowy egrets have favorite feeding areas and a definite pecking order; they displace one another with loud clacking sounds and raised wings.

Though the bird's yellow slippers are its trademark, its brilliant yellow eyes are no less beautiful. In flight, its wing beats are more frequent than those of larger waders.

MRAZEK POND AND CANALS

TRICOLORED HERON

Next to the reddish egret, the tricolored heron (formerly known as the Louisiana heron) is the most active feeder of the wading birds. Like the great egret, it wades through the water slowly, stabbing its prey; at other times, however, it runs frantically, wings outstretched, seizing prey as it tries to escape.

The tricolored heron is a slender bird, with most of its body a blue-gray. Under its wings, its breast and neck are white, with a streak of brown that runs up the neck. During breeding season two white plumes hang from the head. Its eyes are a brilliant red.

The tricolored heron is one of the more widespread herons in the South.

EVERGLADES NATIONAL PARK, J.N. ''DING'' DARLING NATIONAL WILDLIFE REFUGE

WHITE IBIS

A long, reddish-orange curved beak and bright-orange legs are the distinguishing field markings of this handsome bird. This ibis is all white, except for a small black tip on the wing feathers visible only when in flight. Brilliant blue eyes contrast with the colorful beak as the bird feeds — wading slowly and probing the shallow waters for small fish, snails, frogs, crayfish, crabs and insects.

The white ibis is not as vocal as the herons it feeds alongside, but it does make a nasal grunting noise when agitated. Juvenile birds are identical to adults, except for brown eyes and brown splotches on feathers. From a distance, they are sometimes mistaken for the glossy ibis.

The flight of the white ibis is fairly swift, with

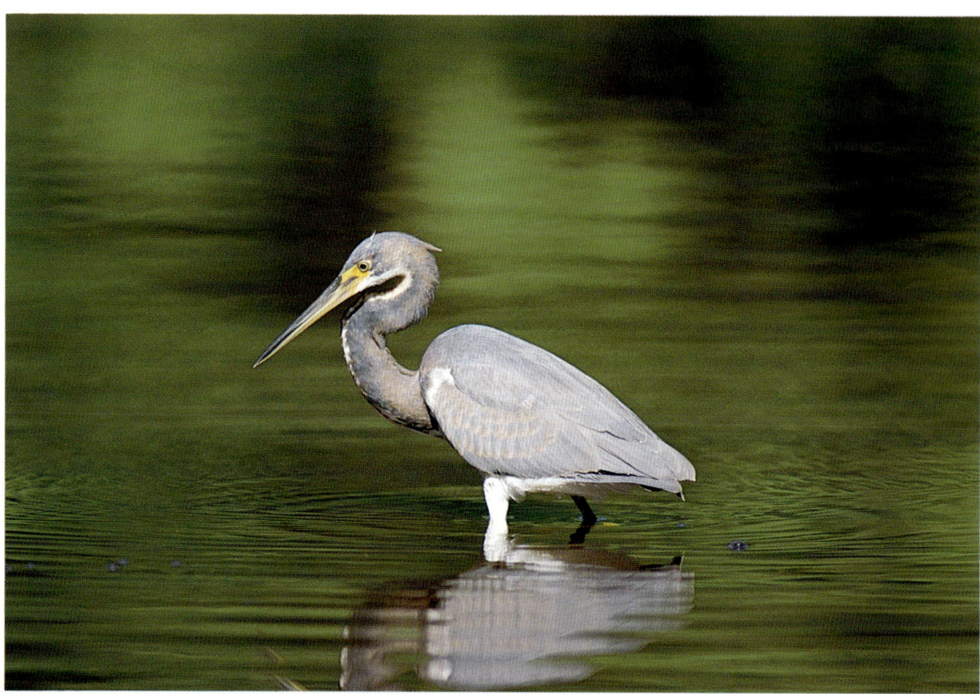

Tricolored heron, Merritt Island, 500mm lens, 1/500 second at f/4

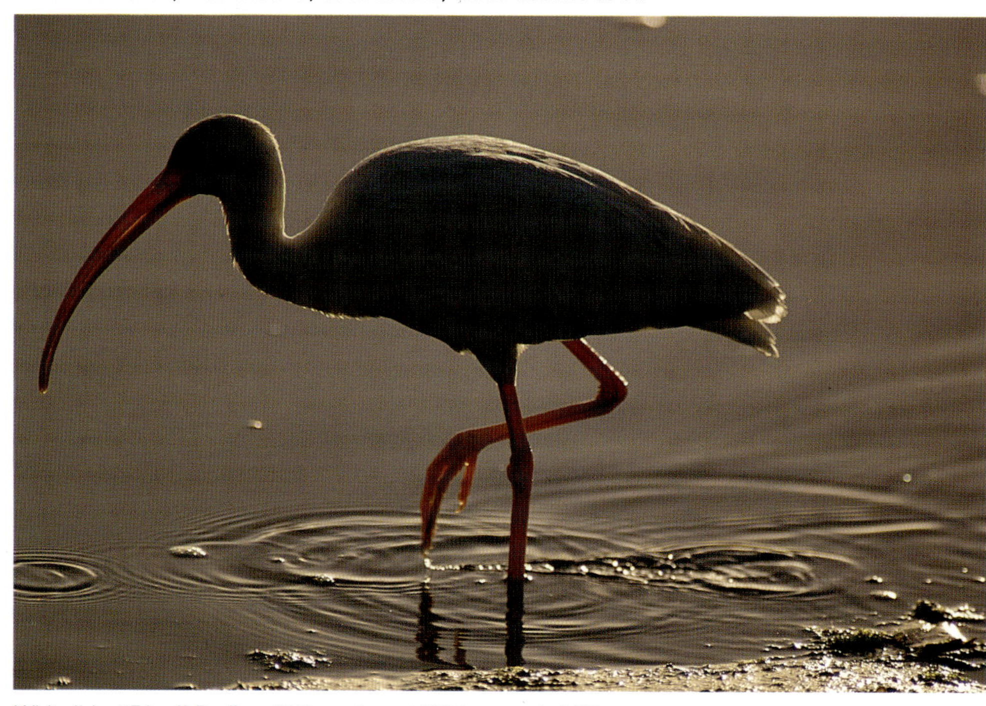

White ibis, ''Ding'' Darling, 500mm lens, 1/250 second at f/4

rapid wingbeats at a low altitude, especially when leaving or returning to a roost. At this time, ibises usually form long, wavering lines that silhouette vividly against the orange sunset.

Since ibises fly low, the wind may be heard streaming through their feathers as they pass overhead.

White ibis will stand patiently in trees along the water's edge for long periods of time, resting and preening.

J.N. ''DING'' DARLING NATIONAL WILDLIFE REFUGE, MERRITT ISLAND NATIONAL WILDLIFE REFUGE

WHITE PELICAN

The white pelican, commonly confused with the woodstork when soaring at great heights, is all white, except for a black wing bar, with a 6-foot wingspan. Unlike

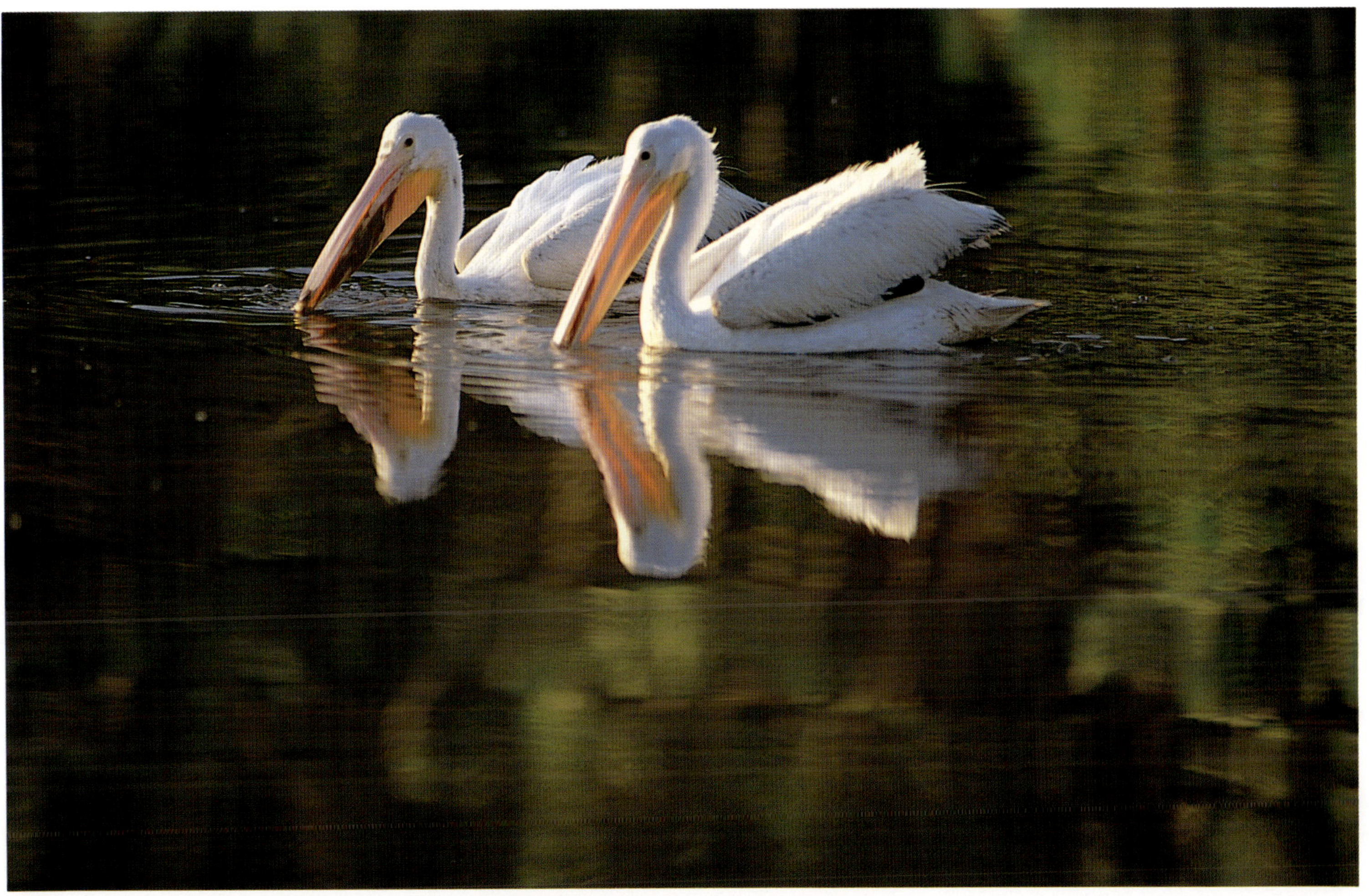

White pelicans, Mrazek Pond, 500mm lens, 1/125 second at f/4

the stork, the white pelican flies with its head tucked back (storks extend their necks and heads). These pelicans winter in Florida but nest in freshwater lakes out West.

When fishing, they do not dive like the brown pelican. They prefer, instead, to feed in groups, swimming in a loose circle, stirring up the water, closing in tighter and tighter. Sometimes two or three will drive fish into shallower water and scoop them up in their baggy pouches, draining the water out slowly before swallowing the fish.

Since the fish these birds eat are of little commercial value, white pelicans are not considered competition by the local fisherman.

MERRITT ISLAND NATIONAL WILD-LIFE REFUGE, SANIBEL, EVER-GLADES NATIONAL PARK

WOODSTORK

Like the spoonbill, the woodstork is both beautiful and ugly. Its gray head is bare of feathers, and it has a large beak. The large, white-feathered body stands about 3 1/2 feet tall. In flight, the woodstork's black-barred wings span 5 feet, and its neck stretches out, unlike the heron's. These storks ride on rising air currents, soaring almost out of sight, and they travel great distances to feed.

Woodstorks can be seen feeding along canal ditches, swamps and ponds. Like herons, they are waders: They feed by sweeping their partially opened bills from side to side while walking. These birds feed by feel; when something touches their beak, it snaps shut. Then, with a quick backward jerk of the head, the bird swallows its prey.

Woodstorks feed in water anywhere from 5 to 20 inches deep, and they will stir heavily vegetated water with their feet to scare fish and crustaceans into the open.

These storks are considered the baro-meter of southern Florida, since nesting is dictated more by the depth of surround-ing waters and the abundance of food than by established season. It is not un-common for the woodstork to abandon nesting some years altogether.

The largest and best-known nesting col-ony occurs in the Audubon Corkscrew Sanctuary near Immokalee. When the birds are actively nesting, a small section of the boardwalk is closed to prevent any disturbance.

Like any parent bird with young, wood-storks can be seen engaged in more feeding at this time.

CORKSCREW SWAMP SANCTUARY CANAL & ROAD DITCHES, HIGHWAY 29

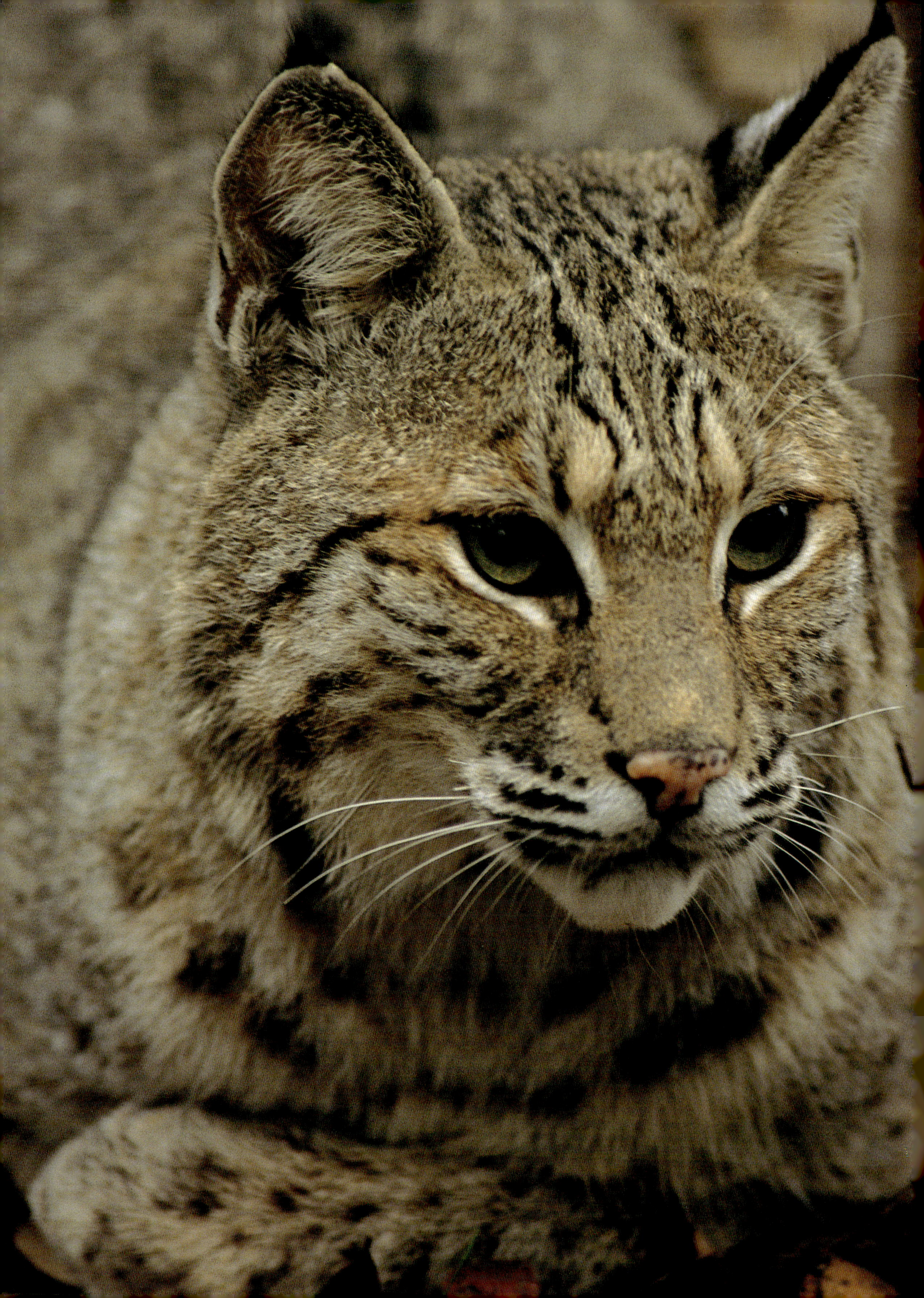

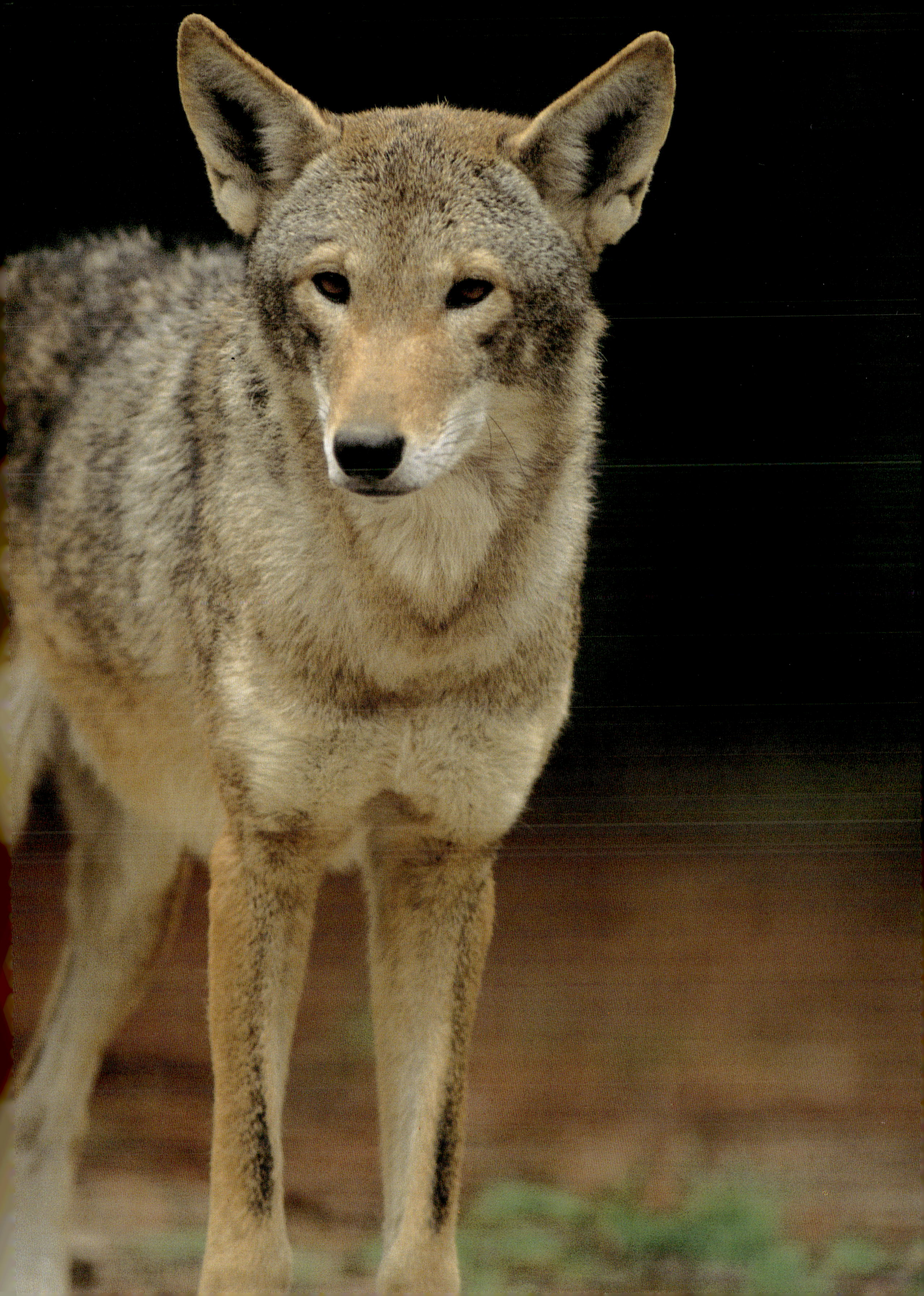

secretive and largely nocturnal cats cross roads at a time when they are most likely to be hit by oncoming traffic. Luckily, panthers generally tend to cross specific roads in their territory at about the same place. This behavioral trait has helped biologists to mark these areas with panther crossing signs to alert drivers to slow down.

Many people confuse the smaller bobcat with the Florida panther. Male panthers, however, can weigh well over 100 pounds, and they can reach a length of 7 feet from their nose to the tip of their long tail.

Deer are the chief food source, but panthers also favor wild hogs. Often they will eat only a portion of their prey, then cover the remainder and return later to finish it off.

Panthers have large territories, which they continually mark to alert other panthers to stay out of, except during mating season.

The majority of the panther population inhabits the Big Cypress preserve and Everglades National Park. Since Big Cypress is a multi-use area, the big cats move north into the agricultural areas during hunting season and return after the shooting ceases.

I have been lucky enough to see the same panther in the wild twice in the last 20 years. There are naturalists who have lived all their lives in the area, however, who have yet to glimpse their first panther.

The Tallahassee Junior Museum has several captive panthers in natural settings that can be seen from an elevated boardwalk.

TALLAHASSEE JUNIOR MUSEUM

KEY DEER

South Florida has its share of endangered animals, and, with habitat destruction and road kills, the tiny key deer is near the top of the list. Only about 260 of these animals are left, roughly two-thirds of the population on Big Pine Key.

These tiny deer can be seen alongside highways, where they sometimes bolt in front of passing cars. The deer look exactly like white-tailed deer, of which they are a subspecies, except they are much smaller — averaging 26 inches in height at the shoulder. They blend in quite well with the dense tropical foliage, camouflaged by thatch palms, palmettos and mangroves.

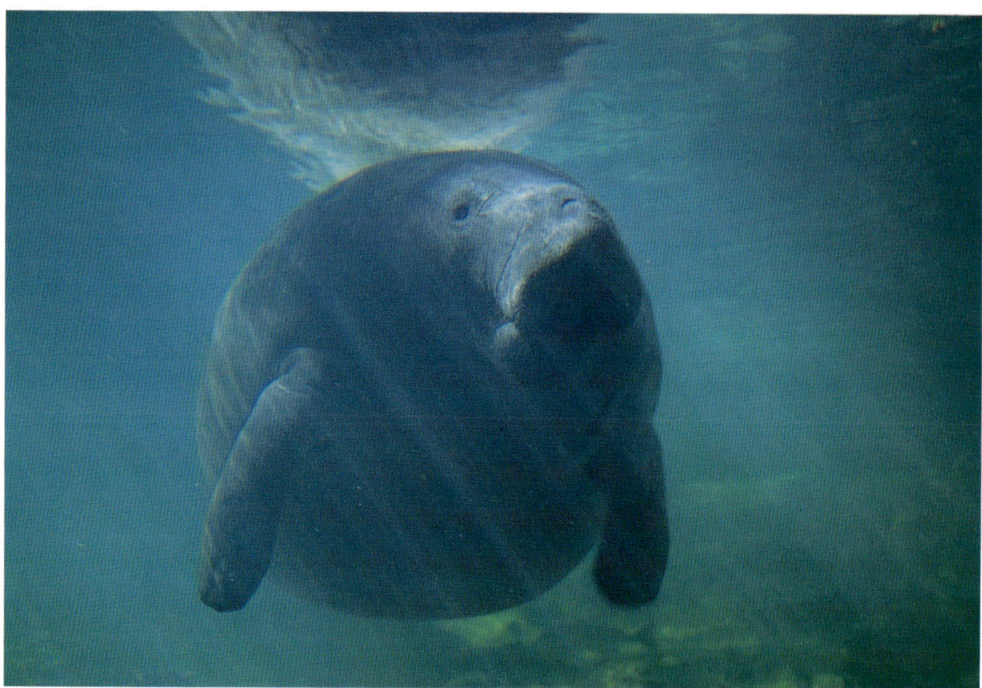

Manatee, Homosassa Springs, 28mm lens, 1/125 second at f/2.8

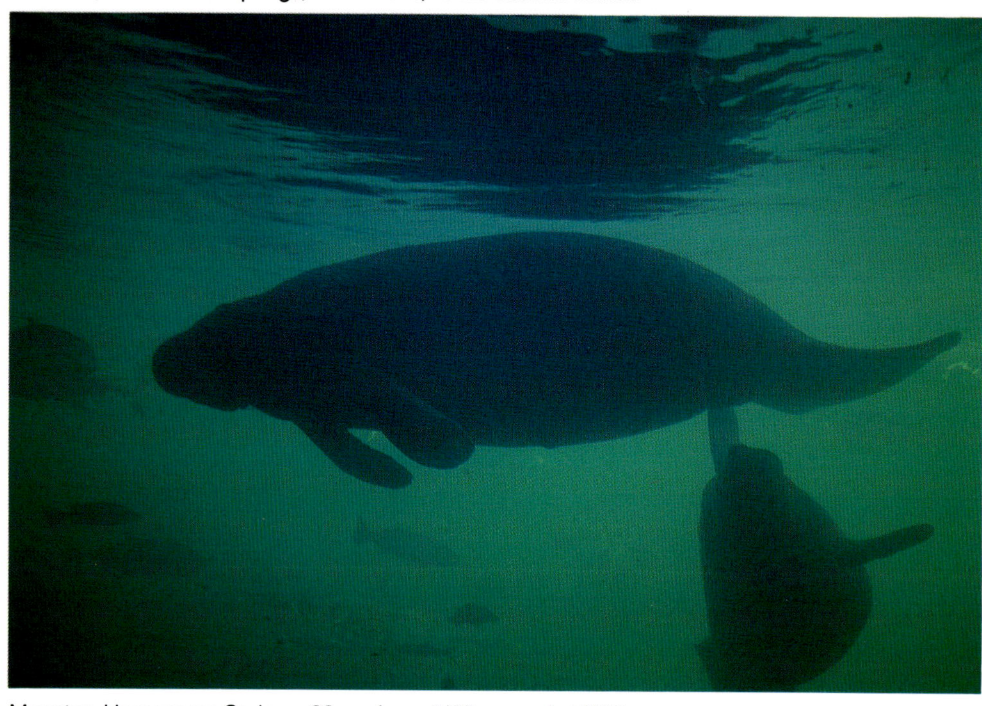

Manatee, Homosassa Springs, 28mm lens, 1/30 second at f/2.8

Key deer obtain their necessary salt intake by eating plants sprayed by ocean water left with a salt residue.

Like the white-tailed deer, the key deer flicks its tail and twitches its ears to let you know when your approach makes it nervous. Since there is nearly always a breeze, traveling undetected is virtually impossible unless you have covered your body odor with a scent.

Rutting season begins around September, and antlers are dropped between February and March. Fawns are born from April to June.

Key deer eat red mangrove leaves and thatch palm berries and graze on grasses in the lawns of local residents. Like most deer, the key deer are primarily nocturnal and are best observed during the early morning or late evening.

On average, 200 speeding citations are issued here every month. If a natural disaster should ever occur here, in conjunction with traffic fatalities, the key deer would likely become extinct.

Please obey all speed limits and heed the strict ban on feeding key deer.

KEY DEER REFUGE — BIG PINE KEY

MANATEE

Northern Florida is genuinely rich in warm springs, spilling millions of gallons of water into its rivers annually. During the winter season, these warm waters are the retreat of the manatee.

These unusual aquatic mammals once ranged from North Carolina to Texas, but today they are restricted to Florida. Manatees weigh as much as a ton and grow to lengths of 11 to 12 feet. As large as they are, they glide gracefully through the clear spring waters, where they feed strictly on aquatic plants.

Since these warm-blooded animals have lungs, they must surface approximately every eight minutes — a factor that has contributed to their demise. Speedboats rip right through the manatees' fleshy backs (usually by accident), with often fatal results.

Manatees suckle their young for approximately the first year after giving birth. Many people snorkel in the springs with these gentle giants, but visitors who prefer to study them without getting wet can do so at an underwater viewing area in Homosassa Springs.

MANATEE SPRINGS STATE PARK, TOMOKA STATE PARK

OPOSSUM

When jokes are made about animals, the opossum is usually at the top of the list. Since this marsupial is primarily nocturnal and wide-ranging, it falls frequent victim to fast-moving automobiles. As mammals go, it is fairly slow, but it can be surprisingly aggressive if cornered — growling and hissing and showing its teeth. To feign death (or "play possum"), it goes limp, with eyes closed and tongue hanging out.

Opossums are fairly nomadic; they often have several dens, with the males traveling farther than females. Though their tails are an aid in climbing, opossums also use them for carrying nesting material. At 10 weeks, the young leave their mother's pouch and begin to ride on her back, where they may stay for another three or four months.

Persimmons are a favorite food, though the rabbit is probably its single most important food source. In residential areas, opossums are flagrant scavengers among garbage cans.

ALONG ROADWAYS

RACCOON

If the opossum is considered one of the dumbest of animals, certainly the raccoon is regarded as one of the smartest. So smart, in fact, that many humanlike characteristics are often ascribed to this highly versatile animal.

It is hard to mistake any other animal for a raccoon, with its dark facial mask and ringed tail, although a lighter-colored species with less distinct markings can be found on No Name Key.

Raccoons usually live near water, and their mistakenly interpreted habit of "washing" food is now thought to be a means of heightening their tactile senses. Their diet consists chiefly of crayfish, frogs, snails, persimmons, insects and, in urban areas, garbage and handouts (both of which can be extremely harmful).

Raccoons are primarily nocturnal and have several den sites — in a cave, crevice or tree cavity. They are expert climbers and can disappear in a palm thicket or mangrove forest in seconds.

Since these night-roaming animals have little color perception, a red-filtered flashlight may enable you to view them without affecting their behavior.

NO NAME KEY, MOST CAMPGROUNDS

WHITE-TAILED DEER

As abundant as this animal is, it usually requires knowing when and where to go to find it, especially since it is still hunted (unlike Florida birds) and thus tends to avoid people as much as possible.

White-tailed deer lie in dense thickets in places like Ocala National Forest and around swamps, where they have no trouble swimming the dark waters. They are active at night, early morning and late evening.

When alarmed, the deer bobs its head up and down, rotates its ears independently and flits its tail. These signs alert the observer to be still. Since deer have relatively poor eyesight, it is movement that they spot and odor that they pick up when the wind direction is in their favor. Although these deer also go by sound, palmettos rustling on a windy day may cover your noise. Position yourself near a tree so you don't stand out.

Deer require freshwater every day, something Florida is not in short supply of yet. Locating a favorite water hole will increase your chances of glimpsing a deer.

In Florida, fawns are born every month of the year. While rutting season in northern Florida is February, in the Everglades it is early August.

Deer are fast runners, and they communicate with one another through body posture. Tracking deer can be difficult, considering all the dense undergrowth and limestone outcrops.

Antlers of males are formed and shed each year, with a velvet material covering them in the beginning stages that is later scraped off to reveal the sharp points.

Adult deer frequently lead a pursuer away from their fawns, which lie motionless in the underbrush.

OCALA NATIONAL FOREST, PINELANDS, SHARK VALLEY — EVERGLADES NATIONAL PARK

REPTILES

AMERICAN ALLIGATOR

Mention Florida to anyone, and the first thing that comes to mind is sun and sand. Then mention swamp, and the image of an American alligator immediately springs to mind. Unfortunately, this remarkable reptile is viewed by many as a horrible man-eating beast. Few predators in North America come as close as the gator to our own predatory status.

Yet the alligator is far from a menace, and it is one of the few remaining animals from an era about which we can only speculate. The American alligator's range includes the entire state of Florida, where it can be found in freshwater ponds, lakes and rivers. Alligators may also turn up in brackish water, but they tend to avoid the ocean areas, which have high salt content. People who report seeing alligators in these areas probably have glimpsed instead the rare American crocodile, now found only in extreme southern Florida.

Since alligators are cold-blooded, they spend much of their time regulating their body temperature by lying in the sun to warm up or by floating in the water — with only eyes and nostrils protruding — to cool off. The ''lazy'' attitude of this seemingly slow-moving creature lulls other animals into a false sense of security, but when a gator needs to move rapidly, it most certainly can. In or out of water, the gator can outrun a human with surprising ease.

The gator's diet consists mainly of fish, frogs, snakes, birds, crabs, mammals and turtles. More than once I have watched an alligator crush a turtle shell with its powerful jaws, throw its head back and gulp down its food. Alligators seldom grab a victim straight on; rather, they prefer to seize their prey from the side and thrash it until the animal has been subdued. Few people ever witness this spectacle, however, since alligators go for long periods without eating and are generally more active at night.

During the dry season, alligators wallow out areas called ''gator holes.'' These deeper pondlike areas are the last to retain the much-needed water for fish and

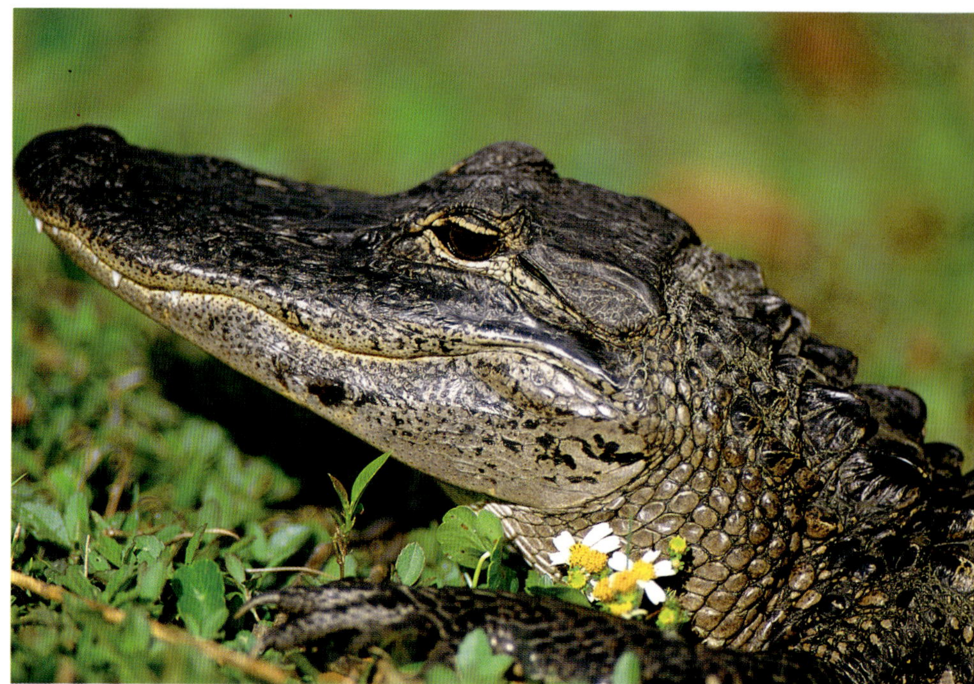

Alligator, Anhinga Trail, 300mm lens, 1/500 second at f/5.6

birds alike. They also keep many waterways clear of vegetation.

During mating season (April-May), male alligators can be heard bellowing a sound not unlike a lion's roar. After mating, the female builds a nest mound, then lays her eggs and guards them until they hatch. The hatchlings remain with their mother during the first few months after birth, and sometimes longer.

This is one of the few times during its life that an alligator is truly vulnerable to attack from natural predators. Blotches of yellow and black help to conceal the baby gators, although raccoons, large wading birds and bobcats take their toll. An ''oinking'' distress call will bring help from any alligator in the area, and on occasion I have imitated this distress signal and had a number of alligators swim towards me. (This technique should be used judiciously, however, for there have been cases reported where alligators that have lost their fear of people from being fed unlawfully have charged out of the water to chase a caller.)

Young gators grow approximately 12 inches per year for the first few years; mature adults average between 8 and 11 feet and live to about 30 years.

SHARK VALLEY — EVERGLADES NATIONAL PARK

AMERICAN CROCODILE

Sightings of American crocodiles in the wild are extremely rare, since this reptile is an endangered species. The last few nesting areas are closed to the public. Even with the majority of the population found in the Everglades National Park (from 150 to 300 total), only 17 clutches were found in 1987 by research biologists.

Crocodiles prefer sandy beaches for nesting; unfortunately, humans have a fondness for beaches too. Beach properties and other developments have contributed to the crocodile's endangered status.

Crocodiles nest approximately 20 feet up from the high-water mark to prevent their eggs from drowning. Their nests may be little more than a depression or as elaborate as a mound built out of vegetation from mangroves.

These salt-water reptiles are restricted to southern Florida. They can be distinguished from alligators by their lighter color and narrower snout.

COOT BAY POND — EVERGLADES NATIONAL PARK, FLORIDA BAY

TREE SNAIL

Florida visitors rarely give much thought to a species as mundane as the snail, but after viewing their first tree snail, that may change. These spiral-shaped snails range from brilliant yellow with brown bands to blue with pink bands. In fact, there are at least 58 color variants in the genus liguus, or ''ligs,'' as the locals call them.

Several thousand years ago, tree snails were blown in by hurricanes, or carried here by other animals or on logs from tropical islands. Cuba has at least 100 color variants, and in the lower Keys snails tend to be more uniform in color than those isolated on hammocks in the Everglades.

Ligs are active during the wet season; during the fall, they lay eggs in the soil at the base of a tree in which they may spend their entire life. Ligs apparently favor certain trees: In the Keys, they prefer Jamaica dogwood, and in the Everglades the lysiloma and buttonwood. Any tree with smooth bark harboring the lichen and fungus these snails feed on is deemed suitable.

Experienced lig hunters look for zigzag patterns eaten in lichen on the side of a tree. After the wet season, these snails seal themselves off to prevent moisture loss — a process called estivation. At this time, they are particularly vulnerable to humans who collect them for their brilliantly colored shells.

It is now illegal to collect ligs. As their habitat gradually shrinks, fewer and fewer species are being found. Natural disasters — such as hurricanes and fires — have eliminated some color forms altogether, and pesticides have taken a further toll.

A species of predatory snail preys on tree snails, and raccoons may eat them too, since there seem to be no ligs on No Name Key, where the raccoon population is unusually large. Tree snails once ranged as far north as Pompano Beach, but today they are confined to the Everglades, Big Cypress Swamp and the Keys.

GUMBO-LIMBO TRAIL, PINELANDS —
EVERGLADES NATIONAL PARK

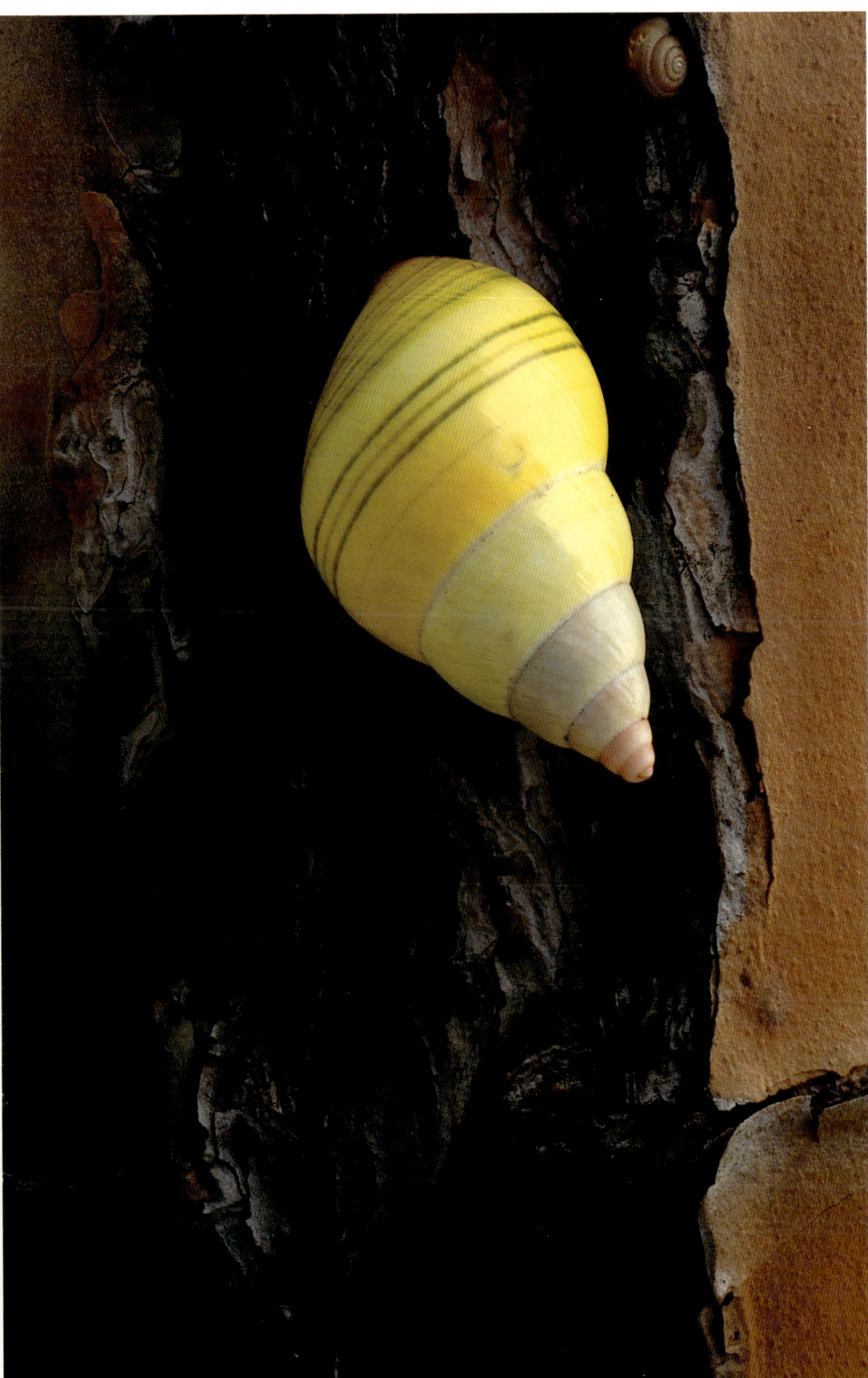

Tree snail, Long Pine Key, 55mm micro lens, 1/2 second at f/16

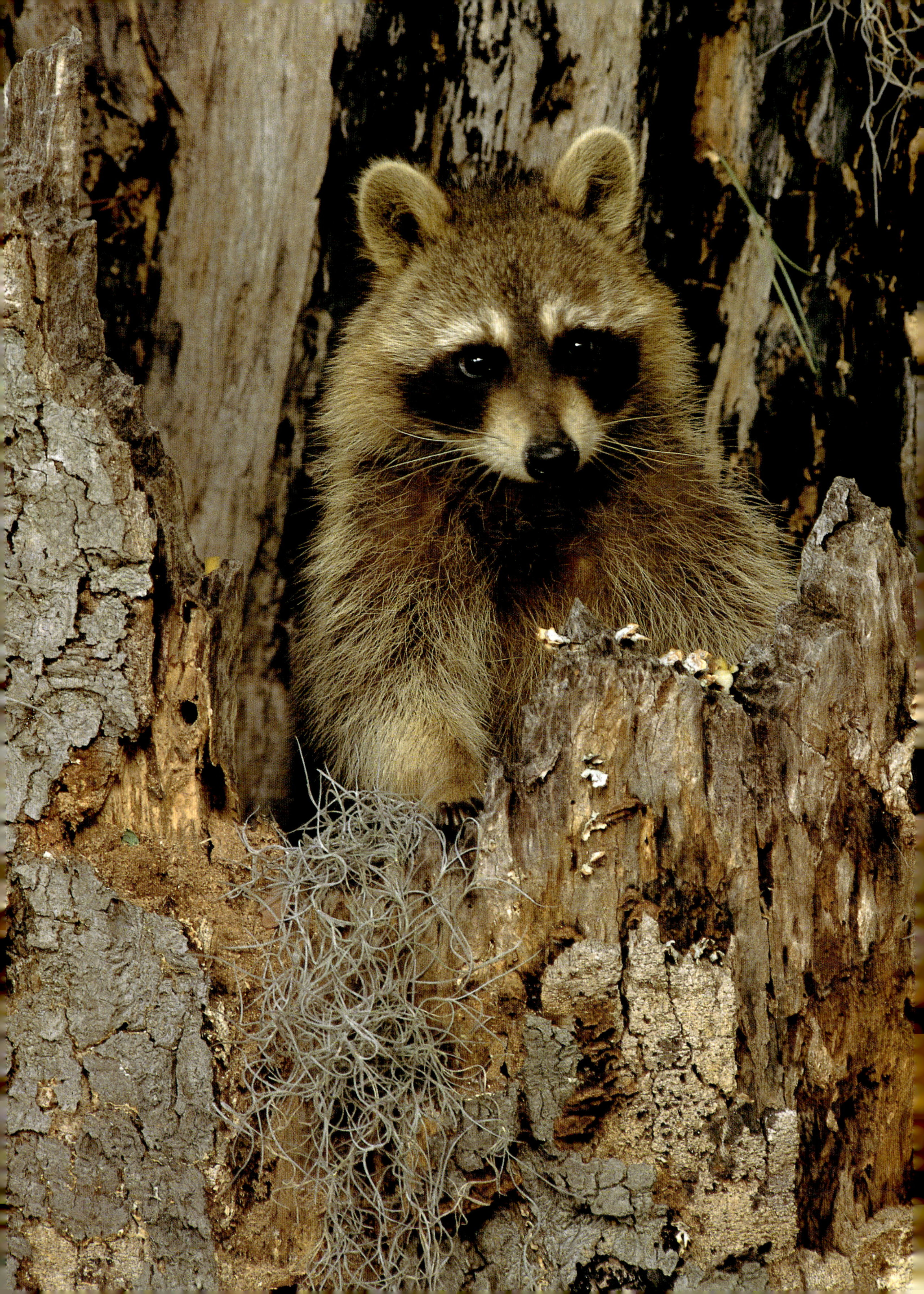

PHOTOGRAPHY

EQUIPMENT

Photographers tend to mystify camera equipment, as if the camera and lens ultimately controlled where and when the photograph is taken. Obviously, more versatile cameras and sharper lenses will improve one's chances of getting good pictures, but ultimately it is the photographer who is responsible for what is produced.

Most camera bodies these days allow for auto and manual exposure; they have TTL capabilities, and, when hooked up with the right lens, they will focus for you. One of the best features I have discovered in the newer cameras is a built-in motor drive. This may not seem like much, especially since most photographers already have motor drives that screw onto their cameras, but if you compare the sound of an external drive to a built-in one, you will hear an incredible difference. Remember: In wildlife photography, the less noise, the more photographs.

To me, the optics are the single most important piece of camera equipment. If a lens is not sharp, or if it is too slow, then the photograph will suffer.

I look for a group of lenses that will do several things: scenics, close-ups and wildlife.

For scenics, use a wide-angle lens from 20mm to 28mm; for the more intimate view, use an 80-200mm zoom that can be converted to a close-up lens by using extension tubes or a bellows. The 200mm micro seems to be the favored lens for close-ups among nature photographers these days.

For years I traveled to the Everglades and photographed birds with a lens no larger than 200mm and obtained good shots. I eventually decided there were some shots I could not get, so I purchased a 300mm; that lens served as my longest focal length up until a year ago, when I began using a 500mm f/4 telephoto. Obviously, I can now get even more shots than before. With this longer lens, my system has become more versatile, though the shorter lens certainly worked well in many situations.

The new generation of telephotos is sharper and faster than ever before, and few lenses manufactured by major camera companies are not acceptably sharp. Accessories like filters, however, should be used for photographic effect, not to protect a lens — that's what a lens cap is for.

Tripods are extremely important in scenic and wildlife photography. Few people hand-hold long telephoto lenses when endeavoring to shoot pictures of birds. A tripod should first be sturdy, and able to collapse to within inches of ground level. It should also be fairly water-resilient.

The tripod head I use is a ball head with a pan mechanism. With one turn of the handle (instead of the three handles so many heads now have), I can make all my adjustments quickly and easily.

Whatever the brand of equipment you ultimately purchase, make sure it is versatile enough to meet your present as well as your projected needs. Many major brands cost a little more (sometimes a lot more). There is a reason: quality.

Coots at sunset, Merritt Island, 80-200mm lens, 1/15 second at f/11

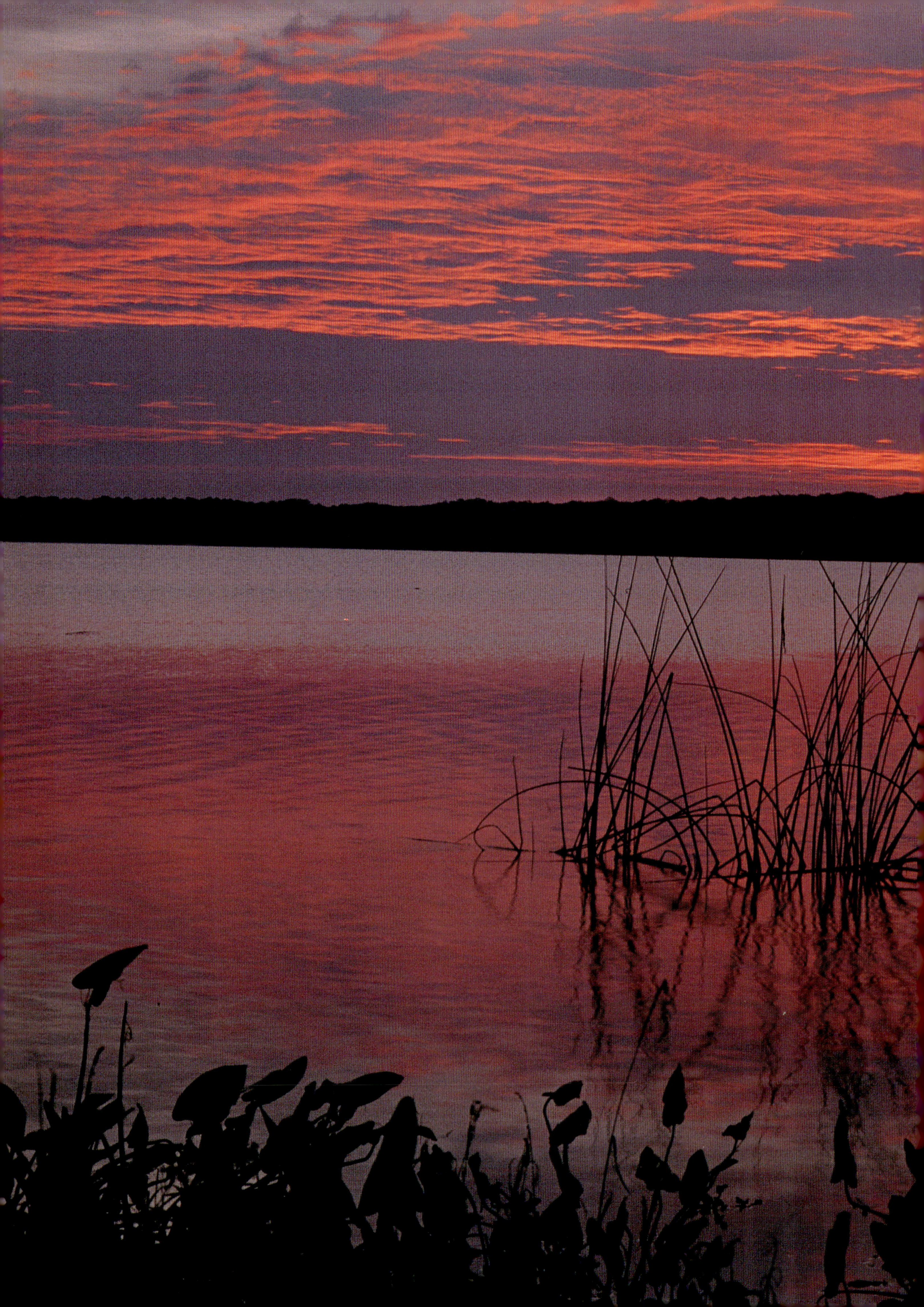

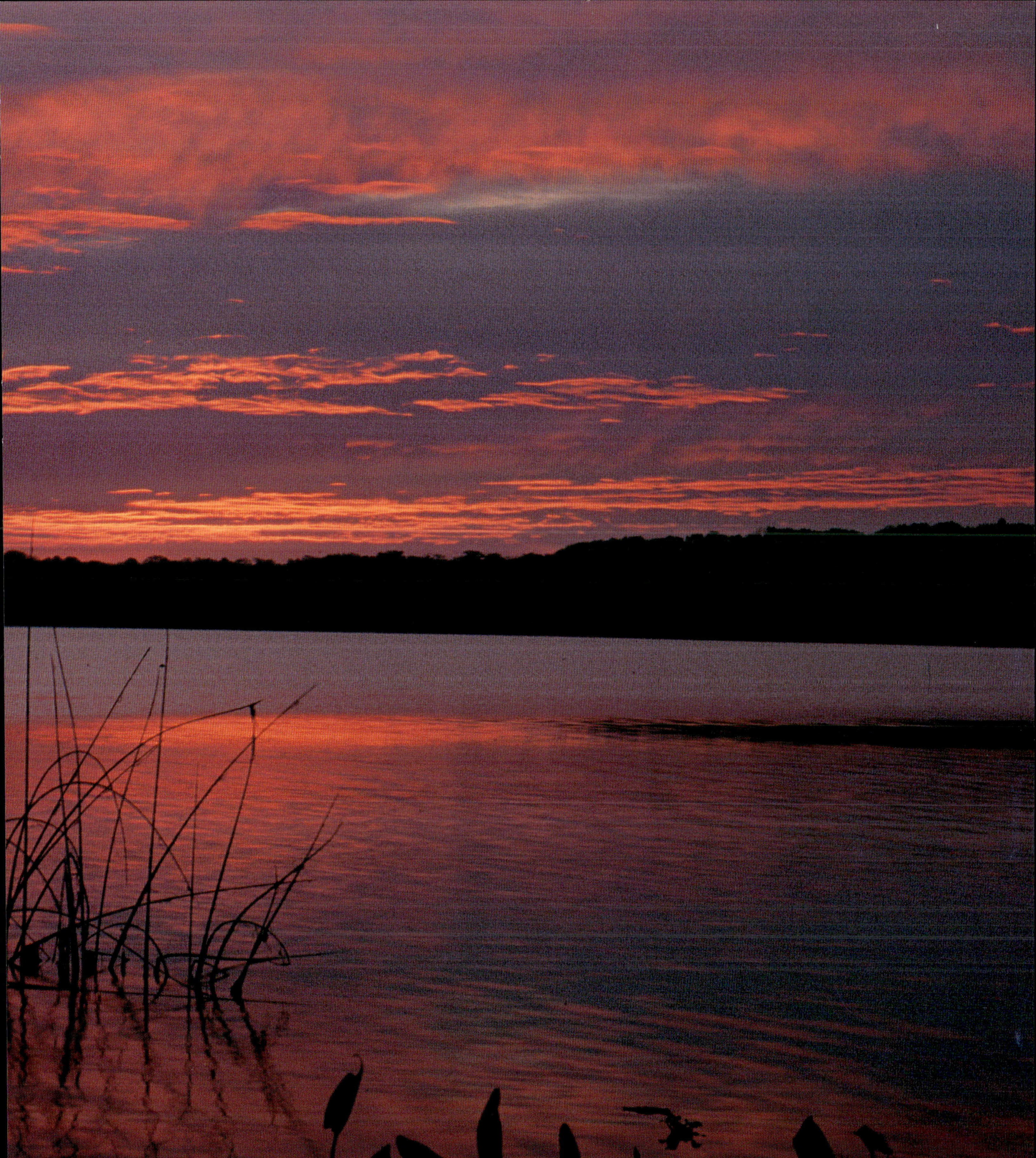

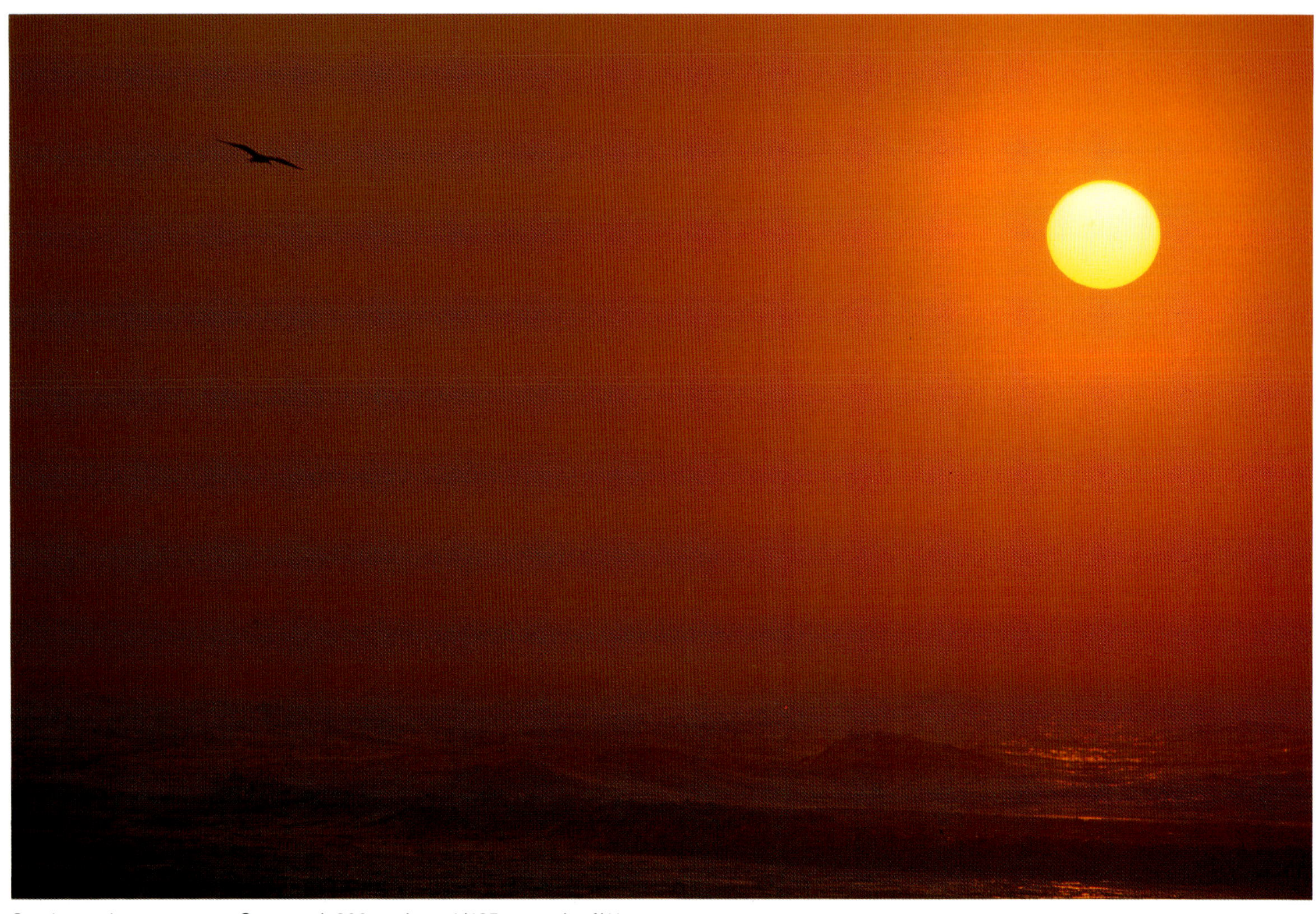

Sunrise and ocean waves, Canaveral, 300mm lens, 1/125 second at f/11

CAMERA CARE

Florida's uniqueness—being surrounded by ocean on virtually all sides — can create real problems for protecting photography equipment. Salt from the air and water is a corrosive agent, so care must be taken to avoid the rusting of even hard plastic cameras and lenses, which have screws and other parts made of metal.

The best way to protect equipment is to keep everything in a carrying case of some sort until ready for use. Wearing a camera around your neck while walking near the surf or leaving it mounted on a tripod may be easier, but you are more likely to have corrosion problems from the salt air. If you must wear your camera or leave it mounted, cover it with a plastic bag and carry a hand towel to wipe the lens barrel and camera body periodically. Ultimately, a damp towel (use freshwater only!) followed by a dry towel is best.

Some photographers use skylight filters to protect the front lens element, but I prefer cleaning the lens periodically with a film-cleansing solution and film-cleaning tissue. In a heavy mist, check your lens every few minutes, for the wind can blow moisture onto the front lens element without your even realizing it.

Salt, of course, is not the only problem at a beach. Sand can cause even more headaches. Never put a camera down directly on the sand; use a camera bag or towel instead. Blowing sand can collect on the rim of your lens. Always use a blower brush to remove sand before cleaning with a tissue, for even a single grain of sand dragged across your lens element can leave a deep scratch. Remember, sand can also enter your camera when you're changing film. Extra caution must be taken, or else scratches may result on your film.

If you are doing a lot of shooting near the ocean, I would recommend that you store film and photo accessories in zip-lock bags. Since tripods often get exposed to more saltwater and sand than anything else, I would suggest you wipe each extension thoroughly — especially the feet, where sand collects — before loading the tripod back into your vehicle.

LIGHTING IN THE FIELD

There are five different ways I use lighting in the field for wildlife photography.

The first, and easiest, is to shoot under natural lighting from the sun. To obtain the best results, shoot in early morning and late evening and capture the warm glow of the light. If, however, the day is overcast, or an animal is backlit by the sun, then use a flash mounted on the camera to provide fill-in lighting and make your subject stand out. To achieve this, take a meter reading and set your flash on automatic where it will put out from one to two f-stops less light than your camera meter indicates. For example, if your camera meter calls for 1/60 second at f/8, then set your flash for an output of f/5.6 or f/4. This technique will also put a glint or catchlight in an animal's eye.

At night I use standard flash units, one mounted on each side of the camera, and a fairly fast lens. To focus more easily in dim light, I use a lamp mounted to my flash or camera (described elsewhere in the section on amphibians). The newer cameras have TTL capability, so no compensation for light loss needs to be made when shooting outside at night.

One of the simplest ways to light relatively stationary subjects, such as caterpillars or flowers, is with mirrors. I always carry a pair wherever I go. Each mirror is made of 1/8-inch plastic and measures 4x6 inches. A wooden frame, built specifically for a mirror to slide in and out of, makes it possible to replace the mirror if it becomes scratched or damaged.

This slot also permits the use of acetate filters. For example, if I need to simulate early-morning light at midday, I simply slide in a warming filter. In addition, I can soften the light by placing a sheet of diffusion material over the mirror.

Screwed onto the bottom of the wooden frame is a small rectangular block of aluminum with a threaded hole, allowing it to be mounted to any standard tripod head. Unlike standard flash units, these mirrors permit me to see exactly where the light hits the subject. With mirrors I can backlight, sidelight or fill in harsh shadows.

There are, of course, times when natural sunlight at any angle will not work. That's when I shade the area with a white photographic umbrella. Obviously, this works only on wildlife that won't run or fly off. (Salamanders are good subjects for this kind of soft lighting.)

Photographing small birds in flight is not a simple task. First of all, the flash units you use must be from 1/5,000 second to 1/10,000 second in duration. Many small units now go to 1/50,000 second, but the light output is so minimal that this often proves unworkable. I would advise using units with flash durations of 1/10,000 second, with sufficient power to allow an f-stop of 16.

The units that I purchased from A. Kenneth Olson of St. Paul, Minn., who makes them himself, are powered in the field by a small 12-volt motorcycle battery. This has the capacity to be used with four flash heads, thus allowing for more creative lighting.

The unit on high power has a flash duration of 1/10,000 second, with an aperture of f/16 at a distance of 3 feet; on low power, it lasts 1/20,000 second at f/11.

These flash units are ideal for photographing birds flying to nests or onto perches. In fact, the whole setup is remarkably simple to use. I customarily include a

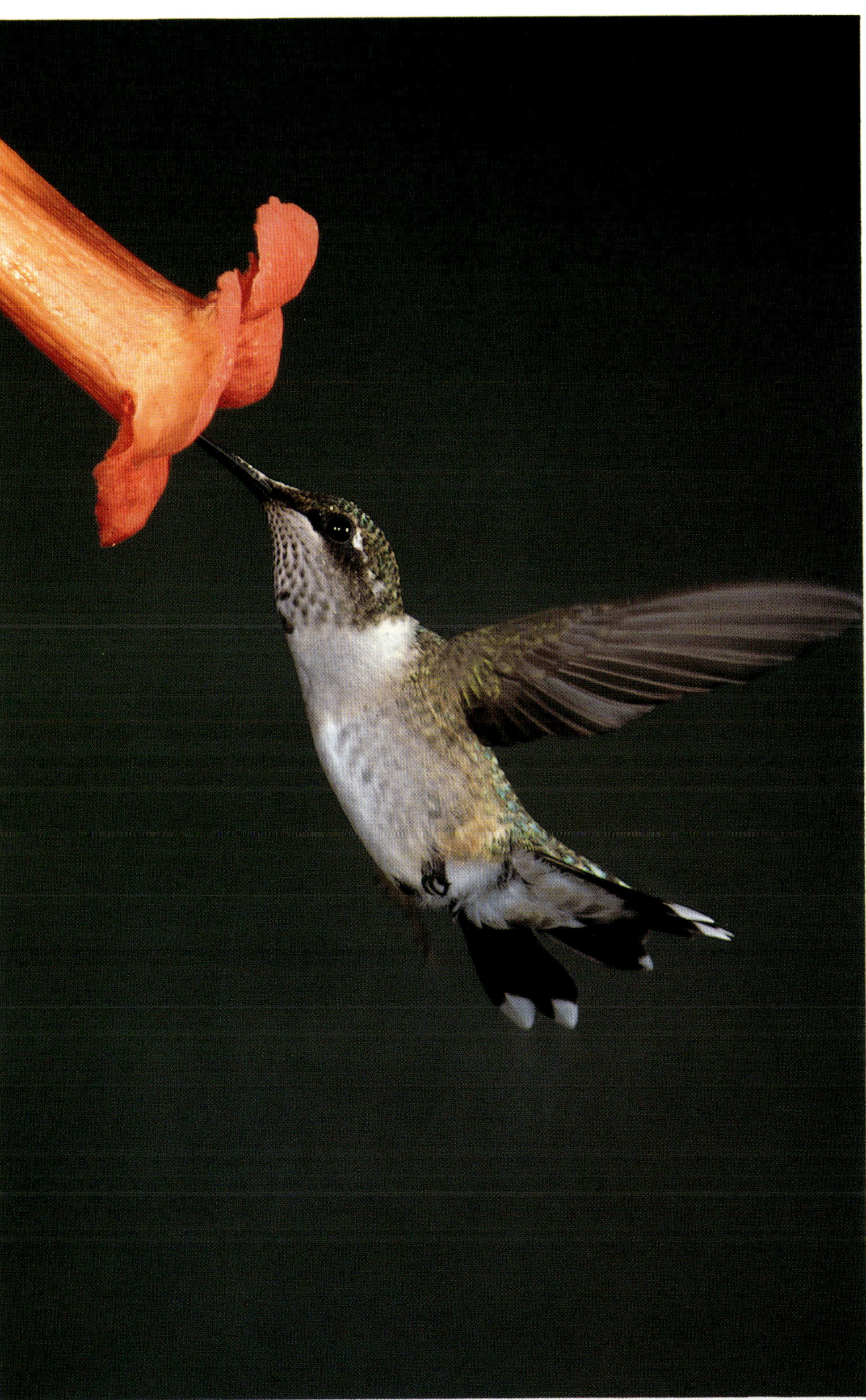

Hummingbird, near Ocala, 200mm micro lens, high speed strobes, 1/10,000 second at f/11

photocell, so that when the bird breaks the beam, it takes its own photograph.

Watching with binoculars, I first study the bird's flight path and behavior to determine where to set up the beam. The particular photocell I use takes 1/10 second after the beam is broken to trigger the entire mechanism.

Accordingly, I must calculate the distance the bird will travel in 1/10 second and prefocus on that area. Here, a small aperture

of f/16 increases my chances of capturing the bird in the field of focus.

A flash meter is essential when setting up the strobes to make sure the f-stop is correct, since you rarely get the same wingspread twice. I have also found that batteries tend to wear down rather quickly.

Whether you are photographing a monarch caterpillar suspended from a leaf or a screech owl in flight, keep in mind that each shot requires different, some-

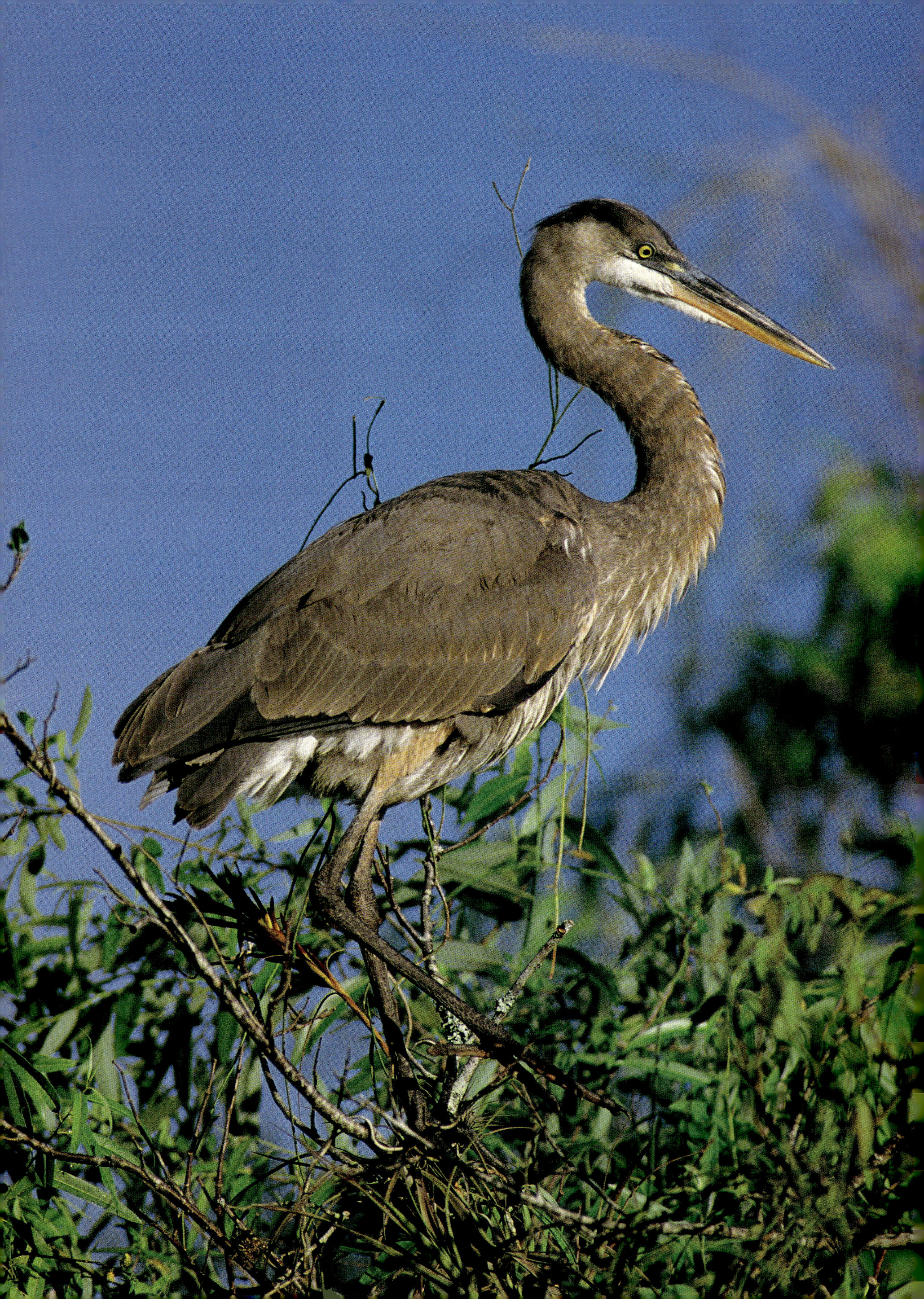

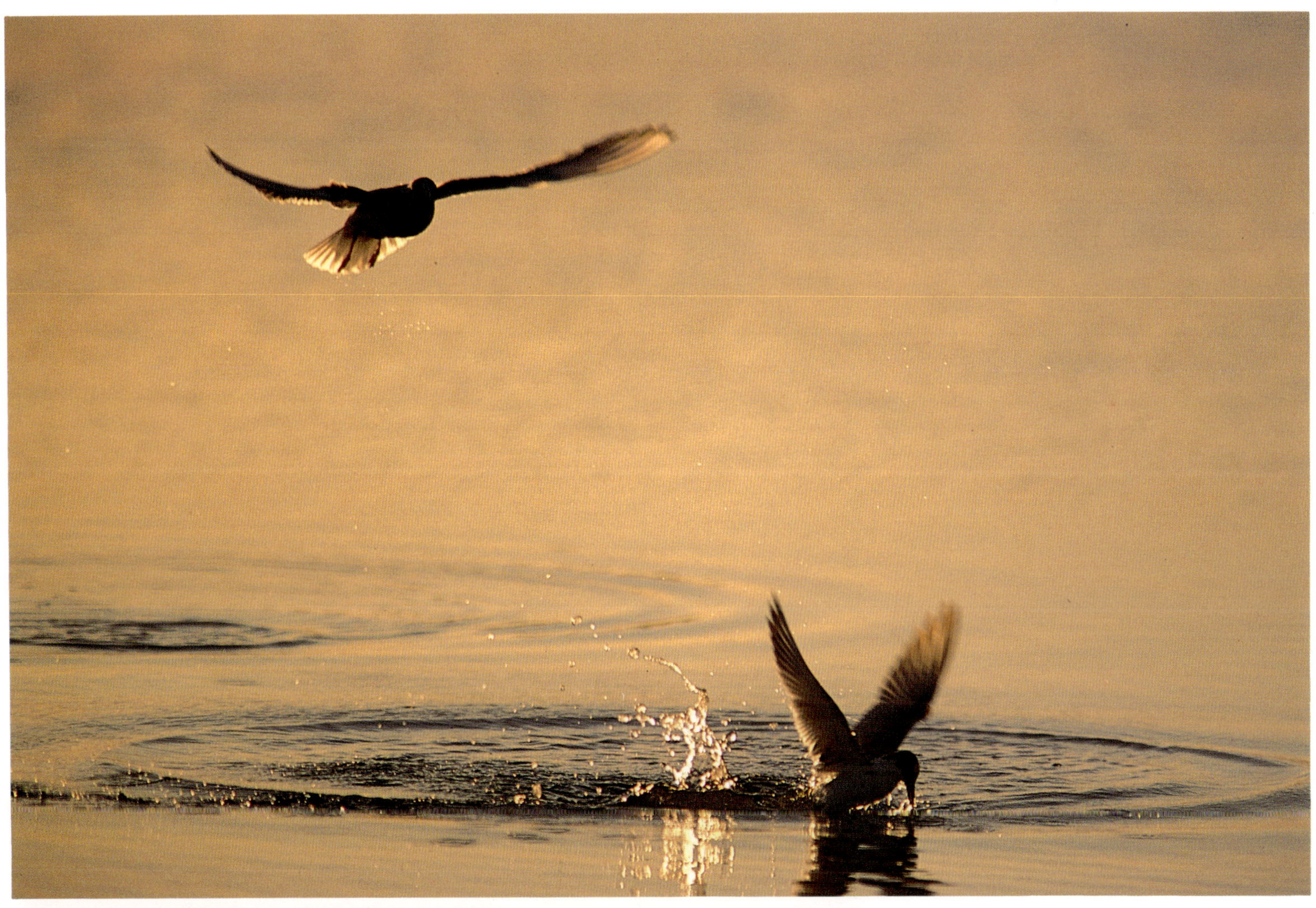

Gulls, Merritt Island, 500mm lens, 1/1000 second at f/5.6

times special, lighting considerations. Too often we tend to shoot fast and take our light as it comes. We should, instead, make a greater effort to create every image as best we can.

SHOOTING FROM A CAR

If your subject is close to the roadside, like many osprey nests and animal feeding areas along the dikes of Merritt Island, then a car is the best blind you can have. Not only can you easily move it to where the animals are, but most birds have learned to accept cars moving and parked. Only when passengers get out of an automobile do the animals get alarmed.

Some birds may grow agitated when first approached, so turn off the ignition and wait until they resume their normal behavior. If you try to shoot while your car motor is running, blurred photographs will result from the vehicle's vibrations.

The best strategy is to have another person drive. While you're shooting, give hand signals instead of verbal instructions; the less noise the better. Tinted windows make it harder for birds to pick up on movement in the car.

There are several ways to support a camera and long lens when your window is rolled down. Novaflex and other manufacturers make window mounts; the model with a monoball head is excellent for stabilizing a camera system. If you don't have a mount, place a jacket or sweater over the window frame to cushion your lens. (This method, however, can become strenuous and tedious.)

Another advantage to using your car as a blind is that you can lay out all your film and accessories on the seat beside or behind you without having to go back and forth to retrieve needed equipment.

Photographing birds in flight from a car window is nearly impossible, due to the short panning range. Instead, concentrate on birds that are feeding, since they are more inclined to ignore your presence in a car.

SHOOTING FROM A BOAT

Many scenic areas in Florida cannot be adequately photographed without use of a boat. Of course, shooting from a boat requires faster shutter speeds and a good deal of hand-held camerawork.

Many birds, especially herons and pelicans, roost among the mangrove trees that line the channel areas of Florida waters. I have discovered it is often wiser to shoot in areas where there is already frequent boat traffic, since the birds there are less skittish and allow closer approach. Long telephotos are thus unnecessary, too.

Always watch the water's current; position the boat where it will drift closer to the birds after you turn off the motor. This technique should enable you to pass within just a few feet of roosting birds.

To be safe, pack your gear in a padded cooler, which will prevent saltwater spray from crystallizing on your equipment. On those relatively rare occasions when a cold front pushes into Florida, you may find yourself engulfed in early-morning saltwater fog along the ocean's edge. Be sure to wipe down your equipment periodically; this moisture is extremely corrosive.

In shallow areas, you will frequently find sandbars where you can leave a boat for a more stable platform (but be sure you do not step onto a coral reef by mistake) from which to shoot. Many of these sandbars are visited by fish-seeking cormorants, gulls and, in the Keys, great white herons. In swampy areas, duckweed or water hyacinth may cover the water's surface.

The low angle the boat affords can contribute to unique shots unobtainable from the swamp's edge. If possible, have someone with you to maneuver the boat while you shoot, or you may lose many photographic opportunities.

LANDSCAPE

Florida's landscape is one of flat land and broad skies. The flat lands may be covered with sawgrass, sand, dwarf cypress, pine forests or cypress swamps. Whichever of these landscapes you select to photograph, make sure the final image is in sharp focus.

To accomplish this, stop the lens down in most cases to at least f-16. If there is little in the foreground, wide-angle lenses can be shot at a large f-stop and still achieve good results.

Whether you are a painter or a photographer, you have probably heard of the "rule of thirds." By placing the horizon where it will either cut across the bottom third of the frame or the top two-thirds, you will determine where the emphasis of the image will be. If there is more land mass, the landscape will become the main subject; if the sky dominates, then the color of the sky, the clouds and the time of day will be the focal point. The word "rule" has always bothered me — particularly in photography — since some of my most successful pictures have been framed

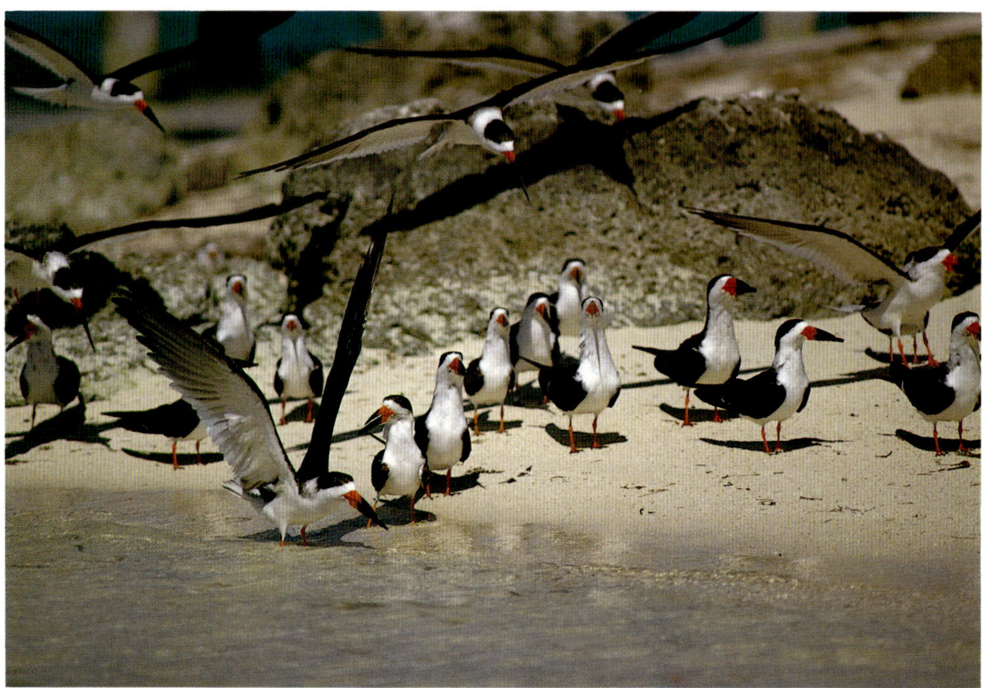

Black skimmers, Keys, 300mm lens, 1/1000 second at f/4

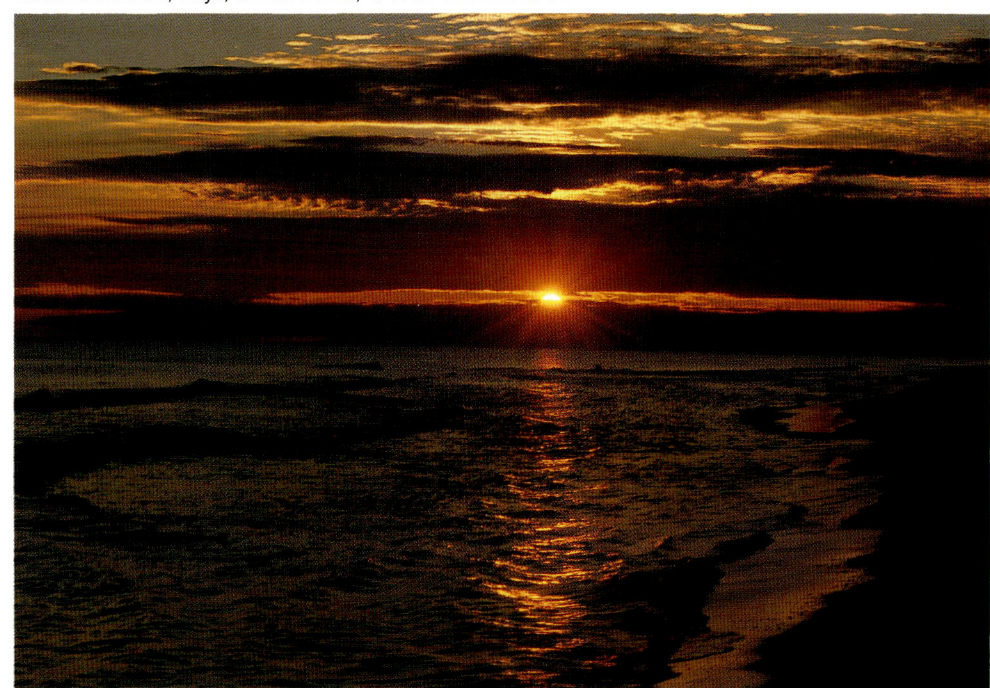

Sunset, Gulf Islands, 80-200mm lens, 1/4 second at f/16

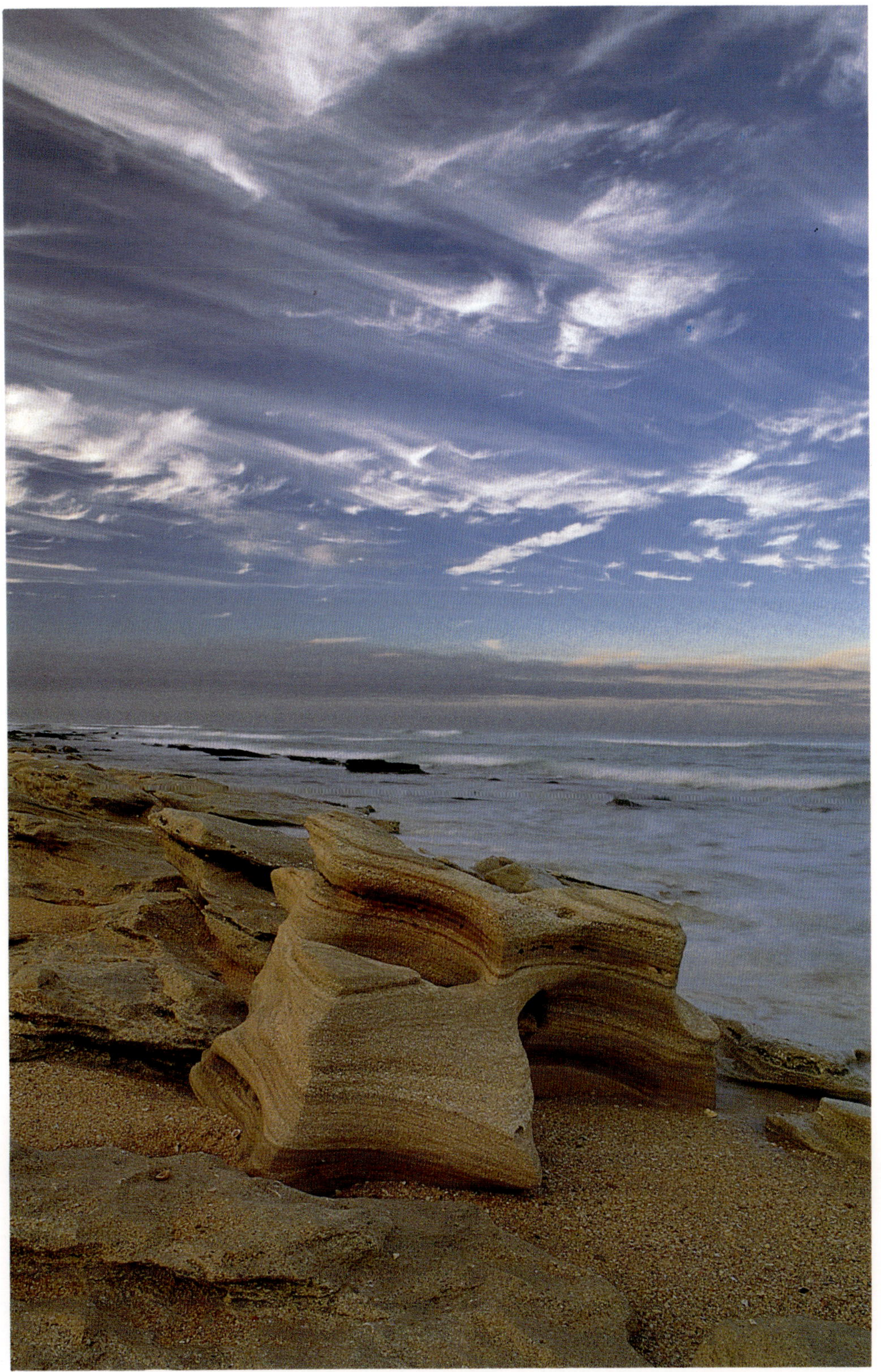

Beach, Washington Oaks, 28mm lens, 1/15 second at f/16

where the horizon cuts the picture in half. The rule of thirds, then, is more of a guideline; don't try to make every image fit within this formula. In fact, don't include the sky at all in your photograph unless you know it will contribute something to the final image.

Cypress trees draped with Spanish moss are ideal subjects for framing a lake covered in fog. In other situations you can add depth to a picture by finding something in the foreground to include in the scenic. If, for example, you wish to emphasize the foreground — a shell on a beach, say, or a spider web in sawgrass — then use a wide-angle lens. If, however, it is the whole of a scene, rather than the individual parts, that you wish to emphasize, then use a medium telephoto lens.

In Florida's flat expanses, horizontal framing emphasizes the horizon; vertical framing requires greater forethought. Look for vertical lines such as trees or sea oats that can lead the eye through the frame.

Shooting in a pine forest on a bright sunny day can be exasperating. I prefer to shoot in softer, overcast light, or during the early morning and early evening, when the difference between light and shadow is not too great. Use of a polarizing filter will eliminate many of the harsher highlights reflecting from the bark, needles and leaves of trees.

Side and back lighting can be far more dramatic in a scene than the customarily harsh frontal lighting of midday. This kind of work demands the use of a tripod and cable release, to avoid any vibration in the camera. (This also allows the photographer to examine the whole image and not just look dead center, as so many people who hand-hold their cameras seem to do.)

Look for shorelines that curve; by adding a land mass to the bottom of your picture, you will also be adding stability.

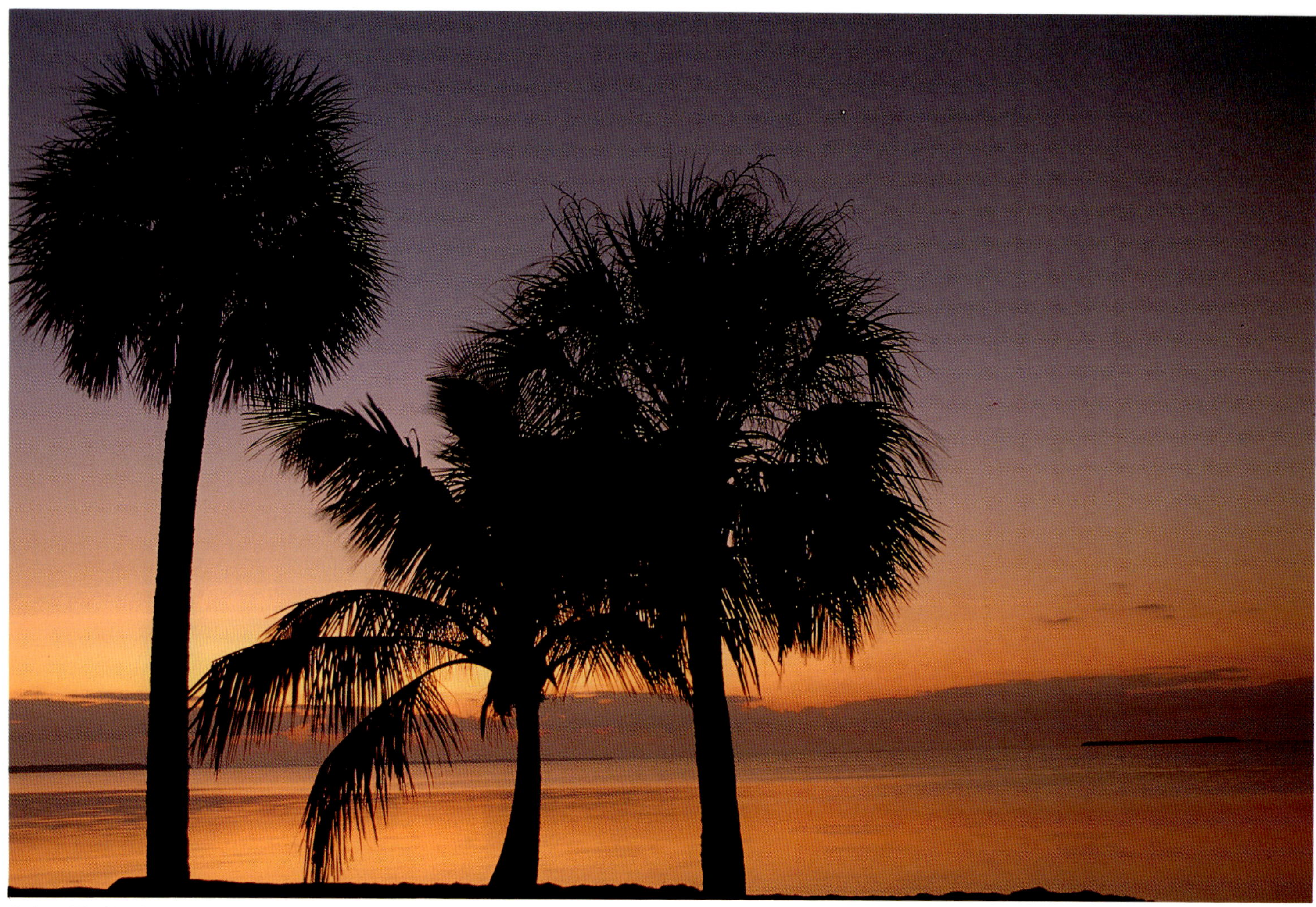

Palms, Florida Bay, 28mm lens, 1 second at f/11

SILHOUETTES

Some of the most magnificent colors in nature's palette begin to appear in the Eastern sky 30 to 40 minutes before sunrise. Yellows, oranges, lavenders, blues and sometimes a mixture create spectacular sky shows. Yet photographers who try to isolate these elements frequently end up with little more than splotches of color.

Some object is necessary with which to contrast the colors. When sparse light spills out over a landscape, shoot silhouettes.

Since trees stand tall against the sky, they provide excellent subjects for silhouetting — especially if you can position yourself at a low angle or if you're shooting in a flat area with little other vegetation to interfere.

When you include water in a shot, the vivid colors will reflect off the water's surface even with strong rolling waves.

If the tree you have selected to photograph dominates the frame, point the camera to include only the sky for metering purposes, then reposition before shooting. Clearly, a tripod and cable release are essential here, since early-morning exposures can range up to several seconds.

Water alone offers a fine background when seabirds stand on short pilings with their wings outstretched, or when they glide just inches over the water's surface.

Before including both water and sky in a shot, take a meter reading off the sky and shoot 1/2 f-stop under or at what the meter reads, depending on the brightness of the sky. Caution should be exercised, however, to avoid losing darker-colored waters if the shot is too underexposed. Palm trees along Florida's bay areas are perfect for silhouetting.

SUNRISE AND SUNSET

Whether land or water, the Florida horizon is fairly flat — and, for photographic purposes, it is hard to beat.

Depending on such factors as the clarity and crispness of the day, or the fog and mist from the ocean, the sun and morning sky will vary in intensity and color. What remains fairly constant, however, is the metering procedure.

Isolate the section of the sky just off to the side of the sun, take your meter reading

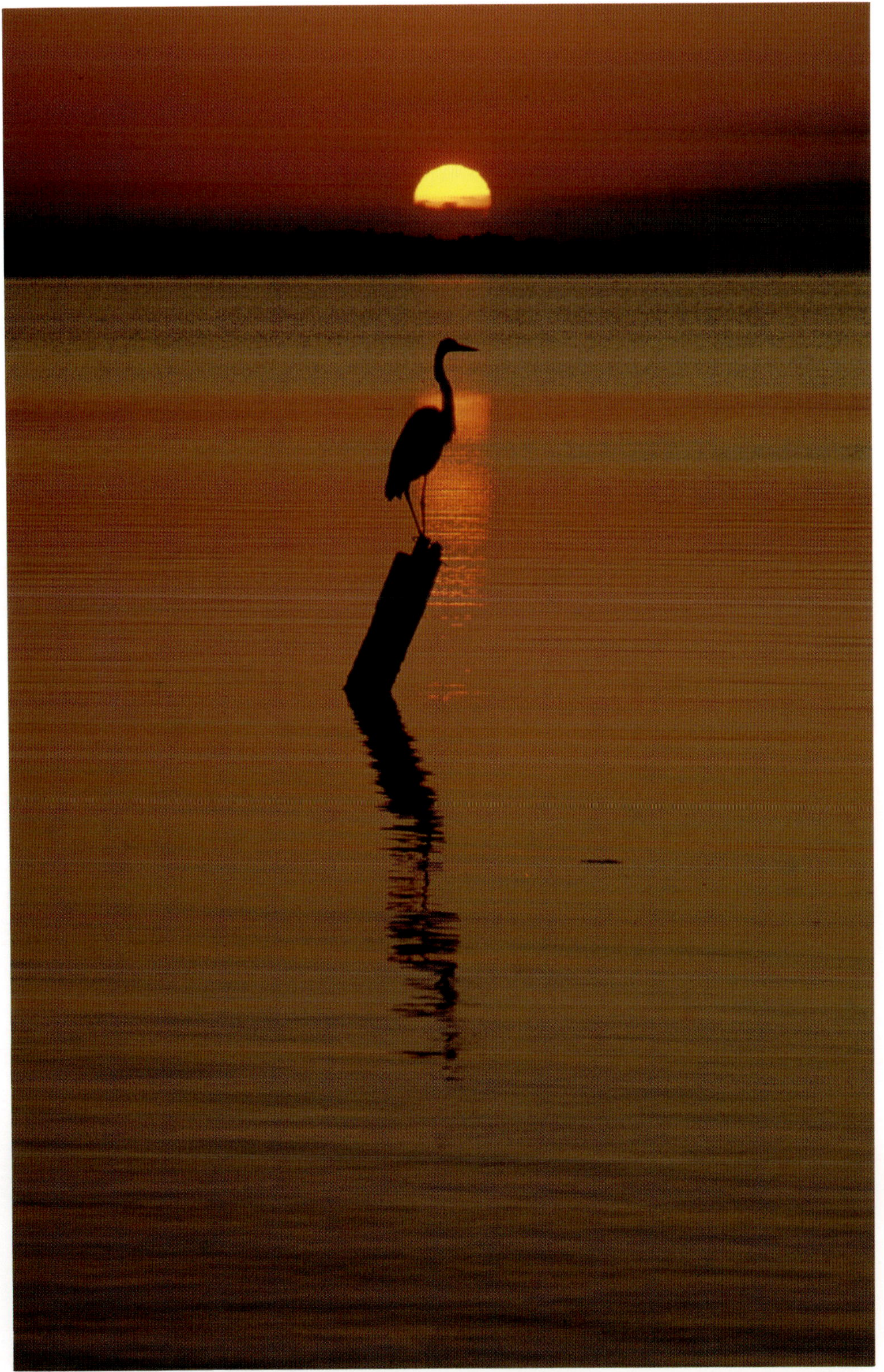

Great white heron, Florida Bay, 80-200mm lens, 1/4 second at f/16

feeling.

If you wish to emphasize the sun when shooting over a lake or the ocean, include more sky; if you prefer to emphasize the reflective colors in the water, pull down and include only a small strip of sky with sun.

The relatively rare days when the morning is cold signal one of two things. Either the morning will be intensely clear and exhibit brilliant colors, or, since the lakes and ocean are warmer, a vaporlike fog will be given off, creating some terrific photographic opportunities. It is rare to be able to shoot wisps of fog backlit by the morning sun with ocean waves in southern Florida, but if you go farther north, the opportunities will increase.

Beaches can work in composing shots of waves washing upon the shores; just as each wave retreats, the wet sand reflects the orange of the sun.

I have had better luck in the Gulf Islands National Seashore area finding and shooting good beach shots at sunset, since the beach is more at an angle to the sun. The eastern beaches are usually fairly straight, and the sun comes up where it must be shot with a straight line. Since the sun is so bright, shooting waves at a fairly small aperture can be accomplished. But beware of lens flare when shooting into the sun.

If you see clouds gathering along the horizon, don't pack up and leave; rather, wait until the sun just starts to break out from the clouds. The clouds will either be strongly lit around the rims, or fingers of light may project vividly across the sky.

Take notice of what is transpiring behind you too, for often when you turn away from the sun you may see softer colors — more pastel, pink clouds — against a pale blue sky with warm light spilling across the landscape. Always look completely around when you are photographing at both sunrise and sunset.

Sunsets usually appear larger than sunrises; unfortunately, more often than not, this is due to the quantity of pollutants

and underexpose about 1/2 f-stop. This will give you a correct exposure. Should you wish to create a more dramatic mood with, say, the bright ball of sun over a dark, reflective ocean, then underexpose 1 to 1 1/2 f-stops, or, when shooting the sun through a bright fog, open up 1 to 1 1/2 f-stops to create a lighter, more ethereal

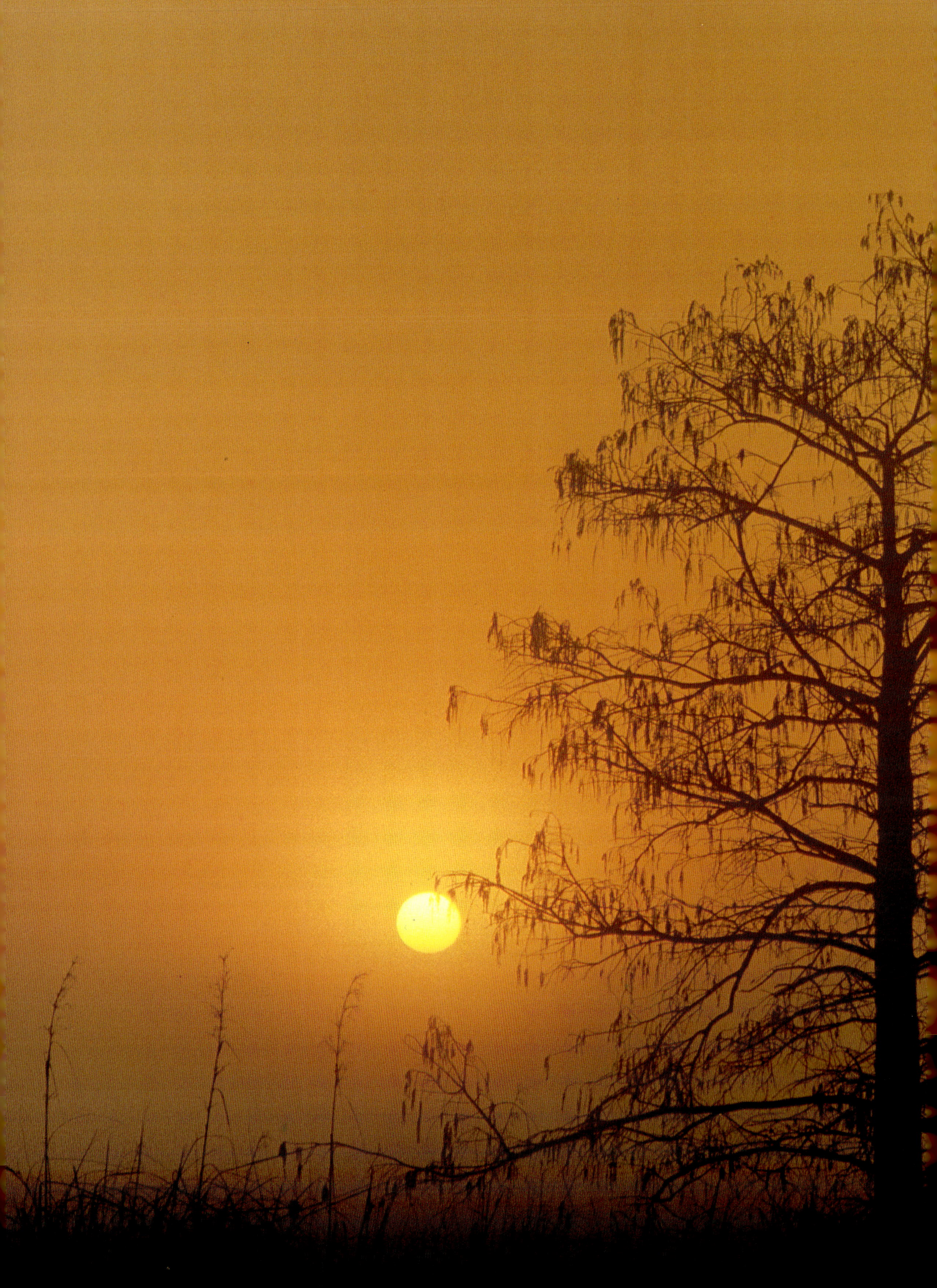

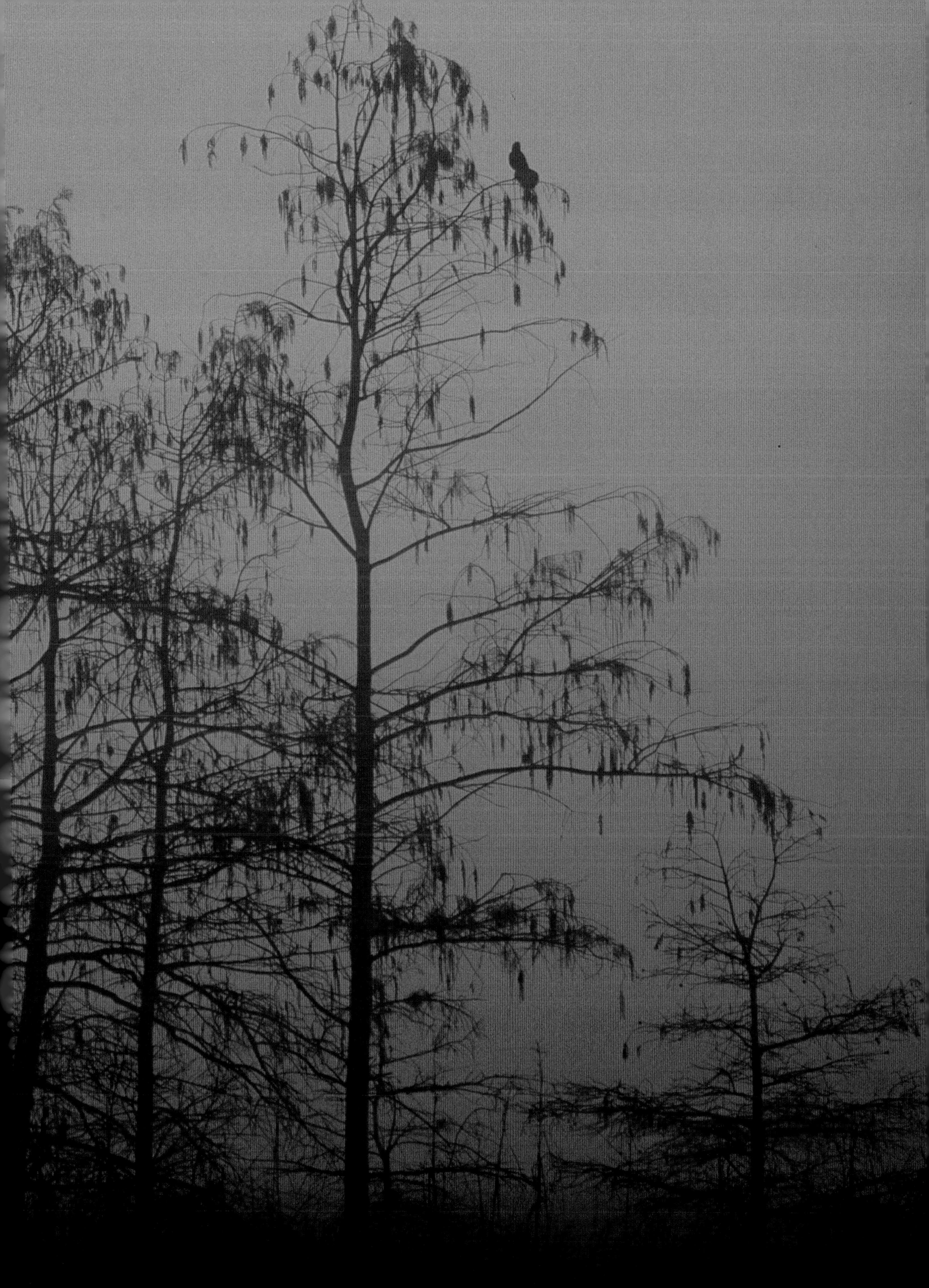

in the air generated by daytime industrial activities.

Patterns in the sand are accentuated when the sun is at a low angle, adding a certain warmth to the sand as well.

Block the sun from hitting your lens by using a sun shade. If that proves insufficient, try a hat to shade your lens. Generally speaking, avoid using a filter, unless it is intended to provide a particular photographic effect, for it will likely increase your chances of getting lens flare.

If you set up your equipment on a tripod in the sand where waves are breaking, be aware that as the waves retreat, the sand will collapse a little at a time, jeopardizing your entire setup.

Replant the feet of your tripod from time to time.

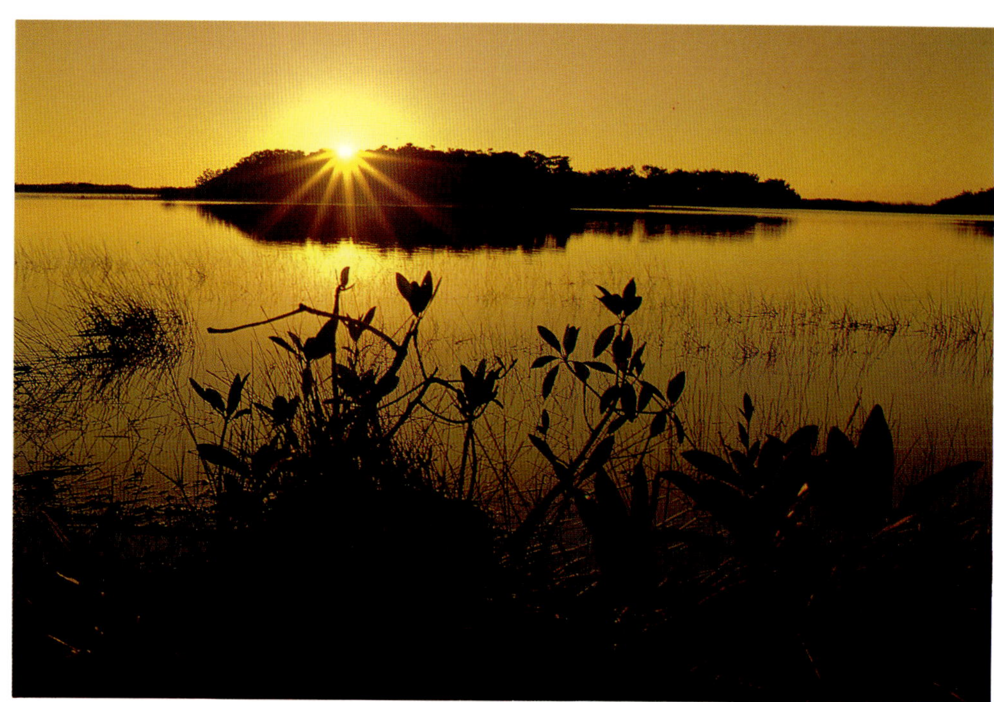

Sunset, Paurotis Pond, 28mm lens, 1/30 second at f/16

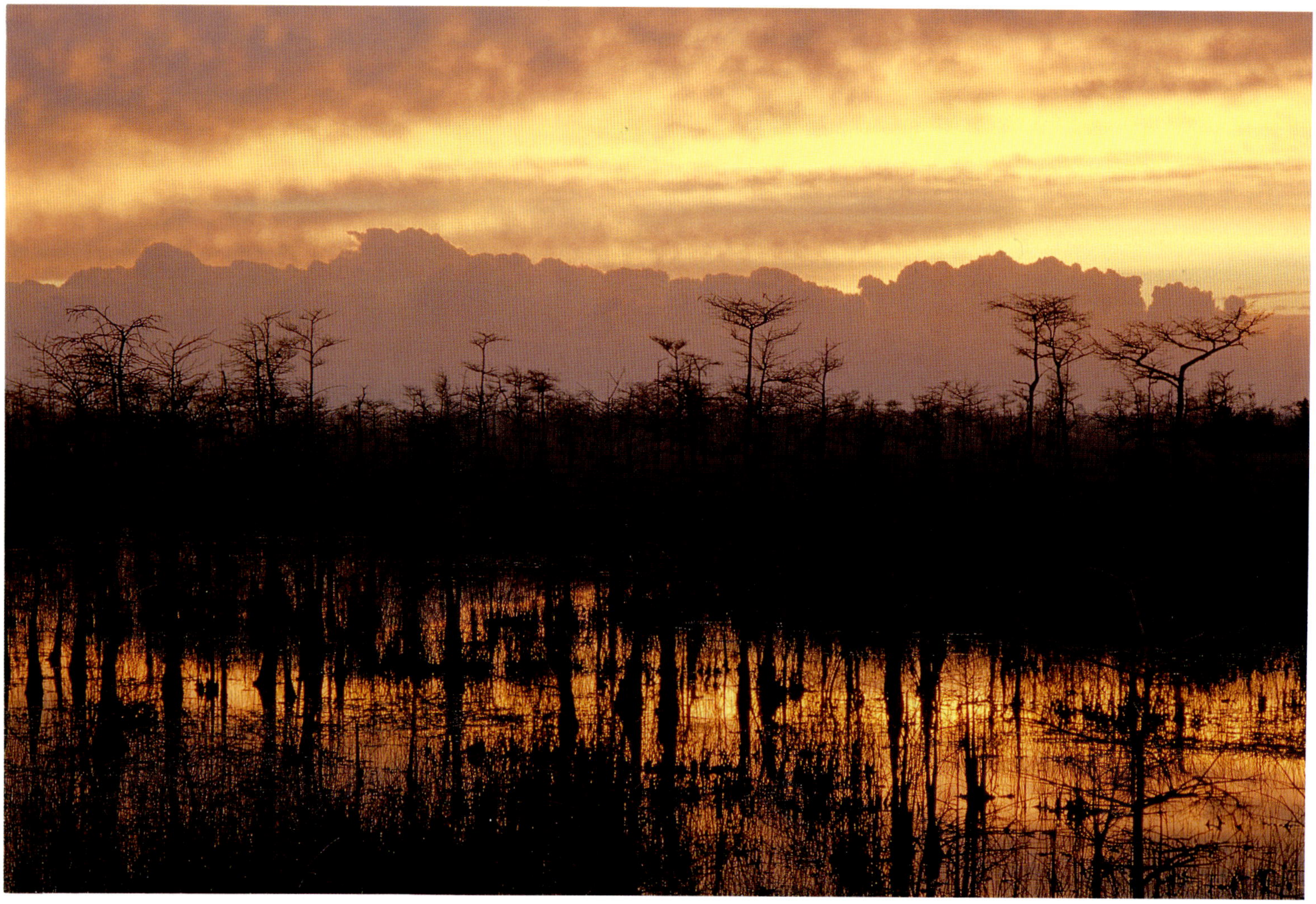

Dwarf cypress, near Pa-Hay-Okee, 80-200mm lens, 3 seconds at f/16

AMPHIBIANS

While extreme caution should be exercised when wading through swamps and lakes — especially at night — this is precisely what is required to get good photographs of frogs and toads. There are at least 39 different species in the state of Florida, including several exotics that have been introduced.

Wait until it is completely dark before entering the water, for any silhouette against the skyline can be seen by frogs and will send them diving under the water's surface or hopping into surrounding thick brush.

In general, most frogs that call are males; during mating season, females respond by the thousands, laying eggs in the surrounding waters.

Frogs are more active during or just after rains. A flashlight is usually required to find the frogs; this same shaft of light will mesmerize the amphibian and make it much easier to photograph. Be careful not to ripple the water when wading, since even with a spotlight on it a frog may dive rapidly and escape.

When photographing frogs, I mount two flashes, one on each side of the camera, and use either a 200mm macro lens or a bellows with an 80-200 zoom. This setup allows me to work anywhere from 1 to 3 feet away from the frog. (A shorter focal length lens would require getting in closer than the frog would tolerate.)

Going one step farther, I attach a flashlight designed for spelunkers and bikers to my flash unit. When I point the camera in any direction, the flashlight's beam illuminates my subject. This beam is usually adjustable, and I prefer the spotlight setting: Unless you are using a fast lens, it can be hard to see how to focus with a dimmer, dispersed light.

Many frogs sit along the water's edge — the first place to scan with your light. Others stay partially submerged, with only their eyes protruding above the water's surface.

Try to get your camera down near the water level when photographing a frog. This will give your pictures a much more interesting perspective.

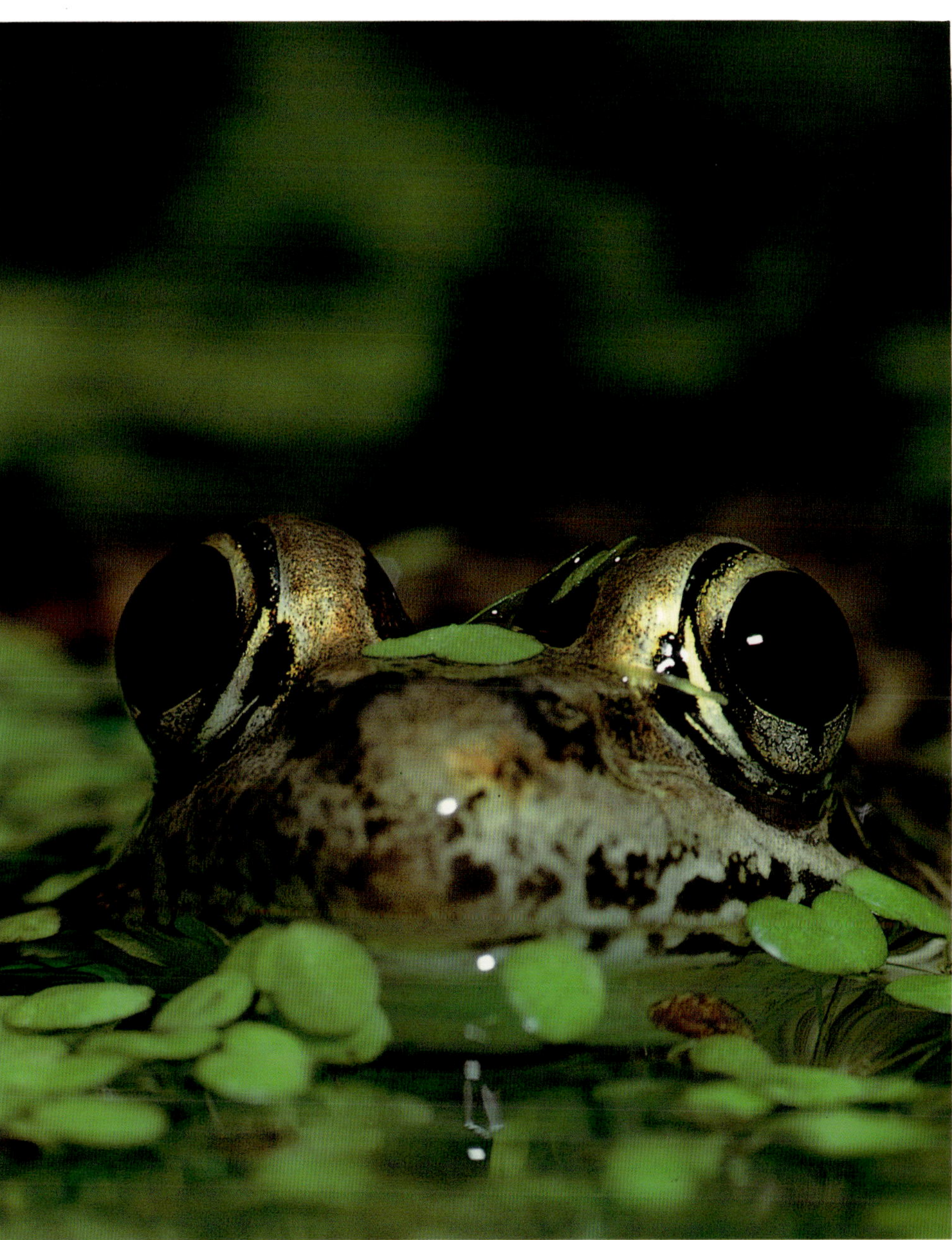

Leopard frog, near Ocala, 80-200mm lens with bellows, 2 flash units, 1/60 second at f/8

Since frogs abruptly stop calling when they think a predator is in the area, you might carry along with you a small tape player with different frog calls. The tape will lure them into resuming normal behavior and make it easier for you to locate them.

Frogs, of course, are not found only in water. Tree frogs, for example, are found (as their name implies) in trees — often in the center of water-filled bromeliads.

The greatest diversity of native species can be found in northern Florida, while the exotics, like the giant marine toad (Bufo marinus), are concentrated in the south. The Everglades are full of frogs, so there is no shortage anywhere in Florida.

Examine the undersides of palmettos for green and squirrel tree frogs. The Southern leopard frog, which is one of the prettiest and fastest of these amphibians, ranges all the way into the Keys.

There are 33 different species of salamanders that live in Florida rivers, streams and woodlands. Most amphibians cannot tolerate saltwater, so during breeding season freshwater ponds may be filled with newts and salamanders carrying out their courtship rituals. Except for newts and their land stage as efts, salamanders must remain moist or they will dry up and die. Many burrow in the ground, live under rocks or in water. During rains, salamanders can often be found crossing back roads. These amphibians are primarily nocturnal.

If you find a salamander that won't slow down no matter how many times you catch it and place it on a patch of moss, try using flash units — one mounted on each side of the camera — and a micro lens. When salamanders are more cooperative but bury their faces in the moss (which is normal behavior when agitated), put your index finger very gently beneath the salamander's chin and raise it slightly. Sometimes salamanders that are agitated will bow their entire body.

BIRDS FEEDING

Feeding birds can be divided into roughly three groups — songbirds, birds of prey and wading birds — each requiring a slightly different approach in photography.

Songbirds are best photographed near a feeding station set up in the yard. Make sure your feeder is continually stocked; any feeder filled for the first time may generate such a frenzy of activity that only high-speed shutters can stop the movement of birds streaking in and out of the frame.

Set up a wooden pole about 6 inches behind your bird feeder. Nail to the top of this pole (which is about a foot taller than the feeder) a 6-inch section of a tree limb, on which birds will land before flying down to the feeder. Pre-focus on the limb with your camera mounted on a tripod. At this point, how you trip the shutter will be determined by the type of system you are using.

There are radio controls that you can plug into a motor drive and trigger from a distance while watching the limb through binoculars, or you can use a very long cable, 20 to 30 feet. Another method is to use the MF-21 back on the Nikon 8008, which I have recently experimented with. This has a freeze-focus mode that allows you to pre-focus on a spot so that when an object comes into focus within a small rectangle in the center of the viewfinder, it will automatically trip the shutter. With this device, it is unnecessary for you to constantly monitor the setup.

In Florida, birds of prey are frequently seen soaring overhead or perched on tree limbs watching for prey. Much of their time is spent on these limbs, especially

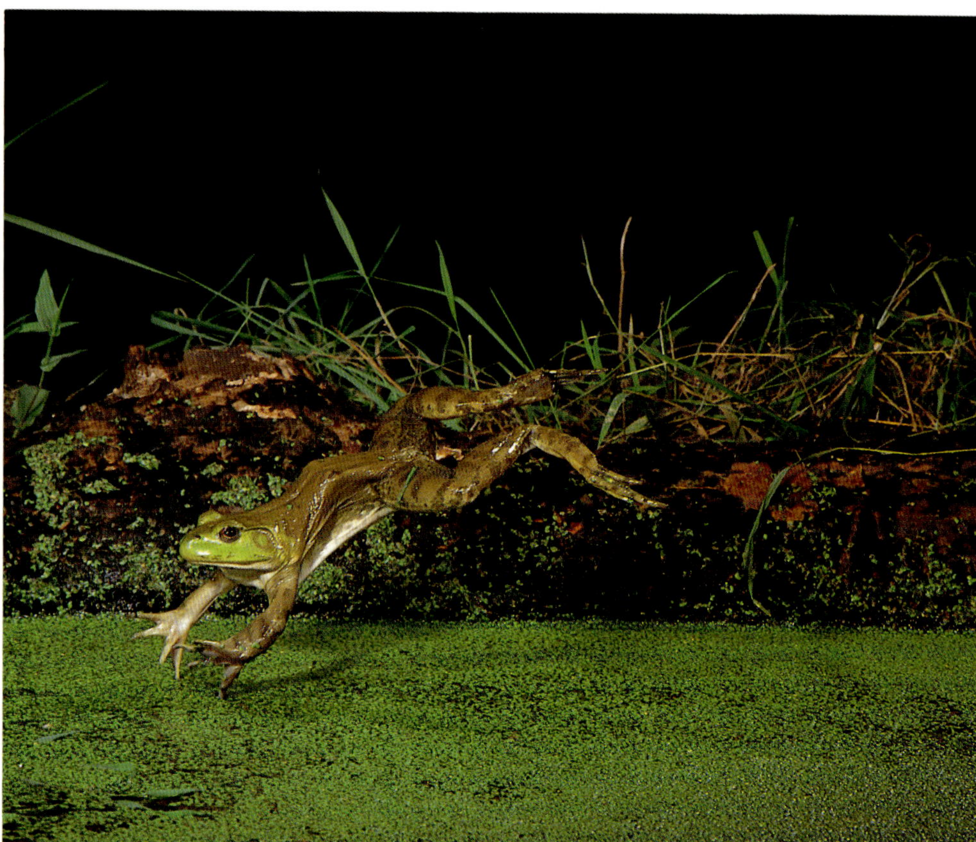

Frog jumping, near Ocala, 105mm lens, high speed strobes, 1/10,000 second at f/11

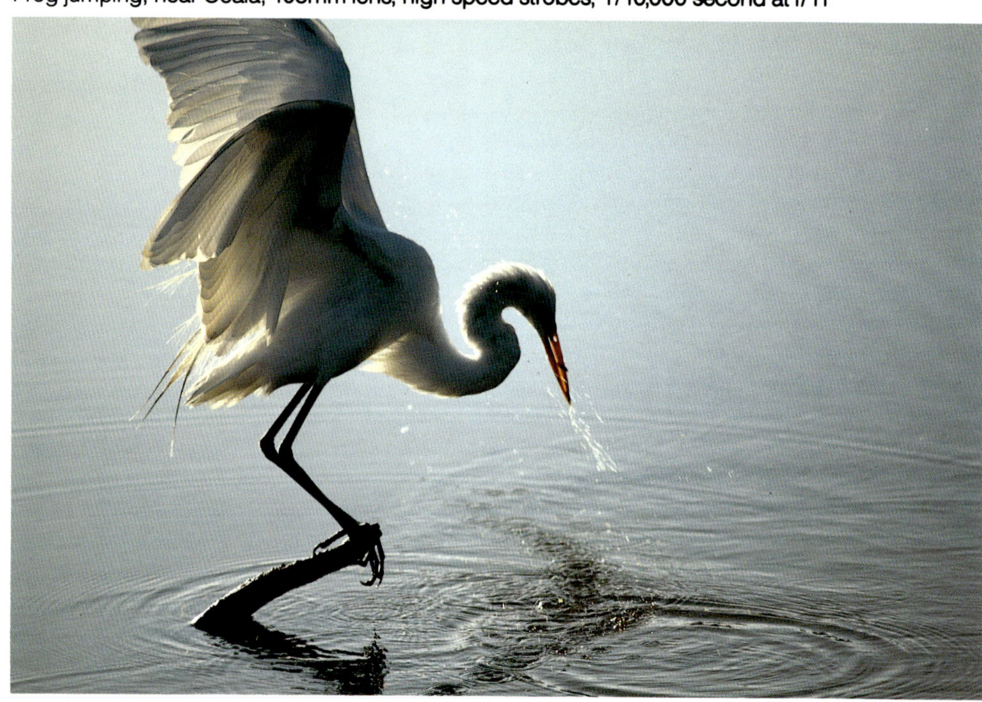

Great egret, Mrazek Pond, 300mm lens, 1/500 second at f/4.5

when people are in the area. This explains why so many photographs are taken of this particular behavior, since we are probably scaring away anything the bird would swoop down on. Osprey can be photographed as they fly over a body of water, hover for a few seconds and dive into the water to catch fish. These birds usually return to a favorite snag to eat their catch.

Carrion eaters such as vultures are much easier to photograph. All one has to do is find a road kill, set up a camera under nearby bushes or in a blind and wait.

Wading birds attract thousands of photographers to Florida's swamps and marshes each year. Southern wading birds include common egrets, snowy egrets, great white herons, tricolored herons, roseate spoonbills, wood storks, white ibis and many others.

Curiously, among these species a variety of feeding habits have evolved. The common egret, for example, often stands motionless for 10 minutes or longer. The spoonbill, on the other hand, kicks up the water, driving crustaceans and minnows toward its spatulate-shaped beak, which it moves back and forth in an arc-like motion (necessitating either greater depth of field or waiting until the head is in line with the body).

The majority of these birds do their feeding in early morning and early evening. At Mrazek Pond in the Everglades, for example, as many as 50 or more wading birds can be seen feeding from just before sunrise until about 8 or 9 a.m. After that, only a handful remain.

Since egrets stand motionless for such long periods of time — and since these birds are often plentiful in lower light conditions — longer exposures work well here. In fact, I have used exposures of as long as five seconds, although 1/8 to 1/4 second is more common. Obviously, a tripod is essential, as well as a cable release.

When photographing an egret, I have found that great depth of field is usually not needed to isolate the bird. When an egret spots a fish, it usually pulls back its head, which then begins to oscillate slightly. Photographers willing to take the time to observe these birds for a while will soon learn to recognize when egrets are about to jab their prey.

One mistake photographers frequently commit when shooting egrets for the first time is framing the birds too tightly. Always leave sufficient room in front of the bird so that when it thrusts its head forward it won't be cut off in the viewfinder. To stop action of this sort, a shutter speed of 1/500 second is required.

When a bird is backlit by the sun, I frequently rely on a flash to fill in. Normally, birds do not react to a flash of light, but I have noted that the simultaneous sounds of shutter, motor drive and flash unit sometimes trigger a response. If this happens, turn the flash unit off.

Most wading birds will alight on dead branches jutting out of the water, allowing

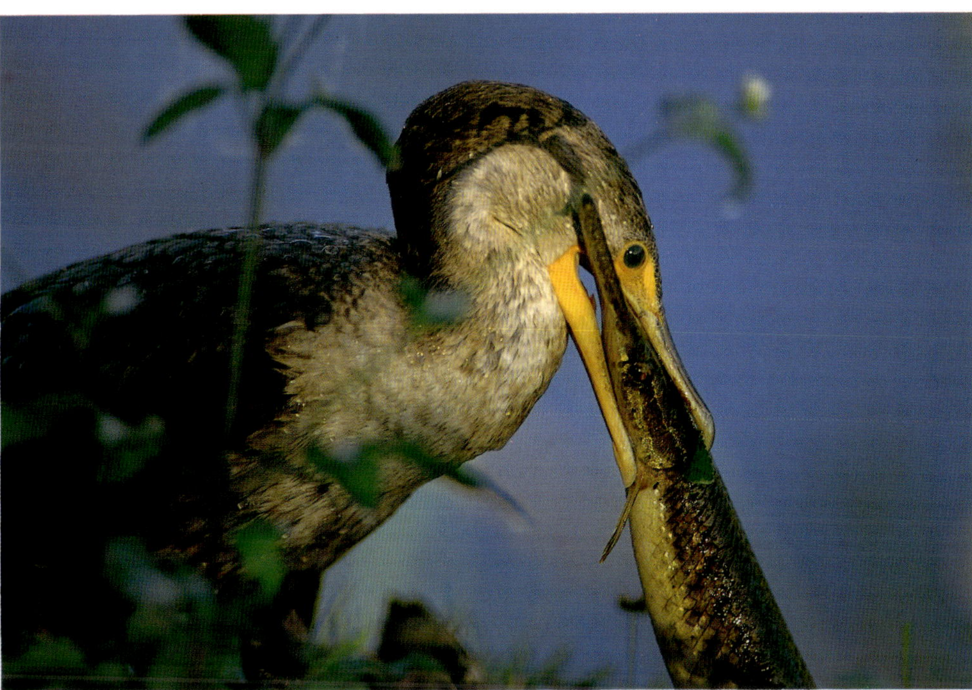

Cormorant with fish, Anhinga Trail, 500mm lens, 1/250 second at f/4

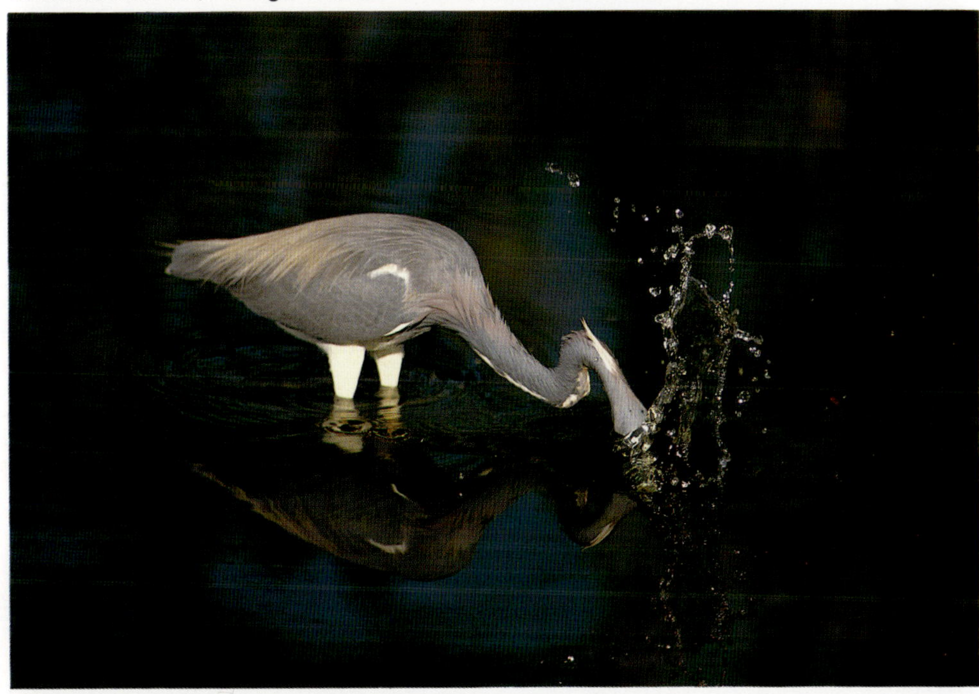

Tricolored heron, Merritt Island, 500mm lens, 1/1000 second at f/4

the photographer to record preening displays with wings outstretched and necks extended. Strong pecking orders exist among these birds, however, so you may witness frequent rearrangement of positions on these perches. By anticipating this kind of action and using a motor drive, you can enhance your chances of obtaining some interesting behavioral shots.

When shooting pictures of egrets and other birds, the photographer will likely be confronted with amazing bursts of speed and bewilderingly hard-to-follow avian action. The snowy egret, for example, may at times walk in the water to feed, while at other times it may fly low over the water and drag its feet, scaring fish into striking range.

Another unusual display of feeding behavior is exhibited by the tricolored heron (formerly known as the Louisiana Heron), which commonly "canopy feeds" — that is, extends its wings and shades the water, catching fish as they dart for cover.

BIRDS IN FLIGHT

Photographing Florida birds in flight will encompass a broad number of species of varying sizes with differing habits — from massive birds that flap their wings slowly (1/250 second) to the delicate ruby-throated hummingbird that requires a special flash of 1/6,000 second. Emphasis will be on medium- and larger-sized birds; see the section entitled "Lighting in the Field" for information regarding smaller species.

One of the first mistakes a photographer usually makes when trying to photograph birds in flight is first framing the bird in the shot and then trying to meter before releasing the shutter. Metering has to be done beforehand.

First take a reading of the sky and underexpose 1/2 f-stop; then, when the bird enters your field of vision, begin to pan while turning your lens-focusing ring to keep the image sharp. A motor drive is essential here.

You need not take more than one or two shots, but just knowing you have that option (rather than having to wind the film manually) will help prevent the mistake of hesitating an instant too long and allowing the bird to fly out of your range of focus.

Some motor drives have continuous and single settings; others have continuous high and low. Use the continuous or continuous high when you require a short burst of shooting, since a bird is usually at its best for only a brief second or two.

Using a longer lens to shoot birds of fast speeds will require an even faster shutter speed. For example, panning with a 300mm lens would require at least a 1/500 second shutter speed. Lead the bird in the frame when you're panning, and make sure there is a little more space in front of the bird than behind. Don't pull the camera down immediately afterwards. If you pull the camera down an instant too soon, you may later discover you have only half a bird.

There are many varieties of soaring birds — vultures and white pelicans, for example — that are easy to photograph as they ride strong thermals with very little wing flapping to worry about. When fishing, the brown pelican hovers for an instant above the water before folding its wings and plunging beneath the surface to catch a fish. When flying in a line with several other birds just inches above the water, these

Woodstorks, Corkscrew Swamp, 300mm lens, 1/500 second at f/5.6

pelicans alternate wing flaps with long glides, enabling you to pan if you have positioned yourself parallel to their flight.

The angle you take to your subject is very important. Generally speaking, a position parallel to the bird is best. Large birds seldom look good coming straight at you, and depth of field is critical (as well as the need to focus a lot faster.)

Avoid using a shorter lens and trying to get closer. A little distance is best, for the closer you are, the faster you will have to pan with your subject.

Many birds fly in formation. White ibis, in particular, can be seen flying in long lines to roost for the evening.

Some of the easiest birds to photograph are gulls, which constantly beg for food at fishing piers and along beaches. A different approach here would be to use a wide-angle lens, since these birds fly so close. Several could be included in the frame, with dramatic cloud formations serving as a background — something a long lens would not allow.

When longer lenses are used, background clouds can be a problem. Although an out-of-focus blue sky works well as a color, a cloudy white background looks lifeless and detracts from the bird. In general, birds in flight should not be photographed on overcast days, although dark storm clouds would offer an exception to the rule.

When a bird soars almost directly overhead, look for several things. An osprey, for example, tilts at an angle, and its wings and body can be fully illuminated by the sunlight. And when a bird such as a great egret flies into the sun, the light that filters through the wings is truly marvelous. Metering will be different here, requiring an overexposure of one to two stops. Most shutter speeds can handle the range flown by egrets, herons, vultures and hawks.

FLOWERS

Visitors who are accustomed to photographing wildflowers in mountain settings where there are natural geological windbreaks quickly discover that Florida's flat landscapes block little wind. In addition, many of Florida's wildflowers grow on tall stems and are thus susceptible to even the slightest of breezes. Of course, the more a flower is magnified by a close-up lens, the more any movement is correspondingly magnified.

One way to increase the chance of finding motionless flowers is to shoot just before sunrise. At this time, flowers may be covered with dew, and the sun's heat has not yet begun to create thermals.

If you plan to shoot pictures of water plants, remember that wind also stirs the water, moving in turn the flowers.

Longer-stemmed flowers can be braced by using a forked stick — or, as several

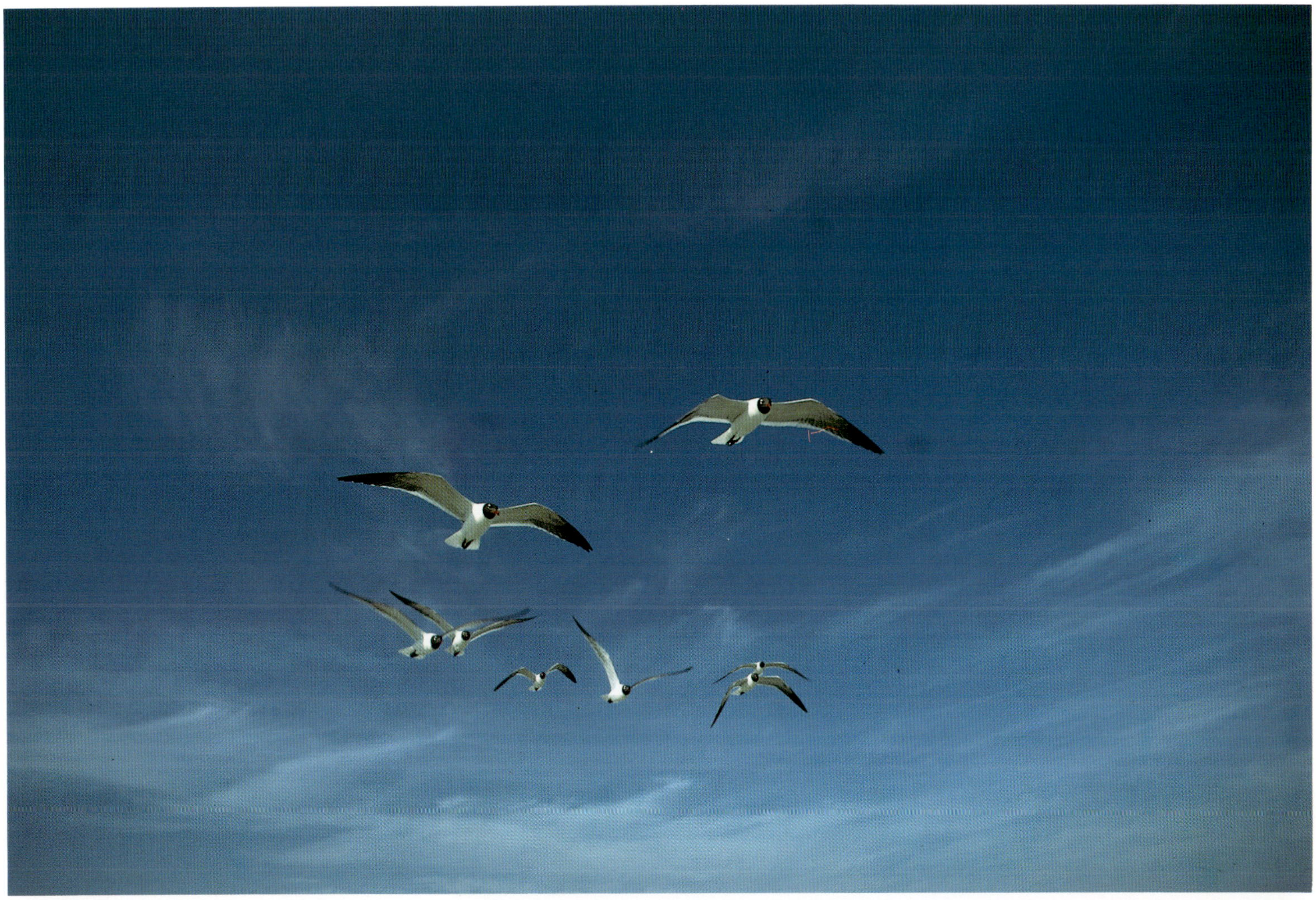

Gulls, Canaveral, 28mm lens, 1/500 second at f/11

workshop students once showed me, by using a hairclip (with no serrated teeth) taped to a gun-cleaning rod. The hairclip can be attached to the flower's stem with no damage; the rod is extended and braced in the soil.

Small apertures are rarely required with flowers such as these, since you usually want to photograph only one, two or three blossoms. This permits you to shoot at a faster shutter speed.

Using a longer telephoto macro lens, such as a 200mm or an 80-200mm zoom lens with bellows or diopter lens, will allow greater control over your background. Too often the use of a short lens creates a cluttered background or washed-out sky.

A set of small mirrors can be used to illuminate flowers, and the background can be controlled by shading areas with an umbrella that are too brightly lit.

Don't use colored matt boards for backgrounds. They invariabley look like what they are: colored cardboard. If one flower has a background that just doesn't work,

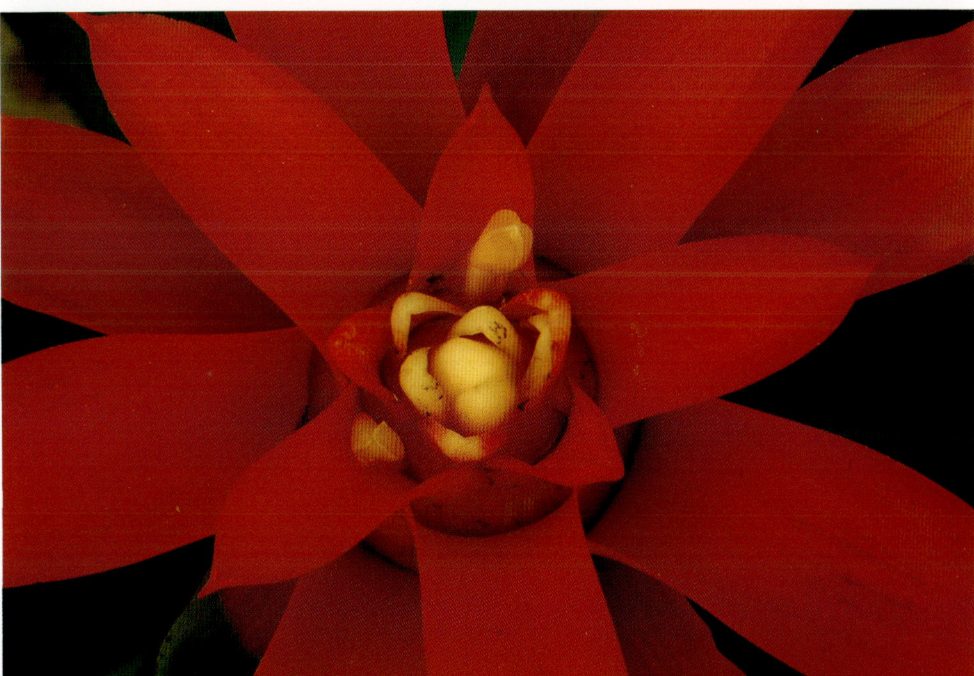

Bromeliad, Homestead, 55mm micro lens, 1 second at f/22

chances are you can find another one by looking in the same general vicinity.

Tabletop tripods seldom work in the field

unless they are placed on a perfectly flat surface (extremely rare, of course, in the wilds). Use tripods like Gitzo that allow the legs to spread and reach to ground level.

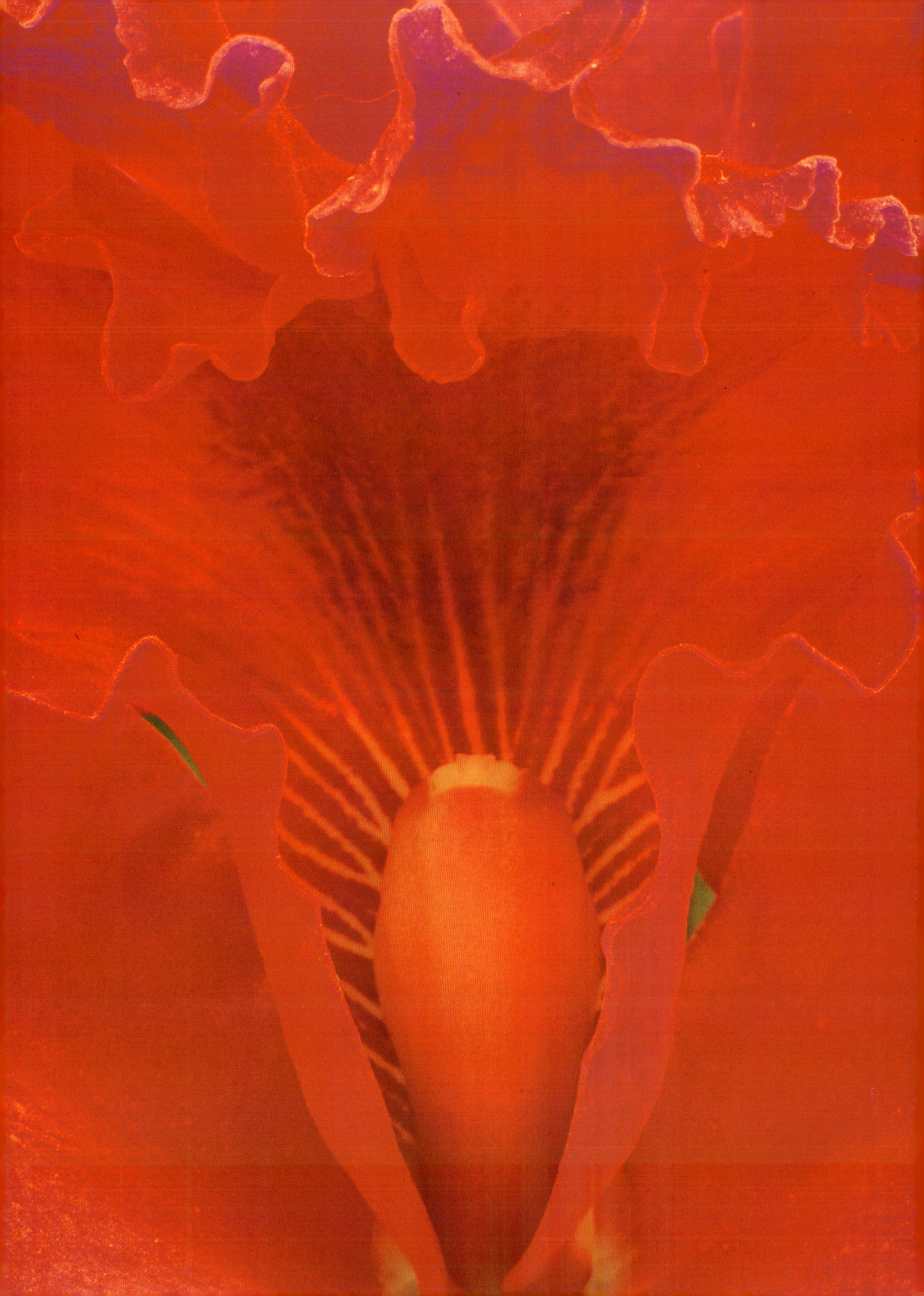

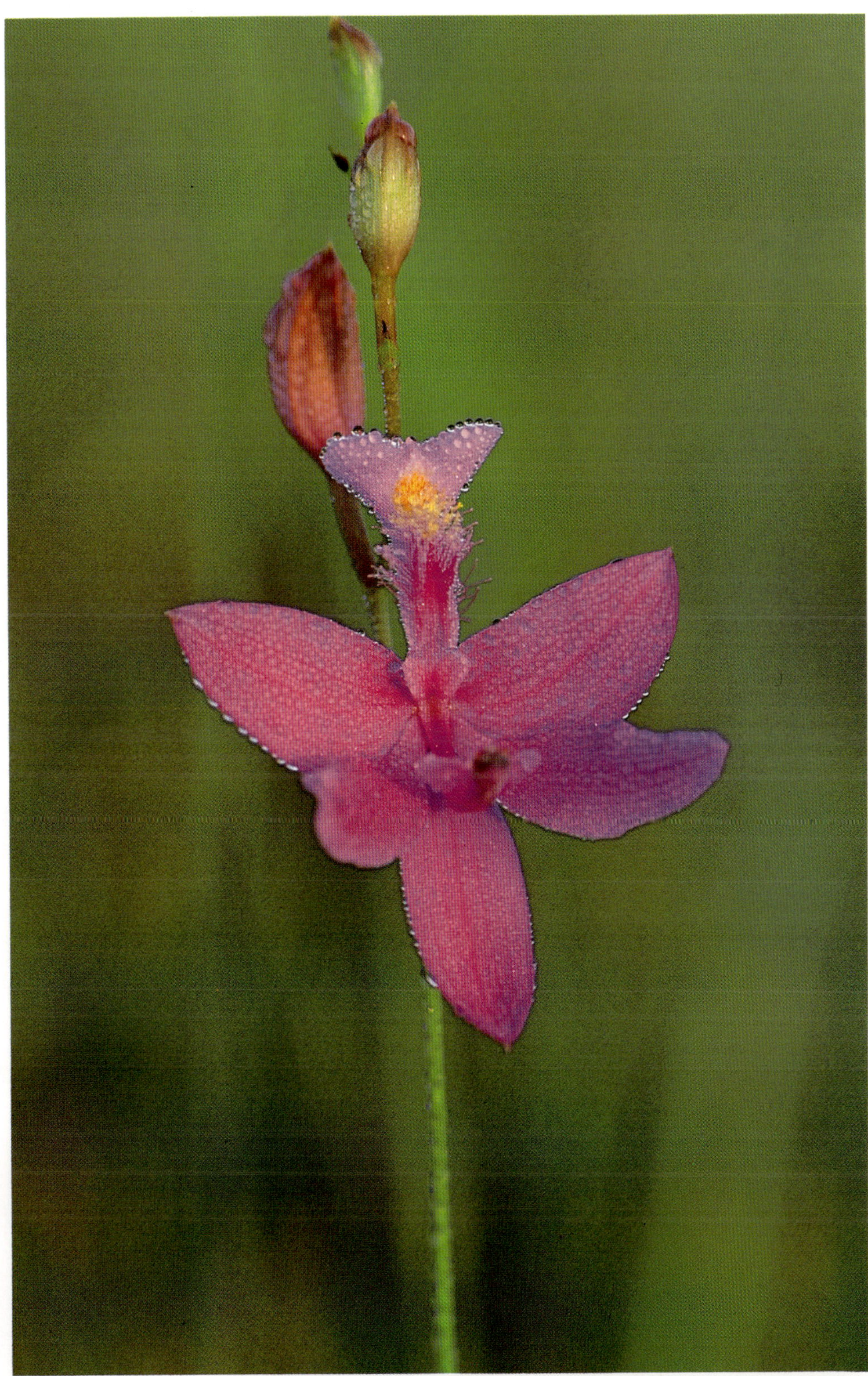

Grasspink orchid, Panhandle roadside, 200mm micro lens, 1/4 second at f/5.6

You might consider experimenting with a right-angle finder that screws into your camera's viewfinder. This device keeps you from having to bury your face in the mud and protects plants you might otherwise flatten.

Some people like to use flash with flowers. This is fine with single blossoms, as long as you balance your light output to the background so it doesn't go black. Few flowers look good (or natural) with black backgrounds unless they are night-blooming species.

Bromeliads, which are fairly sturdy plants that sway very little in the wind, are good subjects to work with.

When photographing waterlilies, a polarizing filter should be used. This will eliminate any harsh reflections on the leaves and turn the water black. On the other hand, there have been occasions when I have photographed lily pads when the sun's bright highlights drew me to the scene. Generally, it is a matter of personal taste whether to use a polarizer or not.

If you have a 300mm lens, find a low angle and shoot through nearby flowers to create a soft, out-of-focus color that frames the sharply focused flowers in the background.

Of course, since wildflowers cannot "escape" like wild animals, they often lull photographers into a false sense of security, for they assume the task will be simple. A few days in the field, however, usually corrects this attitude.

Some photographers carry rolls of plastic to string around an area for a windbreak, permitting them to take pictures after everyone else has packed it in for the day.

INSECTS

Most people consider insects to be pests, but many photographers prefer to view the existence of three-quarters of a million different species as offering special opportunities to photograph something little seen.

In photographic terms, insects can be broken down into just two categories: those that are stationary and those that try to fly, hop or crawl away. The best time of day to shoot insects is in the early morning, when the light is warm and the creatures are still cool (and fairly stationary) from the lower temperatures of night.

Of course, in Florida, it is really only the northern sections of the state that get that cool, except for short periods when the central and southern portions of the state may have a few days of frost. What these warmer sections have that the continental United States does not are tropical insects like the zebra butterfly. Insects, visitors quickly discover, are in abundance in Florida at all times of the year.

Insects that fly — like dragonflies and butterflies — have an advantage, as they can elude us when we try to shoot photographs. Use of a longer focal-length micro lens like a 200mm, however, should increase your chances of getting the shot, since you will not have to get so close. A longer lens also takes in a smaller section of the background, which might otherwise prove distracting.

When you approach a dragonfly, move

slowly; dragonflies have territories that they patrol constantly, driving away insects of their own species and eating others that are not. Dragonflies have favorite perches, so if one flies away, don't give up — it will likely return. The same holds true for butterflies; when one leaves a flower at your first arrival, there's a 50-50 chance it will return shortly.

Although I frequently use flash units when photographing butterflies, there are many times I set up on one particular flower and use small mirrors to reflect sunlight on the subject, permitting higher shutter speeds.

Most ponds have their fair share of dragonflies along the shoreline, and these insects are considerably more active at midday than most other animals.

When photographing a chrysalis, or an insect such as an ambush bug — which takes on the color of its surroundings while waiting patiently for a victim — I use mirrors or ambient light. Often you end up with a black background when using a flash — which looks highly unnatural unless the subject is a moth.

Moths are attracted to light, so if you are photographing at night and shining a white light, they often will smash into your flashlight. You can eliminate this problem by placing a red or yellow filter over the lens of your flashlight.

Certain species of flowers, shrubs and trees will attract one kind of insect more than others. Milkweed, for example, attracts milkweed bugs, milkweed beetles, queen butterflies and monarch butterflies. The latter two spend their larval stage on the milkweed. The passion flower attracts the gulf frittilary, julia and zebra butterfly — and it is also their larval food supply.

Many times it is simply easier to find insects within a city in flower gardens, since in the wilds there are so many thousands of acres over which the insects will be dispersed.

Fort Lauderdale is home to a commercial establishment called Butterfly World, where thousands of butterflies fly about in a simulated tropical rain forest and other native habitats. Species are represented here from all over the world.

In early November, monarch butterflies migrate through St. Vincent National Wildlife Refuge and St. Marks National Wildlife Refuge.

When shooting a butterfly, wait until it opens its wings completely flat. Then all you have to do is line the film plane parallel to the wings; little depth of field will be needed to bring the insect completely into focus.

MAMMALS

Of all the animal groups in Florida, mammals are the hardest to locate and photograph. Most of the "easy" large mammals photographed in the United States are found in national parks out West. The majority of mammals around the Southern swamps are nocturnal, though some may be seen feeding in early morning or late evening. In Florida, many mammals like squirrels, rabbits and deer are game animals; during the hunting season, they are less likely to be seen. Generally speaking, it is the deer, rabbits,

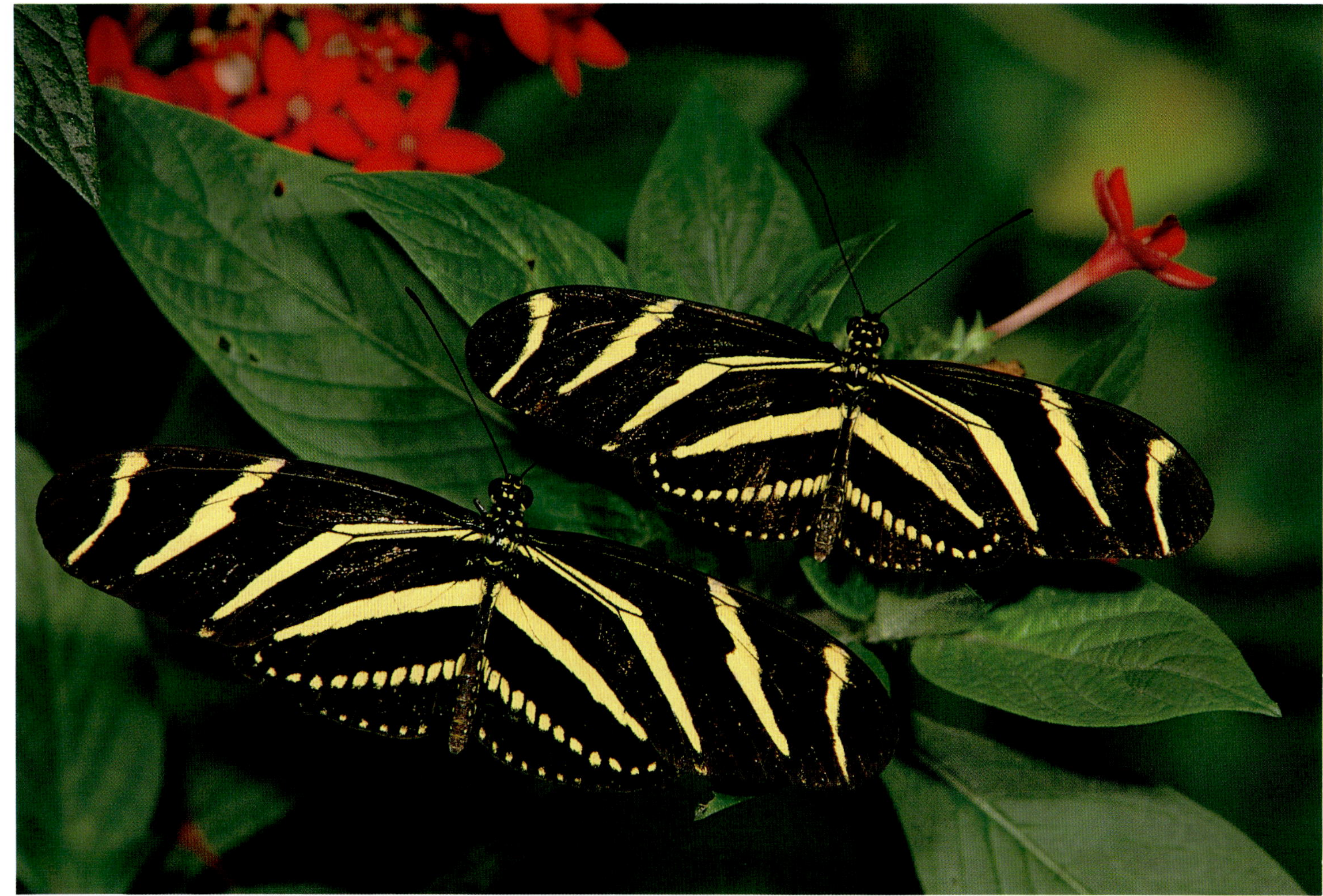

Zebra butterflies, Butterfly World, 80-200mm lens with bellows, 2 flash units, 1/60 second at f/11

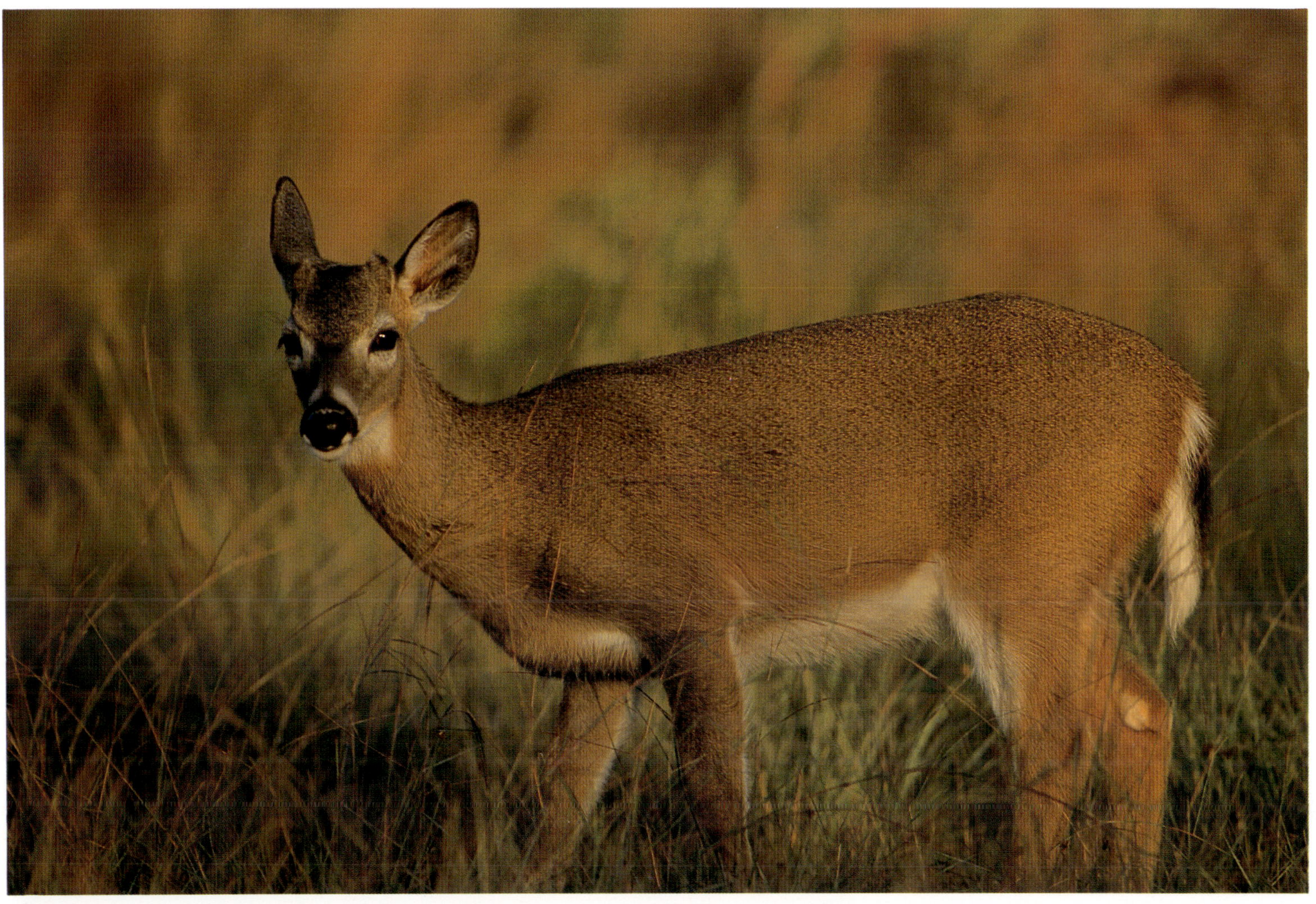

Key deer, Big Pine Key, 500mm lens, 1/125 second at f/4

squirrels and raccoons that one finds easier to photograph — far more so than the elusive bobcat or the endangered Florida panther.

Animals frequent favorite areas. Key deer, for example, frequent the yards of a neighborhood located near the end of Key Deer Boulevard. I use my car as a blind, employing a window mount with my lens mounted to a ball head. The deer accept this, since they are accustomed to cars moving up and down the street.

Focus on the eyes of a mammal when taking photographs. Other parts of an animal can be slightly out of focus, but if the eyes aren't sharp, the photograph just doesn't work.

A motor drive is a must when trying to get action shots or when an animal comes into view for only a few precious seconds. Newer cameras have built-in motor drives, which prove much quieter and less likely to alert an animal to your presence.

I generally use the longest lens available — a 500mm — when shooting pictures of mammals. Since their sense of smell is so highly developed, you might try using a masking scent, available from any hunting supply store. When shooting into an open field, stay back behind any bordering trees and try to avoid making any fast movements.

When stalking a mammal, stop every so often to listen for footsteps. The animal is certainly doing the same — listening for you. If an animal that is feeding looks up suddenly, freeze any movement on your part until it resumes eating.

If you plan to stalk animals in the field, be sure to slip several rolls of film into your pockets. Too often, photographers find themselves in wonderful positions to document extraordinary behavior, only to run out of film mid-shoot.

When you reach an acceptable range, shoot a couple of pictures and then move closer and repeat the process. This way, if an animal bolts, you will at least have taken a few shots.

At the very end of No Name Key there lives a lighter-colored phase of raccoon. People still feed them, so you could find yourself in a potentially dangerous situation. Raccoons can also be found scavenging at night around campgrounds. I recommend using two flash units and a fairly fast lens. (See the chapter on photographing amphibians for more information on this procedure.)

Since squirrels may be found in most city parks, it makes very little sense to stalk them in the wilds.

If you should be lucky enough to glimpse a Florida panther in the wild, do not pursue it. There are, at latest count, only 30 of these cats left in the wild; any undue pressure or harassment could prove fatal to the species.

A good many animal parks with natural settings are to be found in Florida — usually with indigenous mammals and opportunities for obtaining good close-up shots.

REPTILES

Mention reptiles in Florida, and the first species that comes to mind is the alligator. The best advice I would offer for photographing this seemingly sluggish animal is to use a long lens.

For the most part, alligators are not inclined to attack humans. There may come a time, however, when the animal feels threatened; if the distance is breached, the alligator will choose to defend itself or try to escape. Most attacks by alligators have been initiated by animals that have lost their fear of man — usually by having been fed illegally.

A 300mm lens or an 80-200mm zoom will usually suffice to fill the frame, and there are plenty of piers and boardwalks in Florida for photographers to get close enough to this animal to shoot safely. A polarizing filter can be used to eliminate any reflection on the water and enable you to see the alligator's submerged body.

Alligators can be "called" by mimicking the young's distress signal — though only when you are in an area where the gator can't reach you if it should overreact.

Many exotic species of lizards are found throughout Florida, with the greatest concentration in the south. One of the more interesting is the gecko — a lizard that has suction toes similar to those of the tree frog, enabling it to climb on even a slick surface like glass. Geckos are often attracted to windows at night, where insects hover near the available light.

The Texas horned lizard can be found scurrying through the sand in the Panhandle region. Few people are not familiar with skinks, especially the species with the brilliant blue tail, which fools predators into grabbing the wrong end. The tail then breaks off, still wriggling frantically in the jaws of its assailant, while the skink escapes. Later, the skink regenerates a shorter tail.

Since lizards are cold-blooded, they can be found during the early morning warming themselves in bright sunlight. Always approach a lizard slowly. Some lizards immediately try to escape; others remain motionless, which will allow you to take longer exposures. The anole — a lizard popularly but incorrectly referred to as a chameleon — is usually found in trees and shrubs, where it changes its colors from green to brown to blend in with its background.

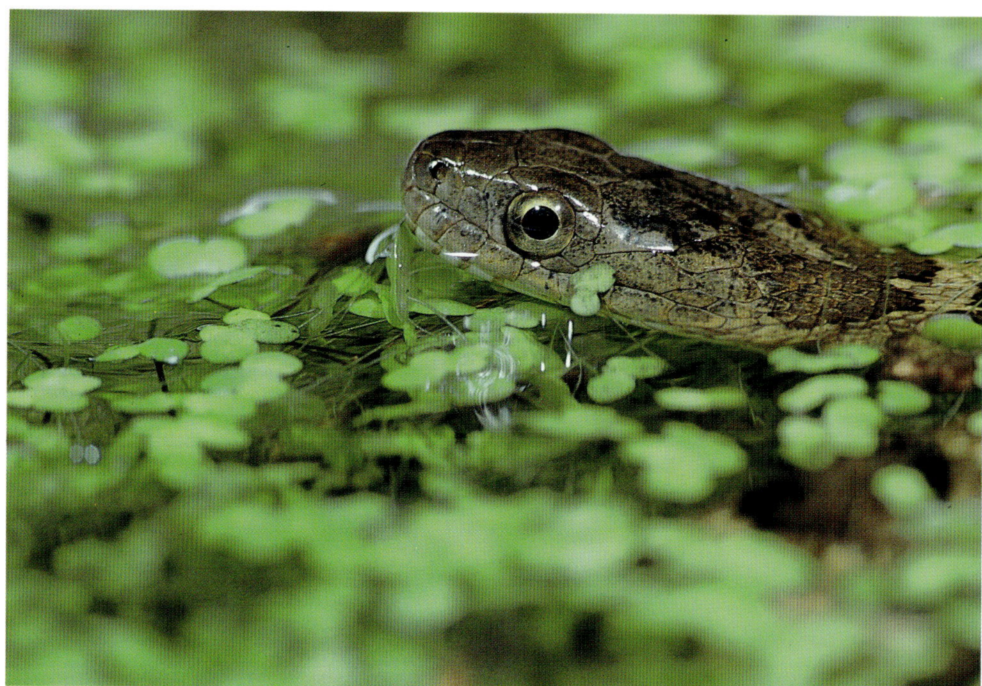

Water snake, near Ocala, 80-200mm lens with bellows, 2 flash units, 1/60 second at f/8

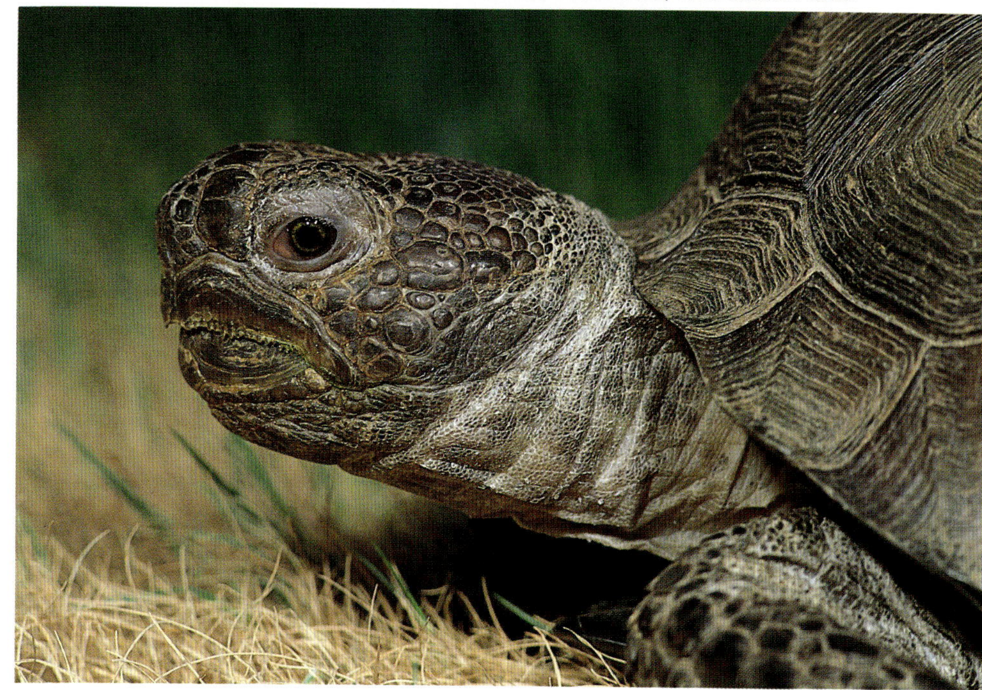

Gopher tortoise, Ocala, 80-200mm lens with bellows, 2 flash units, 1/60 second at f/11

A 200mm micro lens is effective for shooting pictures of lizards, or a bellows and a 300mm lens to allow a greater working distance. Since you will be using a closeup lens of some sort, you should also use a tripod: Magnification of your subject also magnifies movement.

Turtles can be easy or hard to photograph, according to which species you wish to get close to. Water turtles, for example, quickly escape by dropping off into the water upon close approach, while land turtles may find it more difficult to get away.

Cooters and sliders are the true baskers, and they can be seen sunning themselves on logs throughout Florida's swamps. Red-eared turtles prefer lots of vegetation and can be seen pushing up through water lettuce lakes. Snappers can be quite aggressive, but, if given the chance, they usually prefer to escape.

Turtles will swim underwater, surfacing with only the head visible to see if any intruders are in the area. If the coast is clear, they will climb onto a log; if not, they will swim away and return later. Water turtles come up on land to travel to another water area or to lay eggs in a hole dug in the surrounding banks.

A telephoto lens is a must for photographing water turtles. Move slowly and quietly, using trees and bushes close to the water's edge for cover.

Land turtles are at a distinct disadvantage, though a box turtle can "escape" by drawing its head and legs into a tightly closed shell. Some species occur in Florida that are not found in Northern states, such as the Gulf Coast box turtle, largest of all the box turtles in North America. Gopher tortoises are rare and live in pine forests with sandy soil, where they dig burrows. These tortoises can be seen feeding in several areas in the Ocala National Forest in early morning or late evening.

Photography of land turtles can be done with any lens you might have available, since turtles are slow moving and can be handled with relative ease. Shooting at ground level often makes for a more interesting shot. Should you not want to get down flat on your stomach, however, try attaching a right-angle finder on your camera's viewfinder. This will enable you to get the same photograph while kneeling.

SHELLS

Since shells rarely move unless they are tossed about by incoming or retreating waves, photographing them is far more simple than most other subjects. I prefer early-morning or late-evening light, though a mirror can reflect even the noonday sun at a more oblique angle.

Where you are, and the availability and abundance of shells, will determine how you compose your subjects.

When photographing on the beaches of Sanibel-Captiva Islands, I fill the frame entirely with shells, since the beach is virtually nothing but shells. But when photographing shells along Canaveral National Seashore, I prefer to get down at a low angle with a wide-angle lens and compose my shot with a few shells in the foreground and incoming waves and sky in the background.

Many photographers make the mistake of positioning the most colorful shell dead center in their photograph. Instead, try to offset the shell or arrange several where the eye follows the color across the frame in an almost diagonal flow.

Many shells lend themselves to extreme closeups, due to their variety of texture and color.

SPIDERS

Spiders are some of the easiest animals to photograph, since they sit motionless in the middle of their webs or among flowers waiting for their prey to come to them. Although many people have an aversion to spiders, few species can actually harm humans.

I prefer using the same setup I employ for stationary insect photography: a 200mm micro lens or bellows with an 80-200 zoom on a tripod. With extremely high magnification shots, reverse a shorter focal length lens on the bellows and use flash, since any movement will register in a blurred photograph.

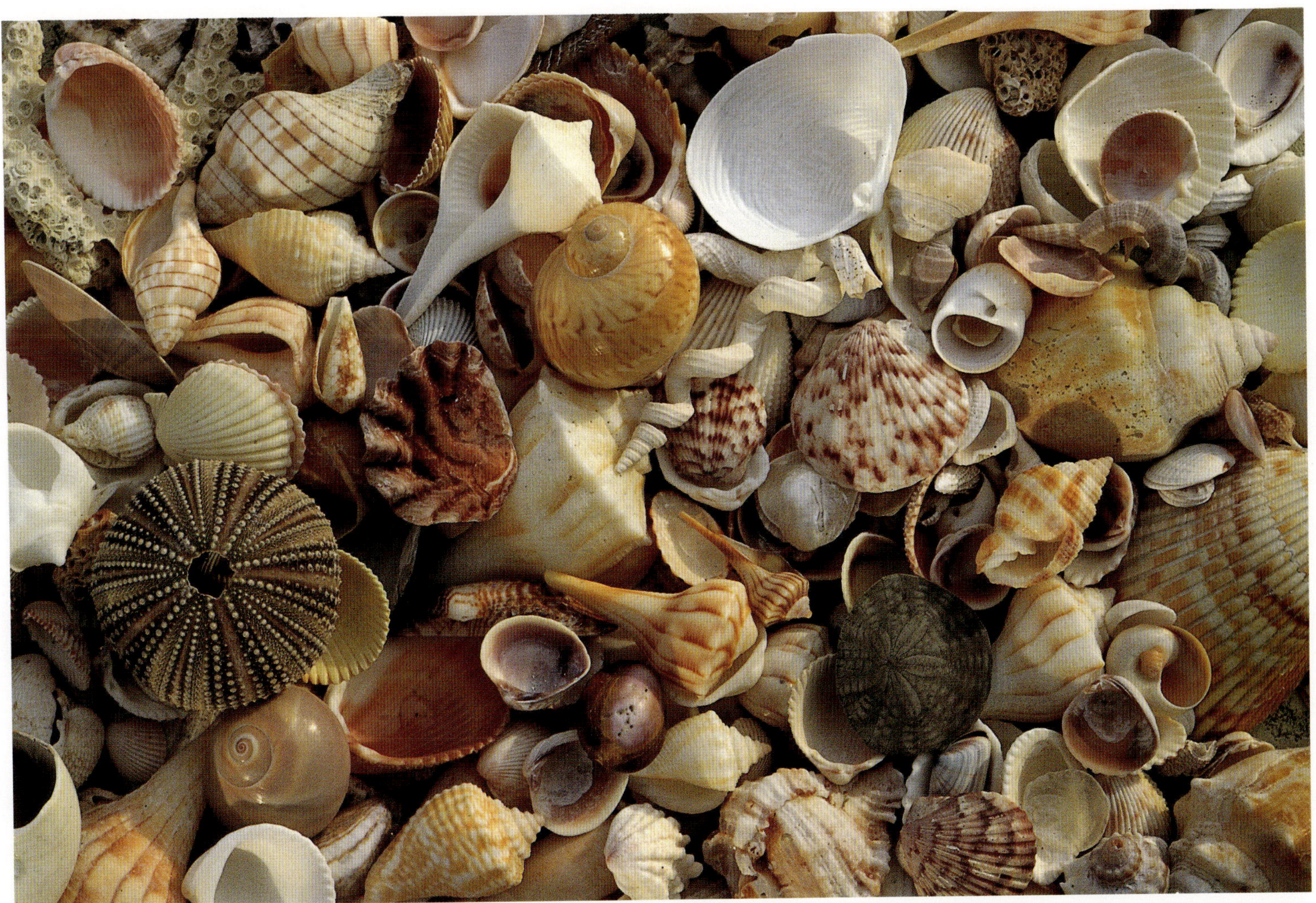

Shells, Sanibel, 55mm micro lens, 1 second at f/32

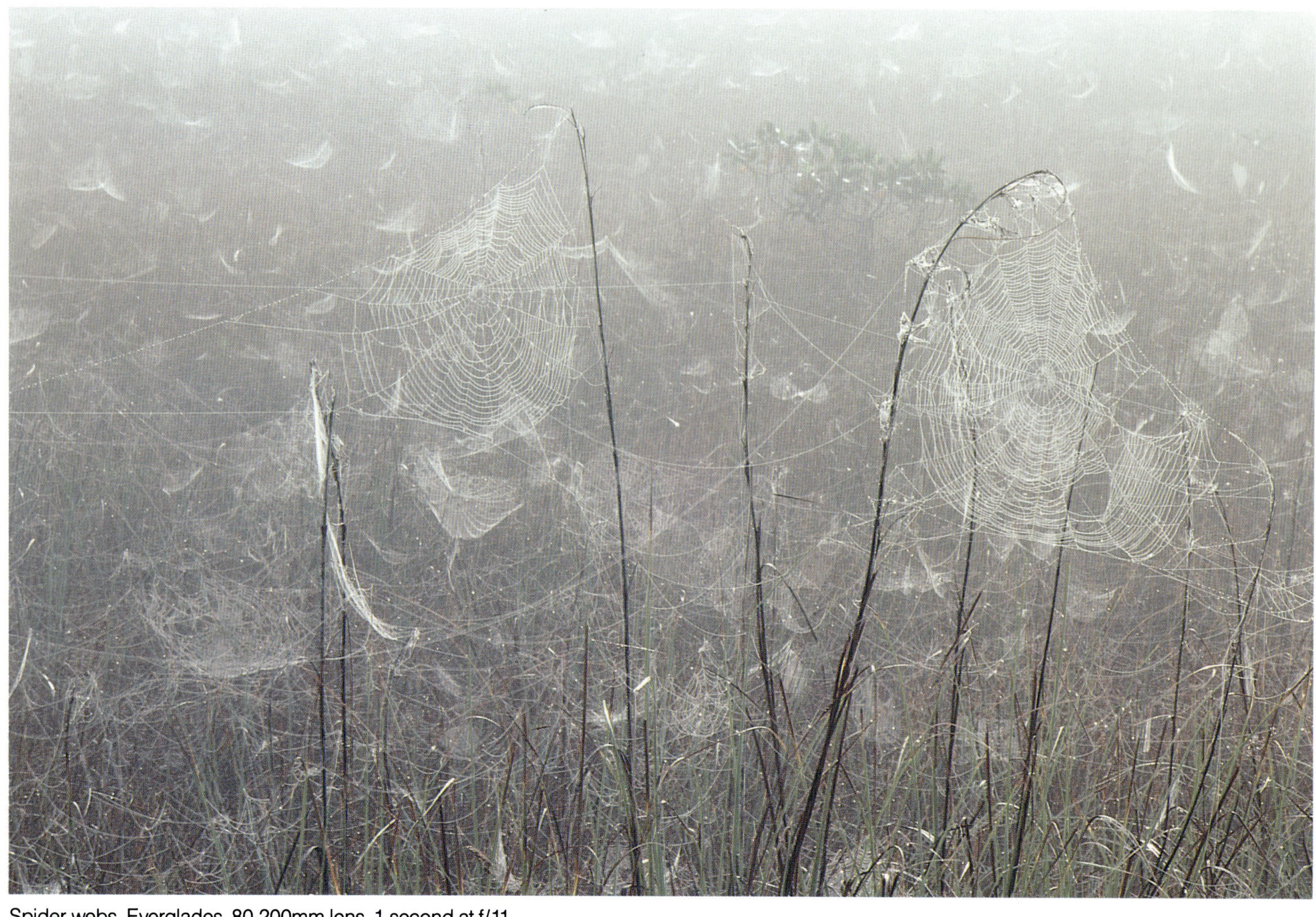

Spider webs, Everglades, 80-200mm lens, 1 second at f/11

When shooting spider webs, I try not to use a small aperture, because I don't want the background to interfere with the web. As with butterflies, I line the film plane parallel to the subject — in this case, the web. On foggy mornings, spider webs stand out when covered with dew, especially ones that are backlit by the sun. Once in the Everglades National Park, between Long Pine Key and Pa-Hay-Okee, I came upon thousands of spider webs draped across the sawgrasses. It appeared as if not a single blade of grass had been left untouched by the strands of silk.

Orb web spiders are the most common, and there are several hundred species worldwide. These spiders do not have good vision; they rely instead on their prey getting snared by their webs. Consequently, these spiders are easier to work with.

One particular species of orb web spider found in many flower gardens — the black-and-yellow argiope — is quite large as spiders go. It is probably the most photographed of spiders.

Spiders are carnivorous and primarily nocturnal. That's another reason we notice webs more in the early morning, for they are probably spun the night before.

Crab spiders are another popular group, due to their ability to change colors depending on the flower they are on. These spiders do not spin webs; instead, they sit in the middle of (or underneath) a flower with their legs held out ready to close on any prey that wanders within reach.

Wolf spiders are active day and night. They carry their egg sacs attached to their spinnerets; after hatching, the babies ride on their mother's abdomen until at least the first molt. There may be well over 100 young in an egg sac.

Jumping spiders have the best vision of all and can be recognized by the arrangement of their large eyes. Their vision is good in making out objects about 12 inches away, which is the distance they can jump quite rapidly.

The Dolomedes, or fishing spider, lives on or near the water's edge, where it catches insects and minnows.

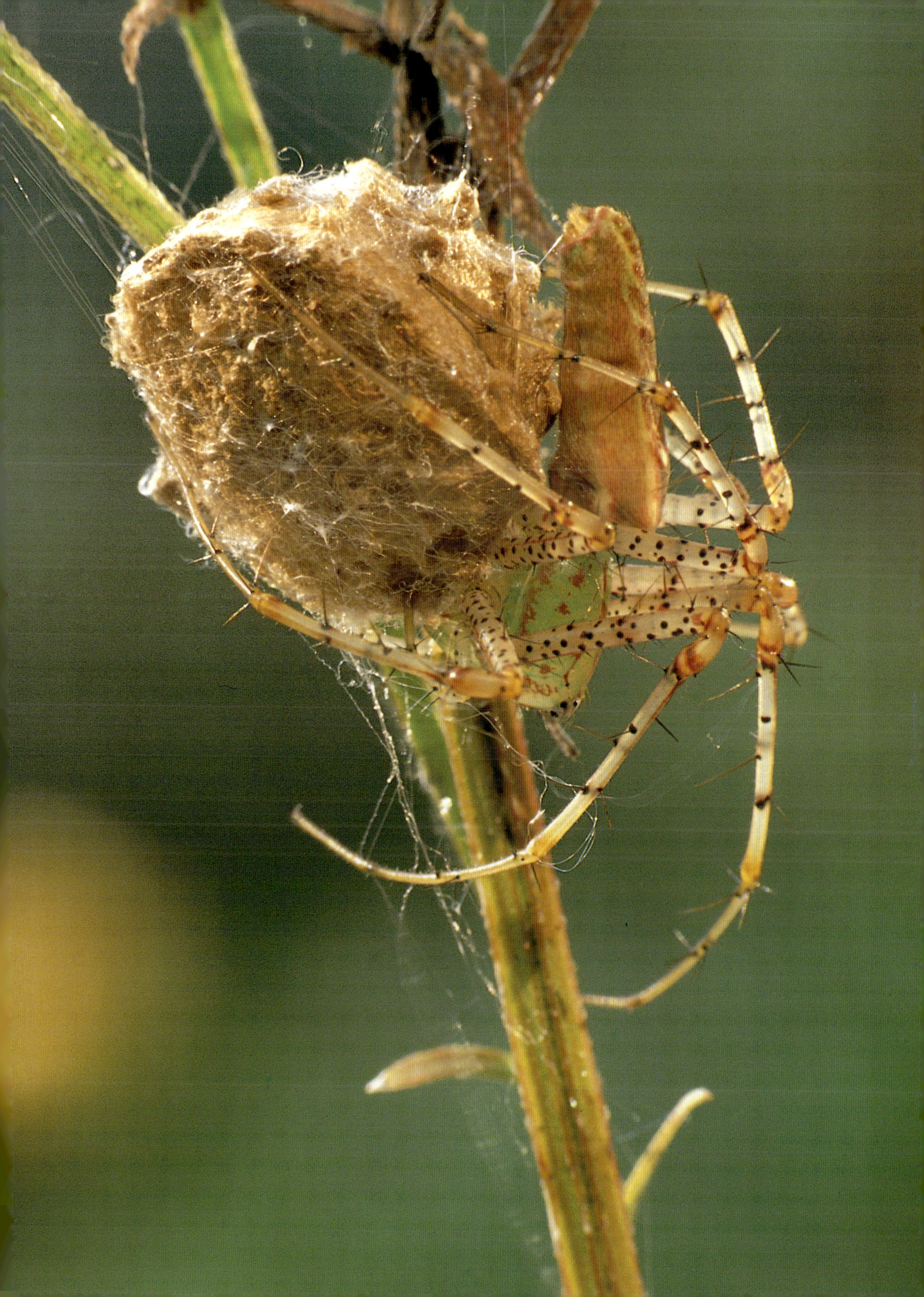

STATE PARKS

1. ANASTASIA RECREATION AREA
STATE ROUTE A1A
ST. AUGUSTINE BEACH
904/471-3033

2. BAHIA HONDA RECREATION
AREA
U.S. 1, BAHIA HONDA KEY
305/872-22353

3. BARNACLE
3485 MAIN HIGHWAY
COCONUT GROVE
305/448-9445

4. BASIN BAYOU RECREATION AREA
STATE ROUTE 20
FREEPORT
904/897-3222

5. BIG LAGOON RECREATION AREA
STATE ROUTE 292
10 MI. SW OF PENSACOLA
GULF BEACH
904/492-1595

6. BLACKWATER RIVER
U.S. 90
15 MI. NE OF MILTON
HOLT
904/623-2363

7. BLUE SPRING PARK
1-4 & U.S. 17
ORANGE CITY
904/775-3663

8. BULOW PLANTATION RUINS
STATE ROUTE S5A
BUNNELL
904/439-2219

9. CALADESI ISLAND PARK
U.S. 19A
DUNEDIN
813/443-5903

10. CAPE FLORIDA RECREATION
AREA
U.S. 1
KEY BISCAYNE
305/361-5811

11. CEDAR KEY MUSEUM
STATE ROUTE 24
CEDAR KEY
904/543-5350

12. CHEKIKA RECREATION AREA
S.W. 237TH AVE. & 168TH ST.
HOMESTEAD
305/253-0950

13. COLLIER-SEMINOLE PARK
U.S. 41
MARCO
813/394-3397

14. CONSTITUTION CONVENTION
MUSEUM
U.S. 98
PORT ST. JOE
904/229-8029

15. CRYSTAL RIVER
U.S. 19-98
CRYSTAL RIVER
904/795-3817

16. DADE BATTLEFIELD
U.S. 301
BUSHNELL
904/793-4781

17. DEAD LAKES RECREATION AREA
STATE ROUTE 71
WEWAHITCHKA
904/639-2702

18. DE LEON SPRINGS RECREATION
AREA
U.S. 17
DE LEON SPRINGS
904/985-4212

19. DELNOR-WIGGINS PASS
RECREATION AREA
COUNTY RD. 901 OFF U.S. 41
NORTH NAPLES
813/597-6196

20. DEVIL'S MILLHOPPER
STATE ROUTE 232
GAINESVILLE
904/377-5935

21. EDEN ORNAMENTAL GARDEN
U.S. 98
POINT WASHINGTON
904/231-4214

22. EVERGLADES RECLAMATION
U.S. 27
LAKE HARBOR

23. FAKAHATCHEE STRAND
PRESERVE
STATE ROUTE 29 AT COPELAND
COLLIER-SEMINOLE
813/695-4593

24. FALLING WATERS RECREATION
AREA
STATE ROUTE 77A
CHIPLEY
904/638-4030

25. FAVER DYKES PARK
U.S. 1
ST. AUGUSTINE
904/794-0997

26. FLAGLER BEACH RECREATION
AREA
STATE ROUTE A1A
FLAGLER BEACH
904/439-2474

27. FLORIDA CAVERNS PARK
STATE ROUTE 167
MARIANNA
904/482-3632

28. FOREST CAPITAL MUSEUM
U.S. 98-27A
PERRY
904/584-3227

29. FORT CLINCH PARK
STATE ROUTE A1A
FERNANDINA BEACH
904/261-4212

30. FORT COOPER PARK
OLD FLORAL CITY ROAD
INVERNESS
904/726-0315

31. FORT GADSDEN
STATE ROUTE 65
SUMATRA
904/670-8988

32. FORT PIERCE INLET
RECREATION AREA
STATE ROUTE A1A
FORT PIERCE
305/461-1570

33. GAMBLE PLANTATION
U.S. 301
ELLENTON
813/722-1017

34. GOLD HEAD BRANCH PARK
STATE ROUTE 21
KEYSTONE HEIGHTS
904/473-4701

35. GRAYTON BEACH RECREATION
AREA
STATE ROUTE 30A S.
FROM U.S.98
GRAYTON BEACH
904/231-4210

36. HIGHLANDS HAMMOCK PARK
U.S. 27-98
SEBRING
813/385-0011

37. HILLSBOROUGH RIVER PARK
U.S. 301
ZEPHYRHILLS
813/986-1020

38. HONEYMOON ISLAND
RECREATION AREA
STATE ROUTE 586 FROM U.S. 19A
DUNEDIN
813/734-4255

39. HONTOON ISLAND PRESERVE
STATE ROUTE 44
DELAND
904/734-7158

40. HUGH TAYLOR BIRCH
RECREATION AREA
STATE ROUTE A1A
FORT LAUDERDALE
305/564-4521

41. ICHETUCKNEE SPRINGS PARK
STATE ROUTE 47 & STATE
ROUTE 238
FORT WHITE
904/497-2511

42. INDIAN KEY
LOWER MATECUMBE KEY
ISLAMORADA
305/664-4815

43. JONATHAN DICKINSON PARK
U.S. 1
STUART
305/546-2771

44. JOHN GORRIE MUSEUM
U.S. 319-98
APALACHICOLA
904/653-9347

45. JOHN U. LLOYD BEACH
RECREATION AREA
STATE ROUTE A1A
DANIA
305/923-2833

46. JOHN PENNEKAMP CORAL
REEF PARK
U.S. 1
KEY LARGO
305/451-1202

47. KINGSLEY PLANTATION
STATE ROUTE A1A
FORT GEORGE
904/251-3122

48. KORESHAN
U.S. 41
ESTERO
813/992-0311

49. LAKE GRIFFIN RECREATION
AREA
U.S. 27 - 441
FRUITLAND PARK
904/787-7402

50. LAKE JACKSON MOUNDS
U.S. 27
TALLAHASSEE
904/385-7071

51. LAKE KISSIMMEE PARK
CAMP MACK ROAD
AKE WALES
813/696-1112

52. LAKE LOUISA PARK
LAKE NELLIE ROAD OFF STATE
ROUTE 561
CLERMONT
904/394-2280

53. LAKE MANATEE RECREATION
AREA
STATE ROUTE 64
BRADENTON
813/746-8042

54. LAKE TALQUIN RECREATION
AREA
STATE ROUTE 20 ON VAUSE ROAD
TALLAHASSEE
904/576-8233

55. LIGNUMVITAE KEY
U.S. 1
LOWER MATECUMBE KEY
305/664-4815

56. LITTLE TALBOT ISLAND PARK
STATE ROUTE A1A
JACKSONVILLE
904/251-3231

57. LONG KEY RECREATION AREA
U.S. 1
LONG KEY
305/664-4815

58. MACLAY GARDENS
ORNAMENTAL GARDENS
U.S. 319
TALLAHASSEE
904/893-4455

59. MADIRA BICKEL MOUND
U.S. 19
TERRA CEIA ISLAND
813/722-1017

60. MANATEE SPRINGS PARK
STATE ROUTE 320 FROM U.S. 19-98
CHIEFLAND
904/493-4288

61. MARJORIE KINNAN RAWLINGS
STATE ROUTE 325
CROSS CREEK
904/466-3672

62. MYAKKA RIVER PARK
STATE ROUTE 72
SARASOTA
813/924-1027

63. NATURAL BRIDGE BATTLEFIELD
STATE ROUTE 363
WOODVILLE
904/925-6216

64. NEW SMYRNA SUGAR
MILL RUINS
U.S. 1, STATE ROUTE 44
NEW SMYRNA BEACH
904/428-2126

65. OCHLOCKONEE RIVER PARK
U.S. 319
SOPCHOPPY
904/962-2771

66. O'LENO PARK
U.S. 41
LAKE CITY
904/454-1853

67. OLUSTEE BATTLEFIELD
U.S. 90
OLUSTEE
904/752-3866

68. OSCAR SCHERER RECREATION
AREA
U.S. 41
OSPREY
813/966-3154

69. PAHOKEE RECREATION AREA
U.S. 441
PAHOKEE
305/924-7832

70. PAYNES CREEK
STATE ROUTE 664A
BOWLING GREEN
813/375-4717

71. PAYNES PRAIRIE PRESERVE
U.S. 441
MICANOPY
904/466-3397

72. PERDIDO KEY PRESERVE
STATE ROUTE 292
PENSACOLA
904/492-1595

73. PONCE DE LEON SPRINGS
RECREATION AREA
U.S. 90 & STATE ROUTE 181A
PONCE DE LEON
904/836-4281

74. PRAIRIE LAKES PRESERVE
STATE ROUTE 523 FROM U.S. 441
KENANSVILLE
305/436-1626

75. RAVINE GARDENS
ORNAMENTAL GARDEN
TWIGG STREET
PALATKA
904/328-4366

76. ROCKY BAYOU RECREATION
AREA
STATE ROUTE 20
NICEVILLE
904/897-3222

77. ST. ANDREWS RECREATION
AREA
STATE ROUTE 392
PANAMA CITY BEACH
904/234-2522

78. ST. GEORGE ISLAND PARK
U.S. 98
EASTPOINT
904/670-2111

79. ST. JOSEPH PENINSULA PARK
STATE ROUTE 30
PORT ST. JOE
904/227-1327

80. SAN MARCOS DE APALACHE
STATE ROUTE 363
ST. MARKS
904/925-6216

81. SEBASTIAN INLET RECREATION
AREA
STATE ROUTE A1A
SEBASTIAN INLET
305/727-1752

82. STEPHEN FOSTER STATE FOLK
CULTURE CENTER
U.S. 441
WHITE SPRINGS
904/397-2733

83. SUWANNEE RIVER PARK
U.S. 90
LIVE OAK
904/362-2746

84. THREE RIVERS RECREATION
AREA
STATE ROUTE 271
SNEADS
904/593-6565

85. TOMOKA PARK
NORTH BEACH STREET
ORMOND BEACH
904/677-3931

86. TORREYA PARK
STATE ROUTE 271, STATE
ROUTE 12
ROCK BLUFF
904/643-2674

87. WASHINGTON OAKS
ORNAMENTAL GARDEN
STATE ROUTE A1A
ST. AUGUSTINE
904/445-3161

88. WEKIWA SPRINGS PARK
STATE ROUTE 436, I-4
EAST APOPKA
305/889-3140

89. YBOR CITY MUSEUM
1818 9TH AVENUE
TAMPA
813/247-6323

90. YULEE SUGAR MILL RUINS
STATE ROUTE 490
OLD HOMOSASSA
904/795-3817

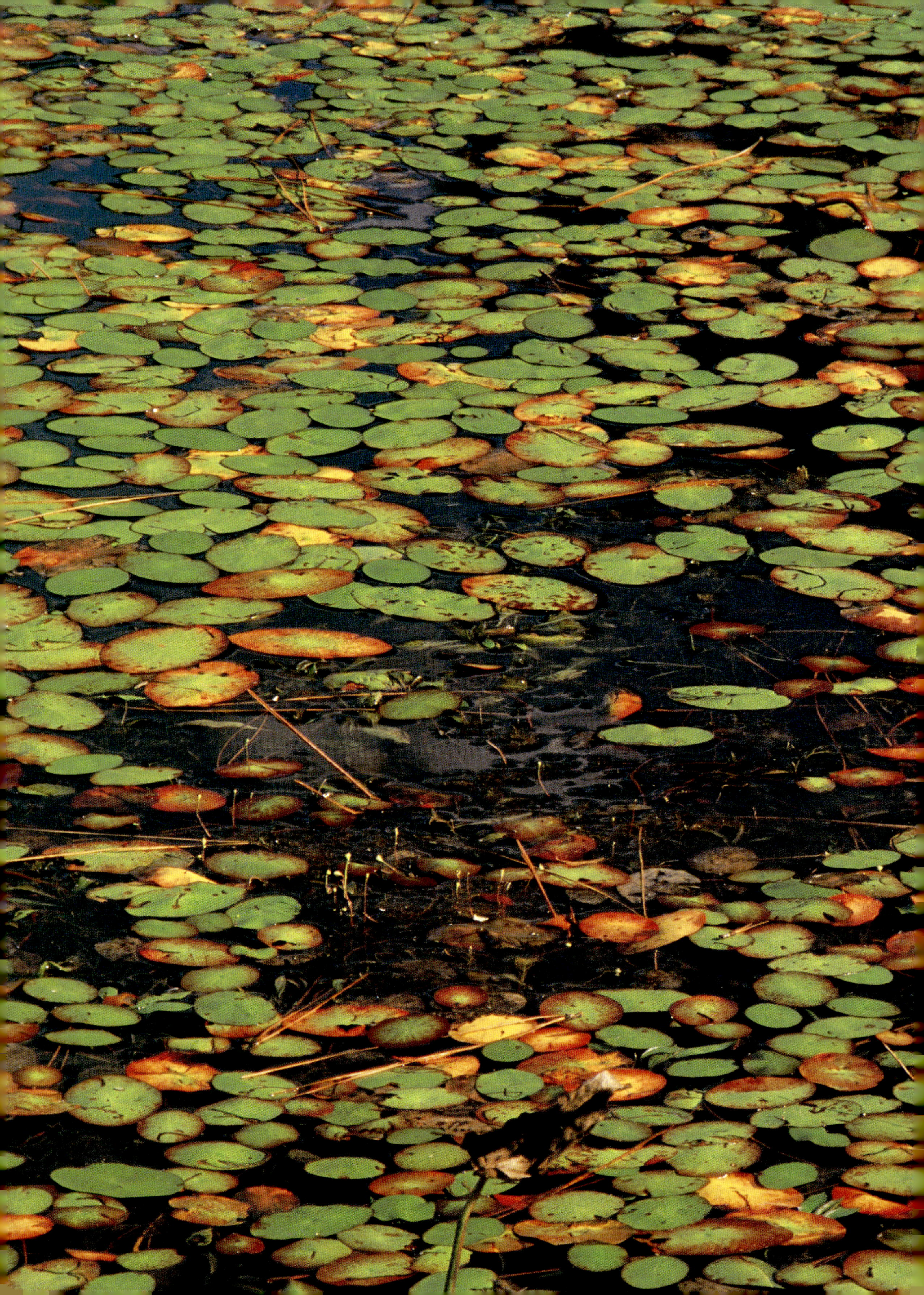

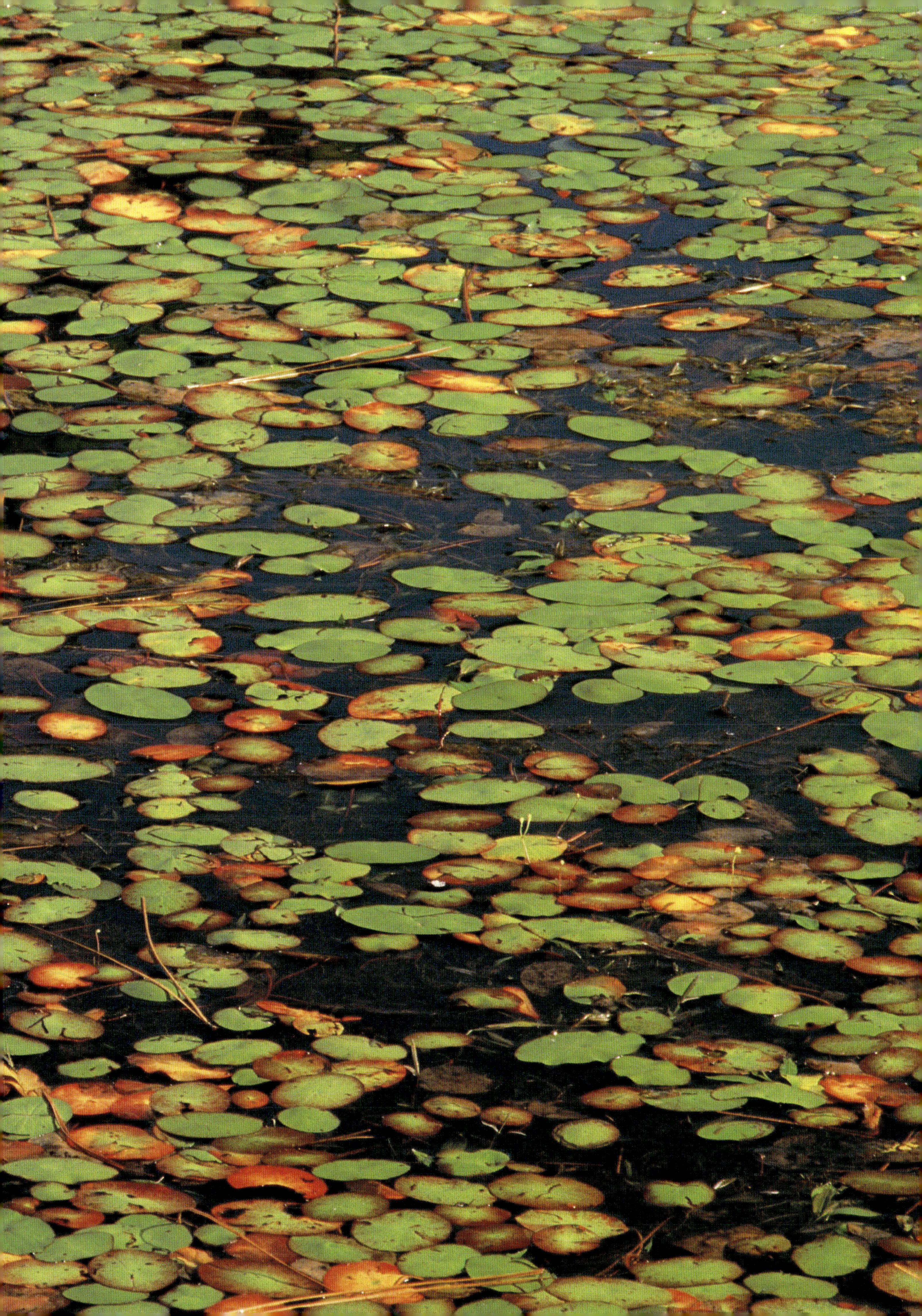

APALACHICOLA

Great egret, little blue heron, green-backed heron, tricolored heron, great blue heron, snowy egret, woodstork, anhinga, cormorant, red-cockaded woodpecker, red-headed woodpecker, red-bellied woodpecker, pileated woodpecker, hairy woodpecker, downy woodpecker, Bachman's sparrow, swallow-tailed kite, osprey, red-shouldered hawk, black vulture, turkey vulture, black bear, bobcat, red fox, gray fox, otter, white-tailed deer, coyote, Florida pine snake, gopher tortoise, alligator.

BIG CYPRESS PRESERVE

Everglade kite, great egret, snowy egret, great blue heron, tricolored heron, green backed heron, little blue heron, yellow-crowned night heron, woodstork, white ibis, anhinga, turkey vulture, black vulture, osprey, limpkin, Florida panther, black bear, white-tailed deer, raccoon.

BISCAYNE NATIONAL PARK

Pied-billed grebe, magnificent frigatebird, great blue heron, great white heron, great egret, little blue heron, tricolored heron, cattle egret, green-backed heron, yellow-crowned night heron, white ibis, black vulture, osprey, Wilson's plover, willet, laughing gull, royal tern, common ground dove, Eastern screech owl, Northern flicker, white-eyed vireo, red-winged blackbird, white-crowned pigeon, manatee, dolphin.

CANAVERAL NATIONAL SEASHORE

Great blue heron, great egret, tricolored heron, snowy egret, white ibis, willet, sanderling, ruddy turnstone, royal tern, laughing gull, ring-billed gull, brown pelican, double-crested cormorant, osprey, turkey vulture, common moorhen, coot, pied-billed grebe, ghost crab.

CORKSCREW SWAMP SANCTUARY

Woodstork, white ibis, little blue heron, great egret, limpkin, American bittern, green-backed heron, tricolored heron, snowy egret, great blue heron, anhinga, pileated woodpecker, barred owl, red-shouldered hawk, swallow-tailed kite, black vulture, turkey vulture, red-bellied woodpecker, pine warblers, raccoon, white- tailed deer, bobcat, fox squirrel, alligator.

EVERGLADES NATIONAL PARK

Pied-billed grebe, horned grebe, white pelican, brown pelican, double-crested cormorant, anhinga, great blue heron, great white heron, great egret, snowy egret, tricolored heron, cattle egret, green-backed heron, black-crowned night heron, white ibis, roseate spoonbill, mottled duck, blue-winged teal, Northern shoveler, lesser scaup, red-breasted merganser, black vulture, turkey vulture, osprey, bald eagle, red-shouldered hawk, clapper rail, king rail, sora rail, purple gallinule, common moorhen, coot, limpkin, laughing gull, ring-billed gull, herring gull, royal tern, black skimmer, Eastern screech owl, barred owl, ruby-throated hummingbird, alligator, bobcat, raccoon, tree snail.

FORT JEFFERSON NATIONAL MONUMENT

Sooty tern, noddy tern, roseate tern, magnificent frigatebird, masked booby, brown booby, black noddy, hawksbill turtle, green turtle, loggerhead turtle.

GULF ISLANDS NATIONAL SEASHORE

Great blue heron, clapper rail, coot, black-bellied plover, killdeer, willet, dunlin, laughing gull, royal tern, Forster's tern, black skimmer, mourning dove, Eastern screech owl, red-bellied woodpecker, downy woodpecker, Northern flicker, fish crow, Carolina chickadee, tufted titmouse, pine warbler, common yellowthroat, red-winged blackbird, boat-tailed grackle, raccoon, nutria, beachmouse, gray squirrel, striped skunk, ghost crab, fiddler crab, armadillo, opossum, alligator.

KEYS

Magnificent frigatebird, great white heron, snowy egret, brown pelican, double-crested cormorant, tricolored heron, little blue heron, cattle egret, roseate spoonbill, turkey vulture, osprey, American kestrel, American coot, ruddy turnstone, herring gull, laughing gull, least tern, royal tern, burrowing owl, white-crowned pigeon, horned grebe, green-backed heron, yellow-crowned night heron, white ibis, blue-winged teal, clapper rail, willet, sanderling, dowitcher, black skimmer, key deer, loggerhead turtle.

MERRITT ISLAND NATIONAL WILDLIFE REFUGE

Pied-billed grebe, white pelican, brown pelican, double-crested cormorant, anhinga, great blue heron, green-backed heron, little blue heron, cattle egret, reddish egret, great egret, snowy egret, tricolored heron, woodstork, glossy ibis, white ibis, mottled duck, blue-winged teal, turkey vulture, black vulture, red-tailed hawk, bald eagle, osprey, common moorhen, coot, willet, laughing gull, royal tern, least tern, black skimmer, fish crow, armadillo, alligator.

OCALA NATIONAL FOREST

Red-cockaded woodpecker, limpkin, bald eagle, king rail, coot, scrub jay, Bachman's sparrow, cattle egret, tricolored heron, river otter, marsh rabbit, raccoon, white-tailed deer, bobcat, gopher tortoise, indigo snake, alligator, black-crowned night heron, glossy ibis, white ibis, black vulture, turkey vulture, marsh hawk.

OSCEOLA NATIONAL FOREST

Anhinga, cattle egret, snowy egret, tricolored heron, great egret, least bittern, great blue heron, woodstork, sandhill crane, little blue heron, great horned owl, barred owl, osprey, red-tailed hawk, ruby-throated hummingbird, red-cockaded woodpecker, black bear, white-tailed deer, raccoon, bobcat, river otter.

SANIBEL

Anhinga, double-crested cormorant, roseate spoonbill, woodstork, great blue heron, white ibis, great egret, snowy egret, little blue heron, tricolored heron, osprey, red-shouldered hawk, turkey vulture, blue-winged teal, mottled duck, brown pelican, common moorhen, willet, ground dove, reddish egret, pintail, red-breasted merganser, yellow-crowned night heron.

ST. MARKS NATIONAL WILDLIFE REFUGE

Bald eagle, anhinga, great blue heron, gadwall, green-winged teal, wood duck, turkey vulture, red-shouldered hawk, clapper rail, least sandpiper, herring gull, Forster's tern, belted kingfisher, Carolina chickadee, marsh wren, tufted titmouse, Northern mockingbird, pine warbler, common yellowthroat, common grackle, opossum, raccoon, marsh rabbit, Eastern cottontail, Eastern fox squirrel, gray fox, white-tailed deer, Atlantic bottlenosed dolphin, alligator, gopher tortoise.

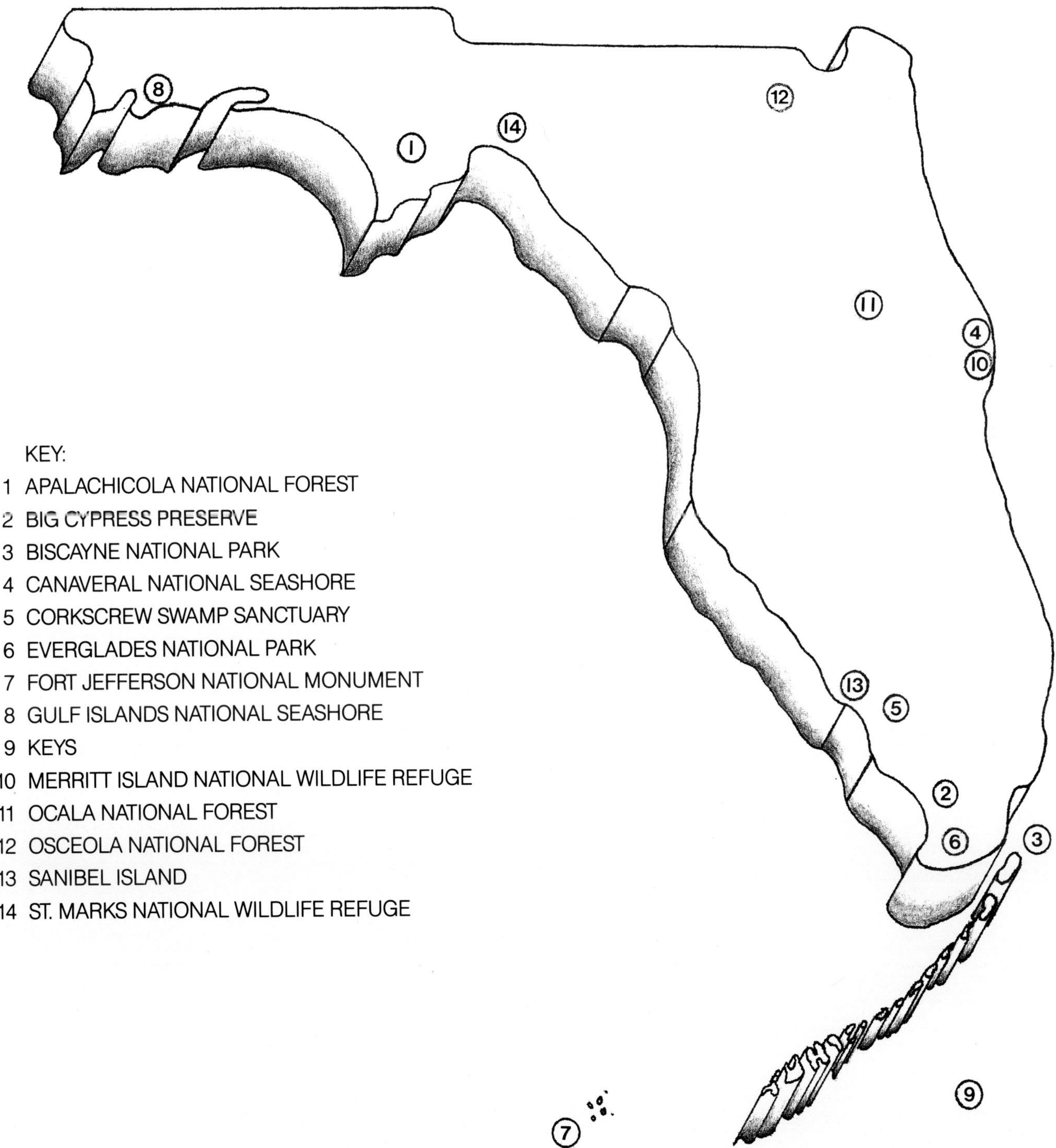

KEY:

1 APALACHICOLA NATIONAL FOREST
2 BIG CYPRESS PRESERVE
3 BISCAYNE NATIONAL PARK
4 CANAVERAL NATIONAL SEASHORE
5 CORKSCREW SWAMP SANCTUARY
6 EVERGLADES NATIONAL PARK
7 FORT JEFFERSON NATIONAL MONUMENT
8 GULF ISLANDS NATIONAL SEASHORE
9 KEYS
10 MERRITT ISLAND NATIONAL WILDLIFE REFUGE
11 OCALA NATIONAL FOREST
12 OSCEOLA NATIONAL FOREST
13 SANIBEL ISLAND
14 ST. MARKS NATIONAL WILDLIFE REFUGE

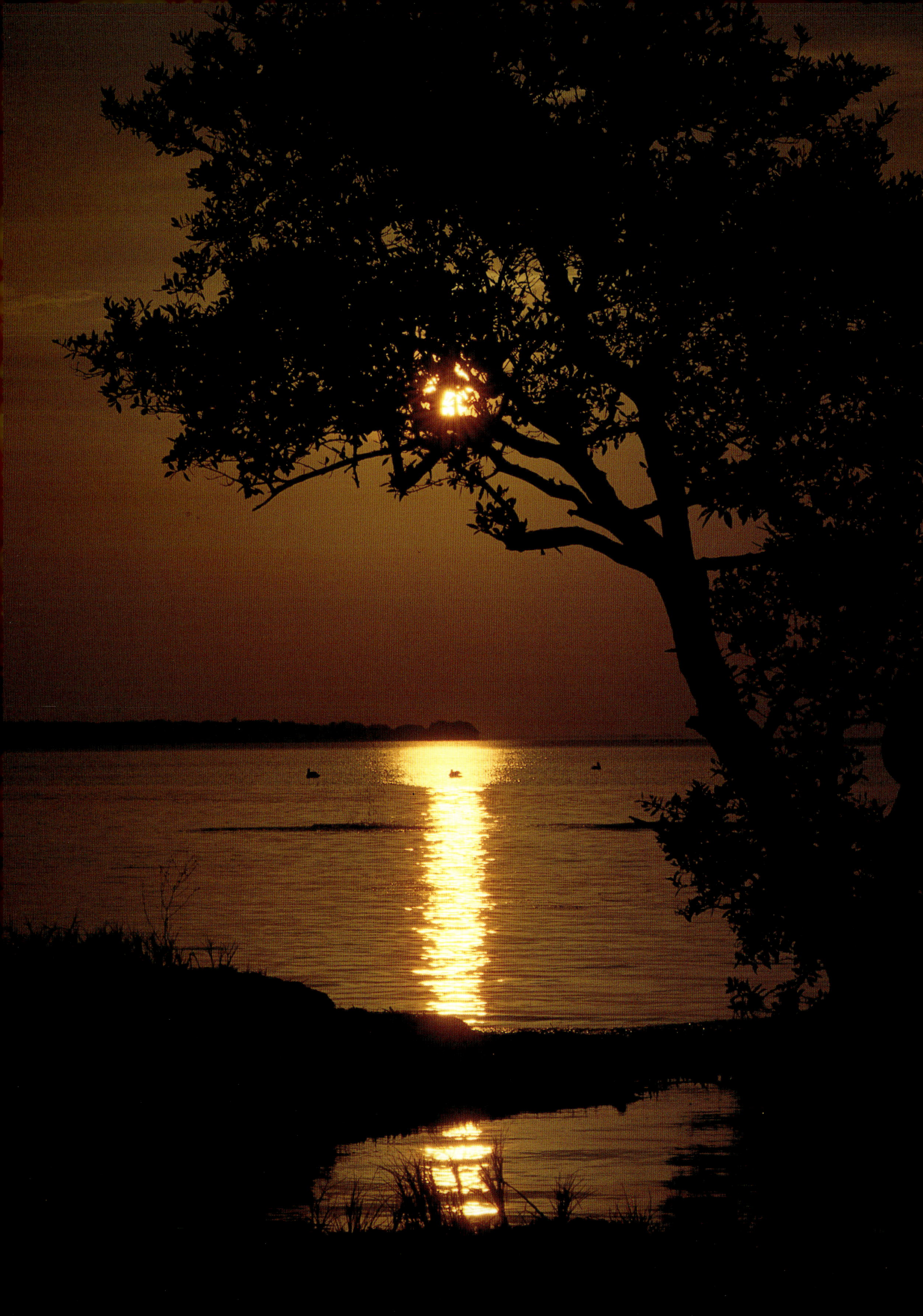